AF902512

The Economy of Chinese Rural Households

Wenrong Qian et al.

The Economy of Chinese Rural Households

ZHEJIANG UNIVERSITY PRESS
浙江大学出版社

palgrave
macmillan

Wenrong Qian et al.
Zhejiang University
Hangzhou, China

The print edition is not for sale in the Mainland of China. Customers from the Mainland of China please order the print book from: Zhejiang University Press.

Based on a translation from the Chinese language edition: 中国农村家庭发展报告（2016）by 浙江大学中国农村发展研究院（CARD）Copyright © Zhejiang University Press, 2017 All Rights Reserved.

ISBN 978-981-13-8590-2　　ISBN 978-981-13-8591-9 (eBook)
https://doi.org/10.1007/978-981-13-8591-9

© Zhejiang University Press 2020
Jointly published with Zhejiang University Press
This work is subject to copyright. All rights are solely and exclusively licensed by the Publisher, whether the whole or part of the material is concerned, specifically the rights of translation, reprinting, reuse of illustrations, recitation, broadcasting, reproduction on microfilms or in any other physical way, and transmission or information storage and retrieval, electronic adaptation, computer software, or by similar or dissimilar methodology now known or hereafter developed.
The use of general descriptive names, registered names, trademarks, service marks, etc. in this publication does not imply, even in the absence of a specific statement, that such names are exempt from the relevant protective laws and regulations and therefore free for general use.
The publishers, the authors, and the editors are safe to assume that the advice and information in this book are believed to be true and accurate at the date of publication. Neither the publishers nor the authors or the editors give a warranty, express or implied, with respect to the material contained herein or for any errors or omissions that may have been made. The publishers remain neutral with regard to jurisdictional claims in published maps and institutional affiliations.

This Palgrave Macmillan imprint is published by the registered company Springer Nature Singapore Pte Ltd.
The registered company address is: 152 Beach Road, #21-01/04 Gateway East, Singapore 189721, Singapore

Preface

China is the biggest developing country in the world; issues of agriculture, rural development and farmers are always the fundamental concern in the modernization of our country. Reform of China started from rural areas. China's rural development has made tremendous achievements in 40 years of reform and opening-up. Total grain output and farmers' net income continue to increase. According to the existing standards in China, namely, per capita annual income of 2300 yuan (2010) in the calculation of the poverty line, poverty population decreased from 770 million in 1978 to 30 million in 2017 and the poverty incidence fell from 97.5% to 3.1%, equivalent to the reduction of nearly 800 million poverty population given the natural population growth factor. However, up to now, China's rural economic development still faces serious problems: the process of factors marketization lags behind the reform of commodity marketization, which restricts the integrated development of urban and rural areas. And the dual economic and social structure of urban and rural areas has not been completely eliminated. Under the background of narrowing the income gap between urban and rural areas, there is still an imbalance in the distribution of social security resources. The trend of widening differences between workers and peasants, between urban and rural areas, between regions and between classes has not yet been fundamentally reversed. The situation that agriculture is a weak industry, rural areas lag behind communities and farmers are vulnerable groups has not been fundamentally changed. Integrated development of urban and rural areas has become a major challenge facing China's rural economy and even China's modernization process, and the effective promotion and implementation of relevant reform measures and policies to a large extent depends on the comprehensive and accurate grasp of the current situation and trend of China's agriculture, rural areas and farmers' development.

The household is the most basic unit of society. It is also the most fundamental social cell constituted by marital, blood and adoptive relationships. Rural households, on the other hand, are the basic organizational unit of rural society that combines production and social lives. Rural households are the basic units of rural consumption and demands as well as the supply side (including labor, capitals) of production factors. The China Rural Household Panel Survey (CRHPS) launched by Zhejiang University (hereafter referred to as ZJU) aimed at setting a baseline for investigating rural issues in China. This comprehensive survey involved complete information on China's rural households, including their basic household structure, employment, income and expenditure, household wealth, agricultural production and management, land utility and circulation, migration of population and urbanization, financial behavior, health and social security, education and training, and so on. The CRHPS could scientifically record and analyze the transition of China's rural households and integrate the multidimensional information of society through rural families at the micro level. It could also help us understand the development of rural China in the dimensions of society, economy, politics, culture, and resources and environment, as well as the basic features of rural consumption and demand, their production factors and the changes in their supply from a micro level. By continuously tracking and investigating all aspects of China's rural households and regularly recording their all directional transitions using micro-statistics, the objective reality of China's rural households could be thoroughly understood and the inner mechanism of the various kinds of social problems could be probed into.

In the final chapter of this report, we further summarized and refined what we think is important and put forward our own viewpoint and the conclusion. Readers may not have to agree to all of our points of view, but we hope it will have a certain reference value for the people who are researchers on the Chinese rural issue and concerned about China's rural development.

The authors of this book are Wenrong Qian, Shaosheng Jin, Jianqing Ruan, Rui Mao, Binlei Gong, Qing Yuan, Xin He, Sitong Chen, Tao Jiang, and Liangyan Guo. Due to the limited level of the author, coupled with the time and energy constraints, there must be unavoidable errors in this book; please let us know if you have any questions.

Hangzhou, China Wenrong Qian et al.

Contents

1 Introduction 1

2 Agricultural Production and Management of Rural Households 11

2.1 Basic Situation 12

2.2 Scope of Production and Management 14

2.3 Agricultural Labor Force 17

2.3.1 Self-Employment 17

2.3.2 Labor Force Employment 19

2.4 Instruments of Agricultural Production 20

2.4.1 Agricultural Machinery Ownership 20

2.4.2 Livestock Ownership 20

2.4.3 Costs of Machinery Hiring or Leasing 21

2.5 Agricultural Land 22

2.5.1 Agricultural Land Ownership 22

2.5.2 Renting of Agricultural Land 24

2.6 Procurement of Agricultural Materials 27

2.6.1 Types and Value of Agricultural Material Procurement 27

2.6.2 Channels of Agricultural Material Procurement 29

2.7 Total Output Value of Family Farming and Sales Revenue 30

2.7.1 Total Output Value of Family Farming 30

2.7.2 Sales Channels of Agricultural Products 31

2.7.3 Sales Revenue of Agricultural Products 33

2.7.4 *Rate of Commercialization* 34
2.8 *Production Subsidy* 35

3 Land Utilization and Circulation of Rural Households 37
3.1 *Basic Situation of Agricultural Land* 38
3.1.1 *General Situation of Samples* 38
3.1.2 *Confirmation and Issuance of Certificates of Land* 39
3.2 *Circulation of Cultivated Land* 41
3.2.1 *General Situation of the Circulation of Cultivated Land* 41
3.2.2 *Effects of Cultivated Land Circulation* 53
3.2.3 *Factors Influencing Agricultural Household Circulation Behavior* 56
3.3 *Confirmation of Rural Land Right and Circulation of Agricultural Land* 64
3.3.1 *Confirmation of Rural Land Right and the Transfer-Out of Cultivated Land* 64
3.3.2 *Confirmation of Rural Land Right and the Time Limit for Transferring Out of Cultivated Land* 66
3.3.3 *The Confirmation of Rural Land Right and the Transfer-In of Cultivated Land* 66
3.4 *Land Expropriation* 67

4 Migration of Rural Households and Citizenization of Migrant Workers 73
4.1 *Population Migration of Rural Residents* 75
4.1.1 *Overview of Population Migration* 75
4.1.2 *Composition of Migrant Workers' Jobs* 75
4.1.3 *Willingness for Urban Hukou* 76
4.2 *The Citizenization of Migrant Workers* 76
4.2.1 *Sample Characteristics* 76
4.2.2 *Basic Structure* 78
4.2.3 *Household Income and Expenditure* 86
4.2.4 *Connection with Agriculture* 87
4.2.5 *Employment and Income* 93
4.2.6 *Education for Children* 106
4.2.7 *Housing Situation* 112
4.2.8 *Healthcare and Social Security* 124

5 **Financial Behavior of Rural Households** 137
5.1 *Basic Situation of Rural Households Participating in Financial Markets* 138
5.1.1 *Risk Markets* 138
5.1.2 *Credit Market* 140
5.1.3 *Inclusive Finance* 143
5.1.4 *Mobile Internet Finance* 150
5.1.5 *Financial Planning Products* 155
5.2 *Agricultural Production and Management Loans for Farmers* 165
5.2.1 *Credit Needs* 165
5.2.2 *Financing Preference* 169
5.2.3 *Credit Gap* 173
5.3 *Private Lending of Rural Households* 175
5.3.1 *Private Lending Participation Rate* 175
5.3.2 *The Scale of Private Lending* 176
5.4 *Financial Knowledge and Financial Behavior of Rural Households* 179
5.4.1 *The Overall Level of Financial Knowledge* 179
5.4.2 *Distribution of Financial Knowledge* 188
5.4.3 *Financial Knowledge and Household Financial Behavior* 194

6 **Research Conclusions** 199

List of Figures

Fig. 2.1	Regions and agricultural production output value, unit: yuan	31
Fig. 2.2	Regions and agricultural gross revenue, unit: yuan	33
Fig. 2.3	Regions and agricultural sales (gross) revenue	34
Fig. 2.4	Agricultural production subsidy	36
Fig. 3.1	Comparison between the area of cultivated land contracted by rural families in the 2015 CRHPS and external data, unit: 10,000 mu. Data source: work report and statistical yearbook of provincial governments	39
Fig. 3.2	Proportion of rent in agricultural income in different regions in 2015, unit: %	47
Fig. 3.3	Costs other than rent	51
Fig. 3.4	Family scale and circulation of cultivated land, unit: %	57
Fig. 3.5	Size of the family labor force and circulation of cultivated land, unit: %	58
Fig. 3.6	Family male labor force ratio and circulation of cultivated land, unit: %	59
Fig. 3.7	The average number of the years of education and circulation of cultivated land, unit: %	60
Fig. 3.8	Proportion of non-agricultural employed labor force and circulation of cultivated land, unit: %	60
Fig. 3.9	Number of minors raised and the circulation of cultivated land, unit: %	61
Fig. 3.10	Total household income and circulation of cultivated land, unit: %	62
Fig. 3.11	Household net asset and circulation of cultivated land, unit: %	63
Fig. 3.12	Whether the urban area has housing and circulation of cultivated land, unit: %	64

Fig. 3.13 Contracted cultivated land per capita and circulation of cultivated land, unit: % 65
Fig. 3.14 Frequency of land expropriation since 2000, unit: time 68
Fig. 3.15 Number of expropriated households in different years (the last time of expropriation), unit: household 68
Fig. 3.16 Area of expropriated land, unit: mu 69
Fig. 3.17 Amount of monetary compensation, unit: yuan 70
Fig. 5.1 General information of household participation in risk markets, unit: % 138
Fig. 5.2 Proportions of households with loans in 2013 and 2015, unit: % 140
Fig. 5.3 Proportions of households with various loans in urban and rural areas in 2015, unit: % 142
Fig. 5.4 The mortgage of household loans in different industries in 2015, unit: % 143
Fig. 5.5 Overall situation of households participating in loan markets in 2015, unit: % 144
Fig. 5.6 Comparison of households participating in private and formal loan markets in 2015, unit: % 144
Fig. 5.7 Comparison of the number of bank outlets around urban and rural households 145
Fig. 5.8 Regional differences in the numbers of bank outlets near the villages/housing estates 146
Fig. 5.9 Comparison of bank card ownership ratio of households, unit: % 147
Fig. 5.10 Forms of financial services received by households, unit: % 148
Fig. 5.11 Satisfaction evaluation of financial services, unit: % 149
Fig. 5.12 Reasons for rural households' unsatisfaction with bank services, unit: % 150
Fig. 5.13 The nearest financial service points to households in rural areas 151
Fig. 5.14 Proportions of owning or using mobile and online bank accounts, unit: % 151
Fig. 5.15 Proportions of households owning mobile and online bank accounts at different educational levels, unit: % 152
Fig. 5.16 Proportions of households owning mobile and online bank accounts with householders at different ages 153
Fig. 5.17 Frequency of using mobile and online banking of rural households, unit: % 154
Fig. 5.18 Main purposes of using online banking, unit: % 154
Fig. 5.19 Main purposes of using mobile banking, unit: % 155
Fig. 5.20 Reasons for not using online banking, unit: % 156
Fig. 5.21 Reasons for not using mobile banking, unit: % 156
Fig. 5.22 Proportions of households owning financial planning products, unit: % 157

Fig. 5.23 Proportions of households owning various financial planning products, unit: % 158
Fig. 5.24 Proportions of financial planning products 160
Fig. 5.25 The beginning time of rural households owning online financial products, unit: % 161
Fig. 5.26 Reasons for holding online financial products, unit: % 162
Fig. 5.27 Reasons for not holding online financial products, unit: % 163
Fig. 5.28 Householders' education level and holding rate of online financial products, unit: % 164
Fig. 5.29 Age of householders and proportions of holding online financial products, unit: % 164
Fig. 5.30 Reasons for not applying for loans, unit: % 166
Fig. 5.31 Reasons for rural households not obtaining loans, unit: % 168
Fig. 5.32 Term of loans 169
Fig. 5.33 Repayment methods, unit: % 170
Fig. 5.34 Loan service satisfaction evaluation 171
Fig. 5.35 The highest acceptable annual interest rate, unit: % 174
Fig. 5.36 Comparison of private lending participation rate, unit: % 176
Fig. 5.37 Household financial knowledge level in China 187
Fig. 5.38 The overall level of China's household financial knowledge 188
Fig. 5.39 Financial knowledge level of people with different educational levels 190
Fig. 5.40 The impact of economic and financial courses on financial knowledge 191
Fig. 5.41 The impact of economic and financial courses on people with different educational attainment 192
Fig. 5.42 Financial knowledge level of people at different ages 193
Fig. 5.43 Years of schooling of different age groups, unit: year 193
Fig. 5.44 The impact of financial knowledge level on household financial market participation, unit: % 194
Fig. 5.45 Financial knowledge level and percentage of households holding risky assets, unit: % 195
Fig. 5.46 National household finance knowledge level and lending, unit: % 196
Fig. 5.47 Rural household financial knowledge level and lending, unit: % 197
Fig. 5.48 The impact of financial knowledge level on household online shopping, unit: % 197
Fig. 6.1 Land area for agricultural production and management 200
Fig. 6.2 The machinery hiring and renting ratio of agricultural families 200
Fig. 6.3 The situation of farmers taking part in land circulation, unit: % 201
Fig. 6.4 The proportion of farmland with 30 years and above rental period 202

Fig. 6.5 The educational attainment comparisons between the old and new generation of migrant workers 203
Fig. 6.6 The distribution of the enrollment in various pension schemes of migrant workers in different age groups, unit: % 204
Fig. 6.7 Distribution of medical insurance varieties of migrant workers in different age groups, unit: % 205
Fig. 6.8 Working time of migrant workers in different age groups (2015) 207
Fig. 6.9 Migrant workers' participation in agricultural production and management, unit: % 208
Fig. 6.10 The employment structure of migrant workers in different age groups (2015), unit: % 209
Fig. 6.11 Proportions of lands transferred out by migrant worker families and rural families 209
Fig. 6.12 Reasons why migrant worker families and rural families transferred lands out 210
Fig. 6.13 The comparison between hired lands of migrant worker families and rural families 211
Fig. 6.14 Nature of housing of migrant workers 212
Fig. 6.15 Furnishing of migrant workers' housing 212
Fig. 6.16 Ownership of migrant workers' housing 213
Fig. 6.17 Vacancy rate of migrant workers' rural housing 213
Fig. 6.18 Reasons for not applying for loans 215
Fig. 6.19 The amount of loans for rural household agricultural production and management that have not been met 215
Fig. 6.20 The scale of private loans 216
Fig. 6.21 Financing preferences of rural families 216

List of Tables

Table 2.1	Household participation in agricultural production and management	12
Table 2.2	Characteristics of the household working population	13
Table 2.3	Rural families and characteristics of the main labor force	13
Table 2.4	Scope of agricultural production and management, unit: %	14
Table 2.5	Scope of food crop production, unit: %	15
Table 2.6	Scope of cash crop production, unit: %	16
Table 2.7	Sown area of the main crops, unit: mu	17
Table 2.8	Self-employment of agricultural production and management	18
Table 2.9	Average participation period in agricultural production and management	18
Table 2.10	Labor force employment in agricultural production and management	19
Table 2.11	Ownership of agricultural production instruments	20
Table 2.12	Livestock ownership	21
Table 2.13	Proportion of machinery hiring or leasing	21
Table 2.14	Machinery hiring or leasing expense, unit: %	22
Table 2.15	Agricultural land ownership	23
Table 2.16	Ownership of cultivated land	23
Table 2.17	Comparison of cultivated land in agricultural production and management	24
Table 2.18	Comparison of cultivated land in agricultural production and management of rural families	24
Table 2.19	Agricultural land renting of agricultural families	25
Table 2.20	Reasons for agricultural families' rent of agricultural land, unit: %	26
Table 2.21	Rental term of agricultural land, unit: %	26

Table 2.22	Sources of agricultural land renting	27
Table 2.23	Types of agricultural material procurement, unit: %	28
Table 2.24	Agricultural material expense per mu	29
Table 2.25	Channels of agricultural material procurement, unit: %	30
Table 2.26	Whether agricultural products are sold or not	31
Table 2.27	Sales channels of agricultural products, unit: %	32
Table 2.28	Online sales of agricultural products, unit: %	33
Table 2.29	Agricultural production subsidies	35
Table 2.30	Rent of agricultural land	35
Table 3.1	Proportion of households with various types of land management right certificates	39
Table 3.2	Proportion of rural families that consider the confirmation and issuance of land certificates can bring benefits	40
Table 3.3	Proportion of reasons why the confirmation and issuance of land certificates cannot bring benefits	41
Table 3.4	Agricultural households' participation in circulation	42
Table 3.5	Transfer-out and transfer-in of cultivated land by agricultural households in 2015	43
Table 3.6	Entities engaged in circulation	44
Table 3.7	Use of circulated agricultural land	45
Table 3.8	Proportion of paid agricultural land transfer	46
Table 3.9	Rents for agricultural land circulation	46
Table 3.10	Village committee intervention and circulation rent in 2015	47
Table 3.11	Regular circulation and irregular circulation of agricultural land	48
Table 3.12	Time limit for agricultural land circulation	48
Table 3.13	Time limit for cultivated land transfer for agricultural use in 2015	49
Table 3.14	Time limit for cultivated land transfer and village committees' intervention in 2015	50
Table 3.15	Proportions of families that have encountered land disputes	50
Table 3.16	Causes of land disputes	51
Table 3.17	Proportion of households using different payment methods in the rent of agricultural land transfer	51
Table 3.18	Proportion of households in need of different types of services in agricultural land transfer	52
Table 3.19	Proportion of households that received different types of services in agricultural land transfer	53
Table 3.20	Proportion of households that received services from various organizations in agricultural land transfer	54
Table 3.21	Land management area per household	55
Table 3.22	Average land management area of labor force	55

Table 3.23	Agricultural land transfer and the agricultural households' input and output in 2015	56
Table 3.24	Family structure and circulation of agricultural land	62
Table 3.25	Confirmation of the rural families' land rights and the transfer-out of cultivated land	65
Table 3.26	Confirmation of the rural families' land rights and the time limit for the transfer-out of cultivated land	66
Table 3.27	Confirmation of the rural families' land right and the transfer-in of cultivated land	67
Table 3.28	Proportion of households with different forms of compensation for land expropriation	70
Table 3.29	Proportion of families receiving different types of non-monetary compensation	71
Table 4.1	Rural population migration rate, unit: %	75
Table 4.2	Nature of migrant workers' jobs, unit: %	75
Table 4.3	Willingness for urban hukou, unit: %	76
Table 4.4	Source structure of migrant workers	78
Table 4.5	Age and gender structure of migrant workers	79
Table 4.6	Genders of the working-age population and their average years of schooling, unit: year	80
Table 4.7	Academic structure of migrant workers, unit: %	80
Table 4.8	Comparison of the academic structure between the new and the old generation of migrant workers, unit: %	81
Table 4.9	Household registration of migrant workers, unit: %	82
Table 4.10	Family migration rate of migrant workers	83
Table 4.11	Number of family members of migrant workers living together, unit: %	84
Table 4.12	Number of family members of migrant workers not living with the respondents (%)	85
Table 4.13	Migrant workers' willingness to obtain an urban hukou	86
Table 4.14	Structure of household income of migrant workers' families	87
Table 4.15	Expenditure structure of migrant workers' families	87
Table 4.16	Migrant workers' participation in agricultural production and management, unit: %	88
Table 4.17	A comparison of agricultural land ownership between migrant workers' families and rural families	89
Table 4.18	Agricultural land area owned by rural families and migrant workers' families and self-use ratio of agricultural land	90
Table 4.19	A comparison of agricultural land transfer-out between migrant workers' families and rural families (Statistics in 2015)	90
Table 4.20	Comparison of agricultural land transfer-out between migrant workers' families and rural families (statistics in 2013)	91

Table 4.21 A comparison of agricultural land transfer-out between migrant workers' families and rural families (statistics in 2011) 91
Table 4.22 Reasons for migrant workers' families and rural families to transfer land, unit: % 92
Table 4.23 A comparison of rented agricultural land between migrant workers' families and rural families 93
Table 4.24 Source of rented agricultural land in migrant workers' families, unit: % 93
Table 4.25 Working hours of migrant workers 94
Table 4.26 Migrant workers' working hours between different generations in 2015, unit: % 95
Table 4.27 Migrant workers' working hours between different generations in 2013, unit: % 96
Table 4.28 Migrant workers' working hours between different generations in 2011, unit: % 97
Table 4.29 Employment structure of migrant workers, unit: % 98
Table 4.30 Employment structure of migrant workers between different generations in 2015, unit: % 99
Table 4.31 Employment structure of migrant workers between different generations in 2013, unit: % 100
Table 4.32 Employment structure of migrant workers between different generations in 2011, unit: % 101
Table 4.33 Distribution of employment industries, unit: % 102
Table 4.34 Distribution of employment sectors, unit: % 102
Table 4.35 Distribution of the nature of enterprises that migrant workers work in, unit: % 103
Table 4.36 Years of education for migrant workers in different industries, unit: year 104
Table 4.37 Years of education for migrant workers in different sectors, unit: year 104
Table 4.38 Income and employment industries, unit: yuan per year 105
Table 4.39 Academic background and income, unit: yuan per year 106
Table 4.40 Expectation for children education in migrant workers' families and rural families, unit: % 107
Table 4.41 Nature of schools that migrant workers' and rural citizens' children are studying in, unit: % 108
Table 4.42 Levels of public school children of migrant workers' families and rural families go to, unit: % 109
Table 4.43 Nature of school migrant workers' children living in different areas study in, unit: % 110
Table 4.44 Levels of public school migrant workers' children living in different areas study in, unit: % 110

Table 4.45	Long-distance education about migrant workers' and rural citizens' children, unit: %	111
Table 4.46	Long-distance education about migrant workers' and rural citizens' children living in different areas, unit: %	111
Table 4.47	Education fees for children in migrant workers' families and rural families, unit: %	112
Table 4.48	Situation of migrant workers' homeownership, unit: %	113
Table 4.49	Proportion of different numbers of houses possessed by family, unit: %	113
Table 4.50	Nature of houses occupied currently by migrant workers, unit: %	113
Table 4.51	Nature of the current housing of local migrant workers, unit: %	114
Table 4.52	Nature of the current housing of non-local migrant workers, unit: %	115
Table 4.53	House decoration of migrant workers	116
Table 4.54	Forms of house leasing of migrant workers, unit: %	116
Table 4.55	The shared housing situation of the migrant workers' family	117
Table 4.56	Situation of migrant workers owning houses with limited property rights, unit: %	117
Table 4.57	Plan of migrant workers to purchase (build) a house, unit: %	118
Table 4.58	Plan of migrant workers living in different types of cities and towns to purchase (build) a house, unit: %	118
Table 4.59	Time planned by migrant workers to purchase a house, unit: %	119
Table 4.60	Time planned to purchase a house of migrant workers living in different types of cities and towns, unit: %	119
Table 4.61	Housing vacancy rate of migrant workers	120
Table 4.62	Housing vacancy rate of migrant workers owning different number of houses, unit: %	120
Table 4.63	Housing vacancy rate of migrant workers in different regions, unit: %	121
Table 4.64	Housing vacancy rate of local migrant workers in different areas, unit: %	121
Table 4.65	Housing vacancy rate of non-local migrant workers in different areas, unit: %	121
Table 4.66	The current vacancy period of the migrant workers' unoccupied housing, unit: %	122
Table 4.67	The current housing vacancy period of the local migrant workers' self-owned housing, unit: %	123
Table 4.68	The current vacancy period of the on-local migrant workers' self-owned housing, unit: %	123
Table 4.69	Situation of migrant workers having chronic diseases, unit: %	124

Table 4.70 Self-assessment of migrant workers over the severity of chronic diseases 124
Table 4.71 Gender differences of migrant workers having chronic diseases, unit: % 124
Table 4.72 Age differences of migrant workers having chronic diseases, unit: % 125
Table 4.73 Distribution of migrant workers and rural residents over ways of living retirement life, unit: % 126
Table 4.74 The comparison between migrant workers and rural residents over distribution of types of social endowment insurance, unit: % 127
Table 4.75 Distribution of the types of social endowment insurance of migrant workers of different ages, unit: % 129
Table 4.76 Comparison between personal payment on social endowment insurance and income of migrant workers 130
Table 4.77 Implementation of the pension system unification in the migrant workers' company, unit: % 130
Table 4.78 Medicare coverage of migrant workers, unit: % 130
Table 4.79 Medicare coverage of migrant workers at different ages, unit: % 130
Table 4.80 Differences in the Medicare coverage of migrant workers of different genders, unit: % 131
Table 4.81 Distribution of the types of medical insurance of migrant workers, unit: % 132
Table 4.82 Distribution of the types of medical insurance of migrant workers at different ages, unit: % 133
Table 4.83 Basic situation of the overall plan for serious illness of migrant workers 134
Table 4.84 Basic situation of housing fund of migrant workers 134
Table 4.85 Reasons for withdrawing the housing fund 135
Table 4.86 Coverage of migrant workers' unemployment, maternity and employment injury insurances 135
Table 4.87 Proportion of migrant workers taking out commercial insurances, unit: % 136
Table 5.1 Situation of household participation in all types of risk markets, unit: % 139
Table 5.2 The participation situation of households in loan markets, unit: % 141
Table 5.3 Distribution of the number of bank outlets near the villages (housing estates), unit: % 146
Table 5.4 Financial planning products and household assets, unit: % 158
Table 5.5 Financial planning products and household income, unit: % 159

Table 5.6 The total market capitalization of financial planning products, unit: yuan 160
Table 5.7 Changes in credit needs, unit: % 166
Table 5.8 Overview of families thinking their application would not be approved, unit: yuan 167
Table 5.9 Different financing preference of rural households, unit: % 171
Table 5.10 Age of the head of household and household financing preference, unit: % 171
Table 5.11 Educational level of head of household and financing preference, unit: % 172
Table 5.12 Gender of the head of household and financing preference, unit: % 173
Table 5.13 Family characteristics and financing preference 173
Table 5.14 The capital amount of unmet needs for lending for agricultural production and management among rural households, unit: yuan 174
Table 5.15 Private lending participation rate, unit: % 175
Table 5.16 Private lending participation rates of different loans, unit: % 177
Table 5.17 The scale of private lending 177
Table 5.18 Private lending for different uses, unit: 10,000 yuan 178
Table 5.19 The scale of private lending per household in different regions, unit: 10,000 yuan 178
Table 5.20 Answers to questions about interest and computing capability, unit: % 180
Table 5.21 Answers to questions about inflation, unit: % 181
Table 5.22 Answers to questions about risks in the financial market, unit: % 182
Table 5.23 The level of attention to economics and finance, unit: % 183
Table 5.24 The load of each factor 184
Table 5.25 Score coefficients on Factors 1 and 2 185
Table 5.26 Distribution of family financial knowledge index 186
Table 5.27 Comparison of Chinese household finance knowledge level between urban and rural areas 189
Table 5.28 Comparison of the overall level of household financial knowledge among eastern, middle and western regions 190
Table 5.29 Financial knowledge level of different genders 194
Table 6.1 The proportion of China's urban and rural working-age population in the total population, unit: % 206
Table 6.2 The satisfaction of rural families' demands for proper fiduciary loans, unit: % 214

CHAPTER 1

Introduction

Rural household is the basic organizational unit of rural society that combines production and social lives. Rural households are the basic units of rural consumption and demands as well as the supply side (including labor, capitals, etc.) of production factors. To obtain the maximum satisfaction, rural households not only need to purchase various types of consumptive goods and the needed household's productive materials from the market but also need to obtain income by utilizing the labor, material and time resources of the whole household. As resources are always scarce and limited, the goal of the decisions made by the entire rural household is to maximize the efficiency of these resources. Therefore, like other rational economic entities, rural households make decisions frequently in terms of production and consumption to maximize profits or efficiency.

The China Rural Household Panel Survey (CRHPS) launched by Zhejiang University (hereafter referred to as ZJU) in 2015 aimed at setting a baseline for investigating rural issues in China. This comprehensive survey involved complete information on China's rural households, including their basic household structure, employment, income and expenditure, household wealth, agricultural production and management, land utility and circulation, migration of population and urbanization, financial behavior, health and social security, and education and training. Moreover, the survey covered the basic conditions of China's rural grass-roots units (village committees), which included information on local public services, social economy, social governance and environmental characteristics, as well as other areas.

© Zhejiang University Press 2020

W. Qian et al., *The Economy of Chinese Rural Households*,
https://doi.org/10.1007/978-981-13-8591-9_1

This report of China Rural Household Panel Survey comprises five parts, including the background, agricultural production and management, land utilization and circulation, migration and citizenization and financial activities, and the conclusion.

It should be noted that the data involved in this report cover not only rural households living in rural areas but also rural families living in urban areas. Taking into account the situation of migrant workers working in urban areas, this report focused on both rural issues concerning agriculture and farmers, and issues concerning life in modern cities. The contents of each of the following chapter are as follows.

Chapter 2 is "Agricultural Production and Management of Rural Households". Agriculture is the foundation of life for human society, and more importantly, it is the fundamental guarantee of continuous development and progress of the overall national economy. Agricultural production and management is the fundamental economic activity of rural households in China, and this chapter analyzes the development and trend of agricultural production and management in China based on the data of the China Rural Panel Household Survey (CRHPS) of Zhejiang University. This chapter consists of eight sections: Basic Situation, Scope of Production and Management, Agricultural Labor Force, Instruments of Agricultural Production, Agricultural Land, Procurement of Agricultural Materials, Total Output Value of Family Farming and Sales Revenue, as well as Production Subsidy. Besides the vast majority of rural households, some urban families are also engaged in agricultural production and management activities (collectively referred to as "agricultural families"), so the sample agricultural families involved in this chapter include rural household samples and urban households engaged in agricultural production and management, totaling 12,035. In addition, in order to get a better understanding of the variation of agricultural families, we divided rural households into three categories, including full-time agricultural family, part-time agricultural family and non-agricultural family in our analysis. The corresponding samples are 11,654 rural household samples. Moreover, survey data prior to 2015, is used in parts of the content to analyze the trends, which comes from the database of China Household Finance Survey (CHFS) of the Southwestern University of Finance and Economics. The results of this chapter indicate that the average age (44.0 years) of full-time agricultural families in China was higher, with females taking a larger share (48.1%) and shorter years of schooling (6.3 years) than other types of agricultural families in 2015. The scope of agricultural production and management indicates that most agricultural households grow food crops. In total, 88.1% of Chinese agricultural families are engaged in food crop production, and 34.8% of agricultural households are engaged in cash crop production. As for the agricultural labor force, it is found that the average number of self-employed persons in agriculture families is 1.9, which accounts for 76.0% of the total working population. In terms of the proportion of agricultural families with an employed labor force, 9.8% of agricultural families nationwide have labor force employment. An average of 46.1% of the agricultural families employed or leased machinery during the production process, but only 30.2% of agricultural households in the western region employed or leased machinery. The ownership of machinery for agricultural production (36.1%) and livestock for agricultural production (21.8%) of agricultural families in the western region are relatively high. Some facts about agricultural land can be seen in the survey data. In 2015, the average cultivated land that Chinese agricultural families produced and managed amounted to 11.3 mu, which was 1.5 mu more than that in 2013. The renting ratio of agricultural households in China is 18.0%. This figure of agricultural households in rural areas is 18.8% and that of urban families is 14.1%. As for the sales channels of agricultural products, 69.6% of the agricultural households in China sell their own agricultural products, of which 64.3% of the urban agricultural families sell their own agricultural products, which is less than the 70.7% of the rural areas. However, only 0.3% of agricultural families sold agricultural products through the Internet in 2015; thus, online sales still have much potential in China.

Chapter 3 is "Land Utilization and Circulation of Rural Households". The household contract responsibility system is a basic rural land system in China, which distributes the agricultural land relatively evenly to rural families. Although the household contract responsibility system ensures the fairness of the agricultural land system to a great extent, with the development of social economy, the average distribution of agricultural land has begun to go against the efficiency of agricultural land utilization. An important factor is the differentiation of rural families in employment. Some rural families prefer non-agricultural employment, which creates idle land; however, agricultural households that are committed to agricultural production and management are facing a shortage of cultivated land. Therefore, the land of rural families should be readjusted to meet the needs of economic development. Under the premise of ensuring that the rural land ownership and the contract system remain unchanged, agricultural land circulation becomes an important readjustment method. This chapter, by using data from the China Rural Household Panel Survey of Zhejiang University (CRHPS) to analyze the land utilization and circulation of China's rural households, is mainly composed of four sections: Basic Situation of China's Agricultural Land, Circulation of Cultivated Land (general situation, effects and influencing factors), Confirmation of Rural Land Right and Circulation of Agricultural Land and Land Expropriation. The sample families involved in this chapter include both rural household samples and urban family samples with a total of 16,373 cases, which are slightly different from the previous chapters. A total of 11,654 rural household samples were used to analyze land expropriation, confirmation and circulation, as well as circulation disputes and circulation services. In addition, data from surveys before 2015 were used in some parts of the content to analyze the trends, and these relevant data were all collected from the China Household Finance Survey (CHFS) database of the Southwestern University of Finance and Economics. The results of this chapter show that 35.9% of Chinese agricultural households were involved in agricultural land circulation in 2015, which is 11.8% higher than that in 2013. In 2013, the rent for transfer-out cultivated land was 383 yuan per mu, and the rent for transfer-in cultivated land was 298 yuan per mu. In 2015, the rent for transfer-out cultivated land had increased to 425 yuan per mu and the rent for transfer-in cultivated land had increased to 443 yuan per mu. For transfer-out cultivated land, the average rent with the involvement of the village committee was 590 yuan per mu, while the average rent without the involvement of the village committee was 388 yuan per mu. For the transfer-in cultivated land, the average rent with the involvement of the village committee was 629 yuan per mu, while the average rent without the involvement of the village committee was 434 yuan per mu. An average of 35.7% of rural households that had purchased houses in urban areas transferred out the cultivated land, which is 21% higher than those that had not purchased houses in urban areas.

Chapter 4 is "Migration of Rural Households and Citizenization of Migrant Workers". This chapter uses the samples of "rural families living in rural areas" and "rural families living in urban areas (migrant workers' families)" from the China Rural Household Panel Survey (CRHPS) by Zhejiang University to analyze the migration of rural families and citizenization of migrant workers. The study found that the average age of migrant workers is 37.7 years old, and the average schooling year is 9.4 years. On average, the working time of migrant workers is 9.1 hours per day and 25 days per month, which is generally higher than the regulations set by the labor law.

The overall education level of migrant workers is not high, but we can see an obvious improvement in the level among the new generation of migrant workers: previously, the illiterate migrant workers accounted for 11.0% of the population, workers with primary school education accounted for 22.4% and workers with junior secondary education accounted for 35.8%. From the old generation to the post-1980s and then to the post-1990s, there is a very clear improvement in the level of education. The proportion of migrant workers with a primary or lower education has dropped, from 47.8% of the older generation to 8.3% of the post-1980s and then to 3.9% of the post-1990s; meanwhile, people with a high school degree or above among migrant workers have markedly increased, from 15.6% of the old generation to 51.4% of the post-1980s and then to 69.8% of the post-1990s. The urban hukou, or household registration, became less appealing to migrant workers that only 17.0% of migrant workers were willing to obtain a non-agricultural hukou. The citizenization of migrant workers has not been marked chiefly by whether they have obtained or been willing to obtain urban hukou. Migrant workers are more or less related to agriculture, but there is a clear trend: in 2015, 27.8% of migrant workers in China engaged in agricultural production and management; however, compared with that in 2013 and 2011, the relationship between migrant workers and agriculture has obviously weakened. The proportion of migrant workers participating in agricultural production and management has dropped from 31.7% in 2010 to 30.4% in 2012 and then to 27.8% in 2014. The number of months which migrant workers are involved in agricultural production has fallen from 6.76 to 6.26 months, and then to 6.15 months. Migrant workers' families have a tendency to rapidly rent out agricultural land: since 2011, migrant workers' families have rented out agricultural land faster and show a trend of continuously renting out land. According to a survey conducted in 2011, the proportion of migrant workers' families having rented out agricultural land was 12.9%, which was higher than that of rural families (6.0%) by 6.9% points. In 2013, that of migrant workers' families became 16.4%, which was higher than that of rural families (10%) by 6.4% points. By 2015, 30.9% of migrant workers' families had rent out agricultural land, which was higher than the 11.3% of rural families by 19.6% points. By 2015, migrant worker families who had rent out agricultural land had, on average, rent out 5.1 mu per household, which is 15.9% higher than the 4.4 mu of rural households. Migrant workers' families generally have higher expectations of their children's education than rural families. The more highly educated migrant workers are, the higher annual income they could get. But no matter what academic background female migrant workers have, their income was significantly lower than that of men. The overall social security level of migrant workers is low: 39.8% of migrant workers do not have any pension insurance and 57.1% of migrant workers are supported by social endowment insurance. Among various social endowment insurances, the new rural social old-age insurance plays a major role, accounting for 66.9%. The coverage rate of medical insurance for migrant workers is 85.2%, but it is still mainly based on the New Rural Cooperative Medical System (NRCMS), accounting for 76.5%. Only 10.7% of migrant workers have registered for the Urban Employee Basic Medical Insurance (UEBMI).

Chapter 5 is "Financial Behavior of Rural Households". It exhibits the characteristics of rural households' financial activities and illustrates the financial participation of rural households by exploring four aspects, namely, the participation in the financial market, agricultural loans, private lending and the financial knowledge and behaviors of rural households. This chapter analyzes the financial behavior of rural households including the participation behavior of rural households in the financial market, agricultural production and management loans of rural households, private lending of rural households, and financial knowledge and behavior of rural households according to the databases of China Rural Household Panel Survey (CRHPS) by Zhejiang University and China Household Finance Survey (CHFS). First, the study found that the development of the current rural financial market was very backward, and the participation rate of rural households in risk markets such as stocks and funds was very low, accounting for only 2.4%, far behind the national overall level of 17.1%. In terms of urban and rural areas, the proportion of rural households participating in various risk markets was much lower than that of urban households. As for the loan market, compared with 2013, in 2015 the ratio of rural households with loans declined from 14.1% to 12%, while that of urban households increased by 18.4% points. Meanwhile, the situation of inclusive finance is also analyzed. The average number of banking outlets of each village revealed the obvious gap in financial service facilities between rural and urban areas. Households with bank cards in rural areas accounted for 55.9% of the total rural households, 23.3% points lower than the national urban households. As for the mobile internet finance, it is found that the proportions of national households owning mobile and online bank accounts in rural areas were only 4.3% and 7.1%, respectively. When it comes to financial planning products, China's households with financial planning products accounted for 9.6% of the total households in the country. Second, some facts about the agricultural production and management loans for farmers are showed from the results. The participation level of rural households in the formal credit market was also low, and the demand proportion of agricultural production and management loans in 2015 was only 12.7%, down by more than 50% compared with 2013. However, rural households actively participated in the private lending market, as there were over 28% of rural households with private loans, far higher than the national level. Private borrowing was mainly used for housing as well as production and management projects, which served as a good supplement to the insufficient formal borrowing. As for inclusive finance, the financial service infrastructure coverage of rural areas, bank account ownership and convenience of banking services still had a great room for improvement. Most agricultural households preferred informal financing channels, while only 22.4% of rural households preferred formal bank loans. Third, survey data also shows households in our country have a higher private lending participation rate in housing and agricultural/industrial and commercial projects, especially in rural areas. In 2015, in rural areas the scale of private lending per household among households in debt was 45,000 yuan, and the proportion of private lending to total liabilities was 77.8%. Fourth, the financial knowledge level of China's rural households was generally low, while financial knowledge has a significant impact on financial behavior. The higher the level of financial knowledge, the higher the proportion of households participating in financial markets, and these households also hold more risky assets. Among households with higher financial knowledge, the proportion of loans will be increased, while the proportion of participation in private finance will be reduced.

Chapter 6 is "Research Conclusions". Based on the statistics of the CRHPS, it summarizes the newly emerged characteristics of China's rural households from seven aspects, including conditions of land use and migration, and sums up the current overall situation of rural households from a micro level. The main results were as follows:

(1) The expansion of household cultivated land management is obvious, and the proportion of agricultural machinery social service is high. In the context of the government making great efforts to promote a modest scale of various forms of agriculture, the expansion of China's rural household agricultural production and management is obvious. With the expansion of agricultural households' production and operation, a higher proportion of agricultural households have purchased agricultural machinery services.

(2) The percentage of long-term cultivated land circulation increased significantly, and the inter-period circulation increased. There has been an obvious increase in the proportion of China's agricultural families taking part in land circulation. It is worth mentioning that the progress of urbanization promoted the circulation of cultivated land. The statistics show that the average rent will increase significantly if the village committee is involved in the process of farmland transfer, whether the land is transferred in or out.

(3) The new generation migrant workers' qualities obviously improved, and there is a considerable change in citizens' manners. The improvement of the new generation migrant workers' moral characters also has an impact on their citizenization. They began to "get out of agriculture" and gradually "fit into" towns and cities. First of all, the proportion of the new generation of migrant workers participating in the New Rural Pension Scheme decreased, and the proportion of those participating in urban employees' pension scheme greatly improved. Second, the proportion of the new generation of migrant workers who participated in the new rural cooperative medical insurance decreased, while the proportion of those who joined the basic medical insurance for urban workers increased significantly. It can be considered that the new generation of migrant workers has begun to change the situation of the old generation that overly relies on the social security provided by their rural place of origin and is gradually integrating into the urban social security system, which will certainly promote the process of farmers transitioning into urban residents.

(4) The new generation of migrant workers' labor supply time declined obviously, which accelerates the shrinkage of demographic dividends. Demographic dividend refers to the positive effect on a country's economic growth brought by the high proportion of working age population and high labor participation rate, which lead to the surplus of labor force, and then a lower labor cost and lower production cost, in the demographic transition process. The CRHPS data further show that the trend of declining demographic dividend is not only manifested in the decline in the working age population, but also in the decline in labor supply time of the new generation of workers.

(5) The trend of migrant workers "leaving agriculture" is obvious, and the circulation of land and increase of the farmland scale are gaining speed. In recent years, the phenomenon of migrant worker households working in agriculture as a part-time job has been gradually reducing, and the trend of farmers "leaving agriculture" has become obvious. This trend of

migrant worker families "leaving agriculture" also contributed to the circulation of land and the large-scale operation of farmlands. At the same time, a small number of migrant worker families started to purchase or rent lands to implement large-scale farmland management. Therefore, it can be argued that as more and more migrant workers are "leaving agriculture", more lands start to be owned by a small number of competent agricultural managers, thus promoting the scale of agricultural land management.

(6) Use and configuration of housing of migrant worker families are dislocated, and housing vacancy in rural areas is serious. At present, the living conditions of migrant workers in urban areas are generally poor. The CRHPS surveyed migrant workers who lived in residential buildings and had relatively stable jobs in urban areas. The CRHPS' samples of migrant workers have the following characteristics. Although the majority of migrant workers have low homeownership rates and poor living conditions in urban areas, most of them have their own houses in rural areas, and the overall homeownership rates are higher. However, the majority of migrant workers' housing in rural areas cannot be transferred. Therefore, the housing of the migrant workers whose families moved frequently has to be vacant, which not only wastes resources, but also reduces migrant workers' ability to purchase apartment in urban areas.

(7) Rural households' needs for formal loans are hard to meet, and private lending becomes the main channel. Demands for formal loans refer to rural families' needs for loans because of production management, housing purchases, daily consumptions and other financial activities. The low availability of formal loaning channels leads to rural households preferring to rely on private lending markets. Private lending refers to the fact that individuals borrow money from relatives, friends or colleagues, as well as private financial organizations other than financial institutions such as banks or credit unions. In fact, private lending markets are more likely to meet demands than formal channels.

CHAPTER 2

Agricultural Production and Management of Rural Households

Agriculture is the foundation of life for human society, and more importantly, it is the fundamental guarantee of continuous development and progress of the overall national economy. Agricultural production and management is the fundamental economic activity of rural households in China, and this chapter analyzes the development and trend of agricultural production and management in China based on the data of the China Rural Panel Household Survey (CRHPS) of Zhejiang University. This chapter consists of eight sections: Basic Situation, Scope of Production and Management, Agricultural Labor Force, Instruments of Agricultural Production, Agricultural Land, Procurement of Agricultural Materials, Total Output Value of Family Farming and Sales Revenue, as well as Agricultural Subsidy. Besides the vast majority of rural households, some urban families are also engaged in agricultural production and management activities (collectively referred to as "agricultural families"), so the sample agricultural families involved in this chapter include rural household samples and urban households engaged in agricultural production and management, totaling 12,035, which is slightly different from the previous chapters. In addition, in order to get a better understanding of the variation of agricultural families, we divided rural households into full-time agricultural family, part-time agricultural family and non-agricultural family into parts of our analysis, using 11,654 rural household samples. Moreover, survey data prior to 2015 is used in parts of the content to analyze the trends, which comes from the database of China Household Finance Survey (CHFS) of the Southwestern University of Finance and Economics.

© Zhejiang University Press 2020

W. Qian et al., *The Economy of Chinese Rural Households*,
https://doi.org/10.1007/978-981-13-8591-9_2

The results of this chapter indicate that the average age (44.0 years) of full-time agricultural families in China was higher, with females taking a larger share (48.1%) and shorter years of schooling (6.3 years) than other types of agricultural families in 2015. About 46.1% of the agricultural families employed or leased machinery during the production process, but only 30.2% of agricultural households in the western region employed or leased machinery. The ownership of machinery for agricultural production (36.1%) and livestock for agricultural production (21.8%) of agricultural families in the western region are relatively high. In 2015, the average cultivated land that Chinese agricultural families produced and managed amounted to 11.3 mu, which was 1.5 mu more than that in 2013. Only 0.3% of agricultural families sold agricultural products through the Internet in 2015.

2.1 Basic Situation

The agricultural production and management items include agriculture, forestry, animal husbandry and fishery management projects which are operated by the family independently, but excluding the agricultural production and management items which are employed by others. From Table 2.1, we can see that 33.8% of household samples in the China Rural Panel Household Survey (CRHPS) are engaged in agricultural production and management. About 73.7% of rural households are engaged in agricultural production, and 9.6% of urban households also carry out agricultural production and management activities. The proportion of households engaged in agricultural production in the eastern region is the lowest with 27.2%, and the proportion of families in the central region engaged in agricultural production is the highest with 61.6%, followed by the western region with 39.7%.

Table 2.1 Household participation in agricultural production and management

Location	*Participation ratio (%)*
National	33.8
Urban	9.6
Rural	73.7
Eastern	27.2
Central	61.6
Western	39.7

Table 2.2 Characteristics of the household working population

Family type	*Proportion of women (%)*	*Age (years)*	*Years of schooling (year)*
Agricultural household	44.0	46.8	7.6
Non-agricultural family	42.0	41.1	11.6

Table 2.3 Rural families and characteristics of the main labor force

Family type	*Share*	*Proportion of women (%)*	*Age (years)*	*Years of schooling (year)*
Full-time agricultural family	33.8	48.1	44.0	6.3
Non-agricultural family	23.2	47.5	37.0	8.0
Part-time agricultural family	43.0	47.2	40.3	7.2

Table 2.2 compares the characteristics of workers in agricultural and non-agricultural families. The gender structure of the workers shows that female workers account for 44.0% in agricultural households, and this proportion is higher than that of non-agricultural households (42.0%). The average age of agricultural household workers is 46.8 years, which is higher than that of non-agricultural households (41.1 years). Comparing the statistics, there are relatively more middle-age and senior people in the labor force of agricultural households. However, the average number of years of schooling of agricultural household workers is only 7.6, which is significantly lower than the 11.6 years of non-agricultural households. It indicates that the educational level of agricultural household workers is generally lower. In conclusion, compared with non-agricultural families, there are more female than male workers in agricultural households as well as an older and less educated labor force. It reflects that the labor force of China that has engaged in agricultural production and management activities is of the relatively low quality.

According to the characteristics of rural (household) members, this chapter further divides rural household samples into three different types: full-time agricultural family, part-time agricultural family and non-agricultural family. Members of rural families that mainly work in agriculture will be defined as the main labor force, and an analysis of the characteristics of the main labor force in the three types of rural households will be conducted. Table 2.3 reflects the proportions of the three types of households and characteristics of their main labor force. Part-time agricultural families occupy the largest proportion, reaching 43.0%, followed by full-time agricultural families, accounting for 33.8%; and the lowest is non-agricultural families for 23.2%. It can be seen that at present, rural households still depend on agriculture for subsistence. Looking at the gender structure of the main labor force, the proportion of women in full-time agricultural families is 48.1%, which is much higher than that of non-agricultural households (47.5%) and part-time agricultural families (47.2%). Looking at the average age of the main labor force, the full-time agricultural family is the highest (44 years), followed by part-time agricultural family (40.3 years), and then the non-agricultural family (37 years). The main labor force of non-agricultural families is the highest in terms of the average years of schooling, reaching 8.0 years, and part-time agricultural family takes the second place with 7.2 years. The education level of the main labor force in full-time agricultural families is the lowest, which is only 6.3 years. Therefore, among the three types of families, full-time agricultural families possess significant weaknesses including a higher proportion of females in the main labor force, higher average age and lower educational level when compared with non-agricultural and part-time agricultural families.

2.2 Scope of Production and Management

The scope of agricultural production and management indicates that most agricultural households grow food crops. As shown in Table 2.4, 88.1% of Chinese agricultural families are engaged in food crop production and 34.8% of agricultural households are engaged in cash crop production. In addition, 5.3% of agricultural families are working in forestry production, 15.7% of agricultural families are involved in livestock production, 1.2% of

Table 2.4 Scope of agricultural production and management, unit: %

Scope of production	*National*	*Urban*	*Rural*	*Eastern*	*Central*	*Western*
Food crops	88.1	84.0	89.0	84.0	92.4	87.6
Cash crops	34.8	26.5	36.4	31.8	31.1	42.6
Forestry	5.3	6.1	5.1	8.1	3.2	4.4
Animal husbandry	15.7	15.6	15.7	8.5	11.5	29.1
Fishery	1.2	1.4	1.2	1.2	1.3	1.0
Other	0.5	1.1	0.3	0.4	0.3	0.8

Table 2.5 Scope of food crop production, unit: %

Scope of production	*National*	*Urban*	*Rural*	*Eastern*	*Central*	*Western*
Rice	37.3	39.7	36.9	28.6	34.9	49.9
Wheat	39.0	45.1	37.8	54.4	35.6	26.4
Corn	72.7	71.1	73.0	73.1	66.1	80.6
Potato	7.9	6.7	8.1	2.9	5.6	16.4
Sweet potato	12.0	8.6	12.6	7.9	10.9	17.8
Other	3.7	2.7	3.9	2.2	3.3	5.9

agricultural households are engaged in livestock production and 0.5% of agricultural households are engaged in other agricultural production and management.

Agricultural families working in food crops production in the central region accounts for as much as 92.4%, which is 8.4% higher than that in the eastern region, while the proportion of agricultural households in the western region engaging in animal husbandry is relatively high, reaching 29.1%.

In the case of agricultural households engaged in food crop production, the proportions of agricultural households growing rice, wheat and corn are high. As shown in Table 2.5, among agricultural households working on food crops, 72.7% produce corn, 39.0% produce wheat and 37.3% produce rice. In addition, 12.0% of food-crop-producing households grow sweet potatoes, and 7.9% of them grow potatoes.

Looking at the regional differences, the proportion of food crop households producing wheat in the eastern region exceeds 50% and reaches 54.4%; the proportions of food crop households producing rice and wheat in the central region are close, with 34.9% and 35.6%, respectively; and 49.9% of the food crop households in the western region grow rice, which is almost half of the regional population. At the same time, the proportion of food-crop-producing households growing potato in the western region is twice the national average level, reaching 16.4%.

In the case of agricultural households engaged in cash crop production, there are a relatively high proportion of agricultural households choosing to grow oil crops (soybean, peanut and rapeseed) as well as fruits and vegetables. As shown in Table 2.6, over 20% of agricultural households engaged in cash crop production grow vegetables and fruits, with 20.2% and 21.9% for each category, respectively, of which the proportion of urban agricultural households is 40.3% and 24.7%, respectively, which is

Table 2.6 Scope of cash crop production, unit: %

Scope of production	*National*	*Urban*	*Rural*	*Eastern*	*Central*	*Western*
Soybean	11.8	14.7	11.4	11.2	16.7	8.1
Peanut	16.3	15.3	27.9	35.9	35.2	10.4
Rapeseed	16.3	17.9	16.1	4.8	14.3	27.8
Tea	4.3	1.0	4.8	3.0	5.7	4.3
Cotton	5.0	3.7	5.2	4.0	11.3	0.2
Beet	0.5	1.1	0.4	0.0	0.1	1.2
Sugarcane	3.3	0.5	3.7	2.0	0.4	7.0
Tobacco	3.4	0.6	3.8	0.4	1.5	7.7
Vegetables	20.2	40.3	17.3	25.4	8.7	25.7
Fruits	21.9	24.7	21.4	22.3	13.5	28.9
Spice crops	2.1	0.7	2.3	0.2	1.4	4.2
Other	13.2	12.6	13.3	11.3	16.6	11.9

much higher than that of rural households with 17.3% and 21.4%, respectively. Nationwide, more than 10% of agricultural households engaged in cash crop production choose to grow oil crops, with 11.8% for soybean, 16.3% for peanut and 16.3% for rapeseed.

Looking at the regional differences of agricultural households engaged in cash crop production, in terms of oil crops, the highest proportion of soybean production is held by agricultural households in the central region with 16.7%; the proportions of agricultural households growing peanuts in the eastern and central regions are quite close, with 35.9% and 35.2%, respectively; while the western region has the highest percentage of rapeseed production with 27.8%. In terms of vegetables and fruits, the proportions of the eastern region are 25.4% and 22.3%, respectively; correspondingly, the proportions of the western region are 25.7% and 28.9%, which are much higher than the 8.7% and 13.5% of the central region. In addition, the proportion of agricultural households growing cotton in the central region is twice the national average, with up to 11.3%, and the proportion of sugarcane and tobacco grown in the western region is twice the national average, with 7.0% and 7.7%, respectively.

Table 2.7 shows the sown area of the main crops (including the sown area of autumn and winter of last year, as well as spring, summer and autumn of this year). From the national statistics, we can see that the average sown area of food crops is larger than that of the cash crops, of which the largest sown area is for corn with 12.5 mu, followed by rice with 8.6 mu. For urban agricultural families, the sown area of rice is 18.5 mu,

Table 2.7 Sown area of the main crops, unit: mu

Scope of production	*National*	*Urban*	*Rural*	*Eastern*	*Central*	*Western*
Rice	8.6	18.5	6.6	5.9	16.3	3.2
Wheat	5.8	5.4	5.9	5.8	6.8	4.2
Corn	12.5	8.2	13.3	5.5	25.9	5.3
Soybean	4.2	8.9	3.2	5.7	4.6	1.5
Peanut	3.6	2.4	3.7	2.4	5.5	1.3
Rapeseed	2.4	2.8	2.3	1.3	2.9	2.4

which is higher than the 13.3 mu of rural agricultural families. As for the sowed area of corn, the rural agricultural families have an average of 13.3 mu, which is higher than the 8.2 mu of the urban agricultural families. At the same time, the urban families' sown area of soybean reaches 8.9 mu, which is much higher than that of the rural families with 3.2 mu.

At the regional level, agricultural families in the central region have the largest sown area of grain, of which the average sowed areas of rice and corn are 16.3 mu and 25.9 mu, respectively, which are much higher than those in the eastern and western regions. The average sown area of cash crops in the eastern and central regions is higher than that in the western region. The average sown area of soybean in the eastern region is the largest with 5.7 mu, while the average sowed areas of soybean and peanut in the central region are both relatively large, with 4.6 mu and 5.5 mu, respectively.

2.3 Agricultural Labor Force

2.3.1 Self-Employment

For agricultural families, the labor force mainly comes from two parts: self-employment (family members involved in agricultural production) and hiring others. On the whole, the average number of self-employed persons in agriculture families is 1.9, which accounts for 76.0% of the total working population. The gap between urban and rural areas is not very large, which indicates that agricultural production and management is still an important channel of employment for agricultural families in China.

The China Rural Panel Household Survey (CRHPS) surveyed the average period of time that family members were involved in agricultural production, and the results are shown in Table 2.8. Looking at the overall

Table 2.8 Self-employment of agricultural production and management

Location	*Self-employed persons (person)*	*Percentage of employed population (%)*	*Average period of participation (month/year)*
National	1.9	76.0	7.0
Urban	1.8	78.3	6.1
Rural	2.0	80.0	7.2
Eastern	1.9	79.2	7.0
Central	2.0	80.0	6.2
Western	2.0	76.9	7.9

Table 2.9 Average participation period in agricultural production and management

Location	*2011 (month/year)*	*2013 (month/year)*	*2015 (month/year)*
National	7.1	6.8	7.0
Urban	6.8	6.2	6.1
Rural	7.2	7.0	7.2
Eastern	7.0	6.8	7.0
Central	6.8	6.0	6.2
Western	7.7	7.6	7.9

national situation, we can see that family members who engaged in agricultural production and management spent an average of 7 months in agricultural production, among which urban agricultural families spent 6.1 months, and rural agricultural families spent 7.2 months. Looking at the regional differences, members of families in the western region spent the longest period of time on average (7.9%) engaging in agricultural production, with the shortest period spent by families in the central region (6.2 months), while the eastern region families only spent 7.0 months. In general, agricultural family members spend more than half of the time in a year in agricultural production and the rest of the time in other economic activities.

Table 2.9 shows the historical comparison of the average participation period of the agricultural families' labor force in agricultural production and management. Nationally, from 2011 to 2015, the average period of the family labor force participation in agricultural production and management has declined slightly, from 7.1 months per year in

2011 to 7.0 months per year in 2015. Among these families, the urban agricultural households' average participation in the agricultural production and management is on a significant downward trend, with 0.7 months of decline per year. However, the rural agricultural households' average period of agricultural production and management has changed little. At the regional level, the average agricultural households' participation period in agricultural production and management shows a downward trend; while that of the western region shows a slightly upward trend.

2.3.2 *Labor Force Employment*

Table 2.10 shows the employment of agricultural families' labor force. In terms of the proportion of agricultural families with an employed labor force, 9.8% of agricultural families nationwide have labor force employment. Looking at the statistics of the urban and rural areas, the proportion of employment in urban areas is 11.5%, while the proportion of employment in rural area is 9.4%, which is 0.7% lower than that of the urban area. At the regional level, the proportions of employment in the western and central regions are relatively high (10.4% and 9.9%, respectively); while the lowest employment ratio is in the eastern region (9.1%).

Among the agricultural households with labor force employment, the average number of agricultural households with employed labor is 12.4, with a median of 5. Agricultural households in urban areas employ an average of 15.5 people, while agricultural households in rural areas employ an average of 11.6 people. Looking at the regional differences, the average

Table 2.10 Labor force employment in agricultural production and management

Location	*Employment ratio (%)*	*Number of employed persons (person)*	
		Mean	*Median*
National	9.8	12.4	5.0
Urban	11.5	15.5	4.0
Rural	9.4	11.6	5.0
Eastern	9.1	11.5	4.0
Central	9.9	13.6	5.0
Western	10.4	11.8	6.0

employed labor force in the eastern and western regions are lower than that in the central region, while the median of employed labor in the western region is higher than that in the eastern and central regions.

2.4 Instruments of Agricultural Production

2.4.1 *Agricultural Machinery Ownership*

We define the instruments of agricultural production as agricultural machinery, which includes pump, thresher, power seeder, harvester, animal husbandry machinery, fishery machinery and forestry machinery. Table 2.11 shows that 32.2% of China's agricultural households own agricultural machinery. The proportion of agricultural household machinery in urban areas is 25.2%, while that of the rural area is 33.6%, which is 8.4 percentage points higher than that of urban families. The ownership of machinery is the highest in the western region, with a proportion of 36.1%, while the eastern region has the lowest proportion of 26.2%.

At the same time, we examined the value of agricultural machinery owned by households. In terms of the median value, the national level is 3000 yuan; the medians of urban and rural areas are both 3000 yuan; the median of the eastern region is 3000 yuan, which is lower than that of the central region, but still higher than that of the western region.

2.4.2 *Livestock Ownership*

Table 2.12 shows that 10.3% of agricultural households in the nation own livestock for agricultural production. The rural livestock ownership ratio is 11.3%, while the urban livestock ownership ratio is 5.6%, which is 5.7 percentage points lower than that rural agricultural households. Among

Table 2.11 Ownership of agricultural production instruments

Location	*Proportion of usage (%)*	*Value of production instruments (yuan, median)*
National	32.2	3000
Urban	25.2	3000
Rural	33.6	3000
Eastern	26.2	3000
Central	35.0	4000
Western	36.1	2650

Table 2.12 Livestock ownership

Location	*Proportion of usage (%)*	*Value of production instruments (yuan, median)*
National	10.3	7500
Urban	5.6	6500
Rural	11.3	7500
Eastern	4.5	7000
Central	6.6	7000
Western	21.8	7000

Table 2.13 Proportion of machinery hiring or leasing

Location	*Proportion of hiring or leasing (%)*
National	46.1
Urban	49.7
Rural	45.3
Eastern	48.2
Central	56.9
Western	30.2

agricultural families in the different regions, the western region has the highest proportion of livestock ownership with 21.8%, which is much higher than in the eastern and western regions; and the proportion of livestock owners in the eastern region is close to that of the central region, with 4.5% and 6.6%, respectively.

Looking at the value of livestock owned by families, the national median is 7500 yuan, while the median of the urban area is 6500 yuan, which is less than that of the rural area (7500 yuan). The medians of the eastern, central and western regions are quite close.

2.4.3 *Costs of Machinery Hiring or Leasing*

It can be seen from Table 2.13 that 46.1% of agricultural families in China hire or lease agricultural machinery for agriculture production, among which the proportion of urban agricultural families employing or renting is 49.7%, which is higher than the 45.3% of rural agricultural households. At the regional level, the proportion of hiring or leasing in the central region is the highest, reaching 56.9%, while that of the eastern and western regions are below 50%, with 48.2% and 30.2%, respectively.

Table 2.14 Machinery hiring or leasing expense, unit: %

	National	*Urban*	*Rural*	*Eastern*	*Central*	*Western*
<2000	75.7	76.0	75.6	77.4	72.8	79.1
2000–5000	18.7	17.5	19.0	17.2	22.0	14.1
5000–10,000	3.6	3.3	3.6	3.5	3.4	4.0
10,000–20,000	1.2	1.4	1.1	1.1	0.8	2.3
20,000–50,000	0.6	1.4	0.4	0.4	0.8	0.3
>50,000	0.3	0.4	0.3	0.5	0.2	0.2

As can be seen from Table 2.14, among agricultural families using machinery for agricultural production, the proportion of households with hiring or leasing costs of less than 2000 yuan is 75.7%; the proportion of households above 2000 yuan and less than 5000 yuan is 18.8%; the proportion of costs above 5000 yuan and below 10,000 yuan is 3.6%, and the families with costs above 50,000 yuan is 0.3%.

Looking at the regions, the western region has the highest proportion of households with mechanical hiring or leasing costs lower than 2000 yuan (79.1%); followed by the eastern region (77.4%); and the lowest in the central region (72.8%). Among families in the central region, the expense between 2000 yuan and 5000 yuan has the highest ratio (22.0%). The lowest percentage is in the western region (14.1%). The proportions of families in the eastern and western regions whose machinery hiring or leasing expense is between 5000 and 10,000 yuan are fairly close.

2.5 Agricultural Land

2.5.1 *Agricultural Land Ownership*

As indicated in Table 2.15, the proportion of agricultural land (cultivated land, forest land, pastureland, etc.) ownership out of all the sample families is 47.4%, of which 97.3% is owned by agricultural families, and non-agricultural families own only 22.0%. In the case of rural families alone, agricultural land ownership reaches 98.5%, and 58% of non-agricultural households have agricultural land.

As shown in Table 2.16, as far as cultivated land is concerned, the area of cultivated land contracted by the Chinese agricultural households is 7.9 mu per household in 2015. From the comparison at the regional level, the differences in the area of contracted cultivated land per household in

Table 2.15 Agricultural land ownership

Sample type	*National ownership ratio (%)*	*Rural ownership ratio (%)*
Overall	47.4	87.8
Non-agricultural family	22.0	58.0
Agricultural household	97.3	98.5

Table 2.16 Ownership of cultivated land

Location	*Mean (mu)*	*Median (mu)*
National	7.9	4.0
Urban	9.1	3.5
Rural	7.7	4.5
Eastern	5.4	4.0
Central	6.1	4.5
Western	7.4	4
Northeast	32.9	20.0

different regions are significant. In the eastern region, contracted cultivated land per household is the lowest at 5.4 mu, followed by the central region and the western region, at 6.1 mu and 7.4 mu, respectively; the cultivated land owned by agricultural households is the largest in the northeast region at 32.9 mu.[1]

As agricultural land can be transferred, the area of cultivated land used for agricultural production and management by agricultural families is different from the area of cultivated land owned. It can be seen from Table 2.17 that compared with 2013, the average area of cultivated land of agricultural households that was used for agricultural production and management in 2015 has increased to a certain extent. Among the area of cultivated land used for agricultural production and management, the national average has increased by 1.5 mu, with that of urban agricultural families increasing significantly, from 7.2 mu in 2013 to 20.4 mu in 2015, while rural agricultural families faced a mild decline in the average area of

[1] In order to thoroughly compare the differences in the area of cultivated land in different regions, this section separates the northeast region from the central region, in which includes Heilongjiang province, Jilin province and Liaoning province.

Table 2.17 Comparison of cultivated land in agricultural production and management

Location	*2013 (mu)*	*2015 (mu)*
National	9.8	11.3
Urban	7.2	20.4
Rural	10.4	10.0
Eastern	6.7	8.9
Central	13.4	7.6
Western	8.8	9.9
Northeast	–	41.4

Table 2.18 Comparison of cultivated land in agricultural production and management of rural families

Sample type	*Mean (mu)*	*Median (mu)*
Full-time agricultural family	9.4	4.0
Non-agricultural family	3.4	2.0
Part-time agricultural family	5.7	4.0

cultivated land.[2] The regional comparison shows that the area of cultivated land used for agricultural production and management has increased by 2.2 mu and 1.1 mu in the eastern region and the western region, respectively, since 2013. The agricultural production and management area of the northeast region reached 41.4 mu in 2015.

As shown in Table 2.18, comparing the three types of rural households in China, the area of cultivated land in agricultural production and management of full-time agricultural families is the largest, with up to 9.4 mu, followed by the part-time agricultural families with 5.7 mu, and then the non-agricultural families with the smallest management area of 3.4 mu.

2.5.2 *Renting of Agricultural Land*

If an agricultural household rents a cultivated land and uses it for agricultural production or animal farming, then the family is defined as a family with rented cultivated land. From Table 2.19, it can be seen that the rent-

[2] Results of the statistics show that the area of agricultural production and management of agricultural families in urban areas has increased significantly, which may be due to the comparatively small number of samples observed in the urban areas, with the total number of samples being only 710 in 2015 and 1744 in 2013.

Table 2.19 Agricultural land renting of agricultural families

Location	*Renting ratio (%)*	*Rented area (mu)*	
		Mean	*Median*
National	18.0	12.8	4.0
Urban	14.1	21.2	3.0
Rural	18.8	11.5	4.0
Eastern	14.8	11.5	3.0
Central	19.3	17.4	7.0
Western	20.2	8.6	2.5

ing ratio of agricultural households in China is 18.0%. In terms of the urban and rural areas, the renting ratio of agricultural households in rural areas is 18.8%, and that of urban families is 14.1%. Regionally speaking, the renting ratio of the western region is the highest at 20.2%, while the proportions of the eastern and the central regions are 14.8% and 19.3%, respectively. By further analyzing the rented area of families with the rented cultivated land, we can see from Table 2.19 that the average rented area per family is 12.8 mu, with the median being 4.0 mu. Looking at the urban and rural areas, the average area is 21.2 mu and the median is 3.0 mu in urban areas, while the average is 11.5 mu and the median is 4.0 mu in rural areas. At the regional level, the central region has an average rented area of 17.4 mu, with the median being 7.0 mu; the eastern region has 11.5 mu, with the median being 3.0 mu; and the western region has 8.6 mu, with the median being 2.5 mu. It is not difficult to find that the rented area of the central region is significantly larger than that of the eastern and western regions.

Table 2.20 shows the reasons why agricultural families rent cultivated land. As can be seen from the table, most agricultural households rent cultivated land to expand production or meet their own needs. On the national level, 38.2% of agricultural households rent cultivated land to expand production, 35.5% rent to meet their own needs and 18.4% rent to gain land subsidies and other revenues generated by land. Looking at the situation of the urban and rural areas, more urban families rent cultivated land to meet their own needs, while more rural families rent to expand the production scale. On the regional level, agricultural families in the eastern and central regions are more focused on expanding production, while those in the western region are more concentrated on meeting their own needs.

Table 2.20 Reasons for agricultural families' rent of agricultural land, unit: %

Location	*Expand production scale*	*Land revenue*	*Meet family needs*	*Expect land appreciation*	*Other*
National	38.2	18.4	35.5	0.1	7.8
Urban	28.8	21.9	42.6	0.0	6.7
Rural	39.7	17.9	34.4	0.1	7.9
Eastern	42.6	18.0	32.0	0.0	7.4
Central	40.4	24.6	28.6	0.0	6.4
Western	31.6	11.8	46.8	0.2	9.6

Table 2.21 Rental term of agricultural land, unit: %

Rental term (year)	*National*	*Urban*	*Rural*	*Eastern*	*Central*	*Western*
<1 year	37.1	37.5	37.0	30.6	46.8	30.8
1–5 years	27.9	26.4	28.1	23.3	25.3	35.5
5–10 years	11.0	10.5	11.0	18.5	8.8	6.6
10–20 years	6.1	4.9	6.3	9.3	4.0	5.7
20–30 years	2.7	4.7	2.4	4.0	2.9	1.3
>30 years	15.3	16.0	15.2	14.2	12.3	20.1

As can be seen from Table 2.21, 37.1% of China's agricultural families have rented cultivated land with a rental term of under 1 year, 27.9% with a rental term of between 1 and 5 years, 11.0% between 5 and 10 years, while 15.3% with a rental term exceeding 30 years. Looking at the different regions, the central region has the highest proportion of households with a rental period of within 1 year (46.8%), followed by the western region (30.8%), and the lowest in the eastern region (30.6%). In the western region, the proportion of agricultural households with a rental period of between 1 and 5 years is 35.5%, which is higher than the 25.3% in the eastern region and the 23.3% in the western region.

We further examined the source and distribution of the renting of cultivated land, as indicated in Table 2.22. About 89.2% of the families with rented cultivated land acquired their land from common agricultural families, while 5.4% and 5.8% of the families rented from large and specialized agricultural families as well as companies or enterprises, respectively. On the whole, the table indicates that the currently cultivated land is mainly circulated from the common agricultural households to the agricultural families.

Table 2.22 Sources of agricultural land renting

Source of renting	*Proportion (%)*
Common agricultural household	89.2
Large and specialized agricultural households	5.4
Family farm	0.2
Cooperative	0.1
Village collective	0.1
Company or enterprise	5.8
Intermediary organization	0.3
Other	0.6

2.6 Procurement of Agricultural Materials

2.6.1 Types and Value of Agricultural Material Procurement

As can be seen from Table 2.23, the proportions of agricultural families that purchase seeds, pesticides, herbicides and fertilizers all exceed 50%, with 87.5%, 88.7%, 74.6% and 93.4%, respectively; 32.1% of rural household chose to purchase agricultural films, 12.4% of agricultural households purchase small agricultural machinery, 10.9% of agricultural households procure seedlings, and only 4.0% of agricultural households purchase young seedling. Statistics of the rural and urban areas show that the proportions of the urban agricultural households' procurement are slightly higher than rural agricultural households, in the types of seedling, young seedling and small agricultural machinery; and that the proportions of commonly used agricultural materials procured by rural agricultural households are mostly higher than those of agricultural households in the urban areas. Among the commonly used materials, the average procurement ratio gaps of pesticide, herbicide, fertilizer and agricultural film are relatively large, which are 7.9 percentage points, 11.3 percentage points, 8.6 percentage points and 6.3 percentage points higher than those of the urban agricultural families, respectively.

At the regional level, the proportion of agricultural material procurement of agricultural households in the central region is generally higher. About 92.4% of the households in the central region chose to buy seeds, which is higher than the 81.3% in the eastern region and 89.1% in the western region; 90.5% of the households chose to buy pesticides, which is higher than the 86.9% in the eastern region and 88.7% in the western

Table 2.23 Types of agricultural material procurement, unit: %

	Seed	*Seedling*	*Young seedling*	*Pesticide*	*Herbicide*	*Fertilizer*	*Agricultural film*	*Small agricultural machinery*
National	87.5	10.9	4.0	88.7	74.6	93.4	32.1	12.4
Urban	86.5	13.7	5.0	82.3	65.3	88.0	26.9	12.9
Rural	87.7	10.3	3.8	90.1	76.6	94.6	33.2	12.4
Eastern	81.3	12.6	5.2	86.9	69.5	91.1	27.4	9.3
Central	92.4	6.1	1.7	90.5	80.5	95.4	22.9	10.8
Western	89.1	14.6	5.5	88.7	73.6	93.7	49.0	18.3

Table 2.24 Agricultural material expense per mu

Location	*Expense (yuan)*
National	1477.6
Urban	1663.7
Rural	1458.6
Eastern	1381.4
Central	1920.9
Western	1225.4

region; 80.5% of the households chose to buy herbicides, which is higher than the 69.5% in the eastern region and 73.6% in the western region; while the proportion of households buying fertilizer is 95.4%, which is higher than 91.1% in the eastern region and 93.7% in the western region. The proportion of households purchasing agricultural film in the western region reached 49.0%, which is well above the 27.4% and 22.9% in the eastern and central regions respectively; and 18.3% of households opted to buy small agricultural machinery, which exceeds the 9.3% in the eastern region and 10.8% in the central region.

As shown in Table 2.24, the national agricultural material expense per mu of agricultural families is 1477.6 yuan. The agricultural material expense per mu for urban agricultural families is 1663.7 yuan, which is higher than that of rural households (1458.6 yuan). Looking at the regional differences, the average agricultural material procurement cost of agricultural households in the central region is 1920.9 yuan per mu, which is much higher than that of the eastern region (1381.4 yuan) and that of the western region (1225.4 yuan).

2.6.2 *Channels of Agricultural Material Procurement*

Agricultural families mainly purchase agricultural materials through the agricultural material market, sales personnel, agricultural material stores/supermarkets, e-commerce platform, and so on. From Table 2.25, it can be seen that most agricultural households in China purchase agricultural materials from agricultural stores/supermarkets, making up 61.4% in total. This is followed by families that purchase agricultural materials through the agricultural market, which accounts for 30.9%; while the channel with the lowest proportion is the e-commerce platform with only 0.2%.

Table 2.25 Channels of agricultural material procurement, unit: %

	National	*Urban*	*Rural*	*Eastern*	*Central*	*Western*
Agricultural material market	30.9	31.5	30.8	25.5	25.3	44.2
Sales personnel marketing in rural areas	6.8	6.4	7.0	8.4	6.4	5.7
Agricultural material store/supermarket	61.4	60.3	61.6	65.3	67.8	48.9
E-commerce platform	0.2	0.2	0.1	0.1	0.1	0.3
Other	0.7	1.5	0.5	0.8	0.5	0.9

At the regional level, the distribution proportion of the channels of procurement in the eastern and central regions is relatively close, with the agricultural market and agricultural stores/supermarkets accounting for 25.5% and 65.3%, and 25.3% and 67.8%, respectively. In the western region, the agricultural material market accounts for 44.2% which is far higher than that of the eastern region and the central region, while agricultural stores/supermarkets account for only 48.9%, lower than that of the eastern region and the central region.

2.7 Total Output Value of Family Farming and Sales Revenue

2.7.1 Total Output Value of Family Farming

The total output value of China's agricultural families is shown in Fig. 2.1. At the regional level, the average output value of agriculture in the eastern region is 38,478 yuan, with a median of 7000 yuan; 46,404 yuan in the central region, with a median of 9000 yuan; and 19,102 yuan in the western region, with a median of 6200 yuan. From the average output values, we can see that the agricultural output value is the highest in the central region, followed by the eastern region; the western region has the lowest value, and the value of central region is about 2.4 times of that of the western region, with a relatively large regional disparity; the middle region has the highest median, while those of the eastern region and the western region are rather close.

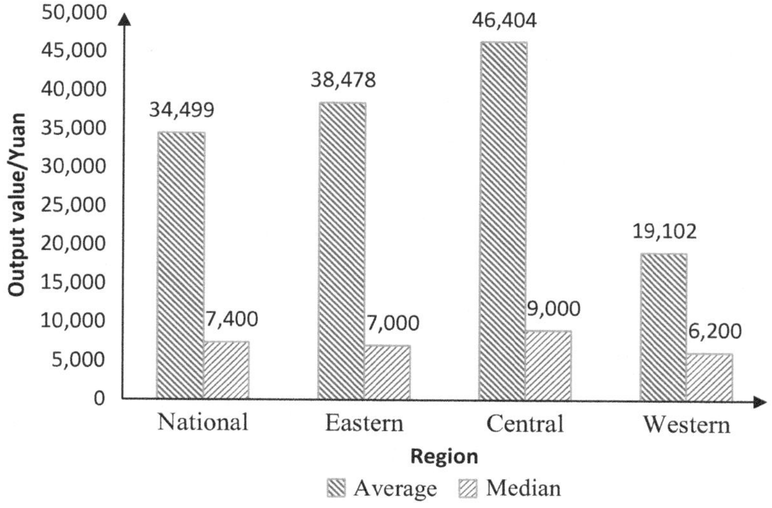

Fig. 2.1 Regions and agricultural production output value, unit: yuan

Table 2.26 Whether agricultural products are sold or not

Location	*Sold ratio (%)*
National	69.6
Urban	64.3
Rural	70.7
Eastern	72.0
Central	77.6
Western	56.8

2.7.2 *Sales Channels of Agricultural Products*

As can be seen from Table 2.26, 69.6% of the agricultural households in China sell their own agricultural products, of which 64.3% of the urban agricultural families sell their own agricultural products, which is less than the 70.7% of the rural areas. At the regional level, the proportion of households selling self-produced agricultural products in the central region is the highest with 77.6%, followed by 72% in the eastern region; and the lowest is in the western region, with only 56.8%.

Table 2.27 Sales channels of agricultural products, unit: %

	National	*Urban*	*Rural*	*Eastern*	*Central*	*Western*
Online sales	0.3	0.6	0.2	0.5	0.1	0
Foreign businessmen's door-to-door acquisition	39.3	35.1	40.2	43.1	37.6	36.2
Self-marketing	23.6	25.5	23.2	22.3	15.7	38.7
Sell to other local big sellers	28.3	29.7	28.0	28.1	33.9	19.1
Sell to processing companies	6.5	5.7	6.6	4.2	7.2	8.8
Consumer door-to-door acquisition	14.7	16.1	14.4	15.5	14.8	13.0
Other	0.9	1.7	0.7	0.9	1.0	0.6

Note: Due to the design of the questionnaire, the proportion of non-online sales add up to 100%

From Table 2.27, it can be seen that in addition to online sales, most of the sales channels of agricultural products are distributed relatively evenly, of which on average, "foreign businessmen's door-to-door acquisition", "selling their own products to the market" and "selling to other big local sellers" are the main sales channels of agricultural products. About 39.3% of the nation's agricultural households sell their agricultural products through the foreign businessmen's door-to-door acquisition channel, which takes the largest share, followed by selling to other big local sellers and selling their own products to the market, which accounts for 28.3% and 23.6%, respectively.

Looking at the regional differences, in the eastern region, the channel of agricultural product sales with the highest proportion is the foreign businessmen's door-to-door acquisition, accounting for 43.1%; in the central region, the proportion of "foreign businessmen's door-to-door acquisition" and "selling to other big local sellers" are relatively close, which are 37.6% and 33.9%, respectively; the western region mainly sell products through the channels of foreign businessmen's door-to-door acquisition and selling their own products to the market, which accounts for 36.2% and 38.7%, respectively.

The situation of agricultural families selling agricultural products through the Internet is shown in Table 2.28. The statistics show that the proportion of agricultural households selling agricultural products through the Internet in 2015 is less than 1%, thus, online sales still have much potential in China. Looking at the results of the urban and rural areas, the proportion of agricultural households in urban areas selling agricultural products through the Internet is higher than that of rural agricultural households. According to the statistics of the urban agricultural

Table 2.28 Online sales of agricultural products, unit: %

	National	*Urban*	*Rural*	*Eastern*	*Central*	*Western*
All	0.0	0.0	0.0	0.0	0.0	0.0
Most	0.0	0.0	0.0	0.0	0.0	0.0
Half	0.1	0.1	0.1	0.1	0.0	0.0
Small part	0.2	0.5	0.1	0.4	0.1	0.0
None	99.7	99.4	99.8	99.5	99.9	100.0

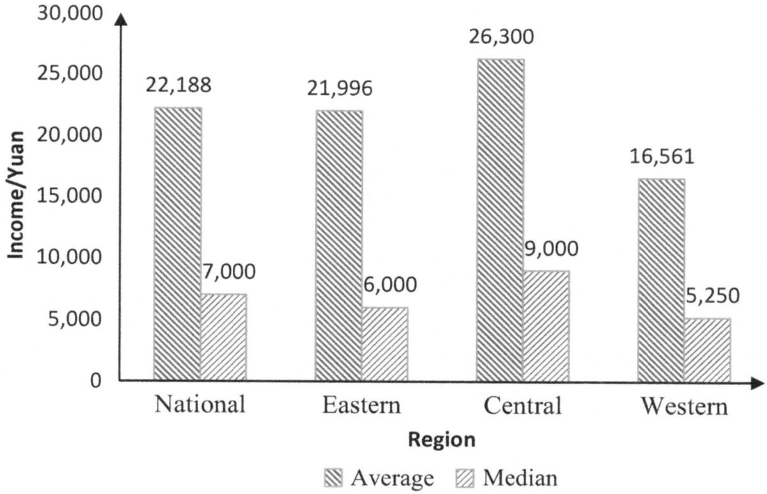

Fig. 2.2 Regions and agricultural gross revenue, unit: yuan

families in different regions, the proportion of agricultural products sold online in the eastern region (99.5%) is higher than that of other regions, while there are barely any agricultural products sold through the Internet in the western region.

2.7.3 Sales Revenue of Agricultural Products

The (gross) sales revenue of agricultural products of China's agricultural families is shown in Fig. 2.2. In 2015, the average (gross) sales revenue of agricultural products of China's agricultural families was 22,188 yuan, with a median of 7000 yuan. Looking at the regional differences, the average (gross) sales revenue of agricultural products of the eastern region valued 21,996 yuan, with a median of 6000 yuan; 26,300 yuan in the central region, with a median of 9000 yuan; 16,561 yuan in the western region, with a median of 5250 yuan. The central region has the highest average sales revenue, followed by the eastern region; and the western region has the lowest revenue. The highest median is the central region, which is approximately twice the amount of that in the western region.

2.7.4 *Rate of Commercialization*

By dividing the agricultural sales (gross) revenue of the samples by the total output value of family farming, we calculated the rate of commercialization of agricultural products produced by agricultural households, as shown in Fig. 2.3. The average rate of commercialization of agricultural products produced by agricultural households in China was 62.0% in 2015. The rate of commercialization of agricultural products by rural agricultural families was 62.1%, which is higher than that of the urban agricultural households (61.2%). At the regional level, the agricultural products' rate of commercialization of the central region is the highest, which is 66.9%; and the commercialization rate of agricultural products of the eastern region is slightly lower than that in the central region, for 63.2%; the western region has the lowest rate of only 54.9%.

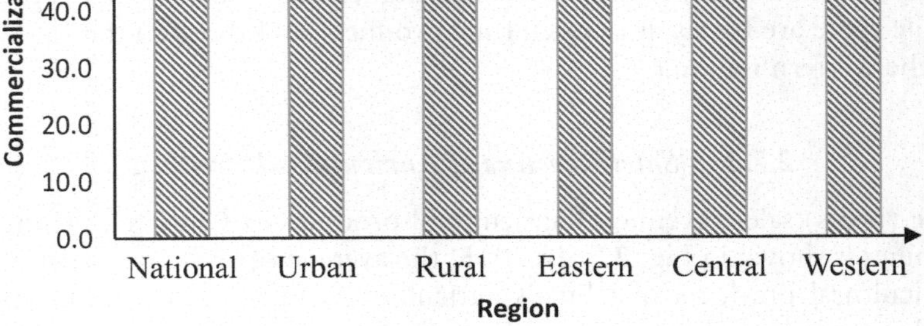

Fig. 2.3 Regions and agricultural sales (gross) revenue

2.8 Production Subsidy

As indicated in Table 2.29, 72.4% of China's agricultural families receive agricultural production subsidy, with a median subsidy amount of 400 yuan. The proportion of rural and urban families acquiring subsidies is 73.2% and 68.6%, respectively, and the median subsidy amount for rural areas is higher than that of urban areas, which are 400 yuan and 360 yuan, respectively. In terms of the different regions, the proportion of subsidy acquisition in the eastern region is 68.1%, the median of subsidy is 363 yuan; the highest percentage of subsidy acquisition is 80.8% in the central region, which also has the highest median subsidy amount of 500 yuan; while in the western region where the economy is comparatively backward, 67.2% of families receive subsidy and the median subsidy amount is 350 yuan.

We have further examined the situation of agricultural subsidies of agricultural families in food crop and cash crop production. It can be seen from Table 2.30 that the proportion of agricultural households that only plant food crop receives the highest subsidies, reaching 79.4%, as well as receiving the highest subsidy, with the median of 450 yuan; and 47.1% of agricultural families that grow cash crops alone receive subsidy, with the median subsidy amount of 300 yuan.

Table 2.29 Agricultural production subsidies

Location	*Subsidy ratio (%)*	*Subsidy amount (yuan, median)*
National	72.4	400
Urban	68.6	360
Rural	73.2	400
Eastern	68.1	363
Central	80.8	500
Western	67.2	350

Table 2.30 Rent of agricultural land

Crop type	*Subsidy variable (%)*	*Subsidy amount (yuan, median)*
Food crops only	79.4	450
Cash crops only	47.1	300

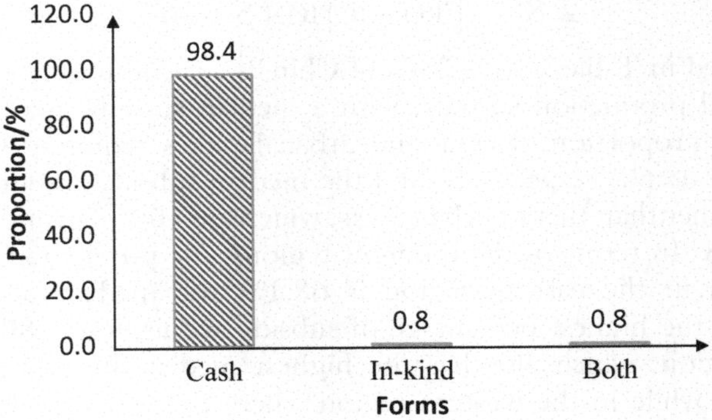

Fig. 2.4 Agricultural production subsidy

There are three main forms of agricultural production subsidies for agricultural families: cash subsidy, subsidy in kind or both. As shown in Fig. 2.4, in 2015, 98.4% of agricultural households received monetary subsidies, and only 0.8% households were subsidized in kind, while 0.8% of the agricultural families received both cash and in-kind subsidies.

CHAPTER 3

Land Utilization and Circulation of Rural Households

The household contract responsibility system is a basic rural land system in China, which distributes the agricultural land relatively evenly to rural families. Although the household contract responsibility system ensures the fairness of the agricultural land system to a great extent, with the development of social economy, the average distribution of agricultural land has begun to go against the efficiency of agricultural land utilization. An important factor is the differentiation of rural families in employment. Some rural families prefer non-agricultural employment, which creates idle land; however, agricultural households that are committed to agricultural production and management are facing a shortage of cultivated land. Therefore, the land of rural families should be readjusted to meet the needs of economic development. Under the premise of ensuring that the rural land ownership and the contract system remain unchanged, agricultural land circulation becomes an important readjustment method. This chapter, by using data from the China Rural Household Panel Survey of Zhejiang University (CRHPS) to analyze the land utilization and circulation of China's rural households, is mainly composed of three sections: Basic Situation of China's Agricultural Land, Circulation of Cultivated Land (general situation, effects and influencing factors) and Land Expropriation. The sample families involved in this chapter include both rural household samples and urban family samples with a total of 16,373 cases, which are slightly different to the previous chapters. A total of 11,654 rural household samples were used to analyze land expropriation,

© Zhejiang University Press 2020
W. Qian et al., *The Economy of Chinese Rural Households*,
https://doi.org/10.1007/978-981-13-8591-9_3

confirmation and circulation, as well as circulation disputes and circulation services. In addition, data from surveys before 2015 were used in some parts of the content to analyze the trends, and these relevant data were all collected from the China Household Finance Survey (CHFS) database of the Southwestern University of Finance and Economics.

The results of this chapter show that 35.9% of Chinese agricultural households were involved in agricultural land circulation in 2015, which is 11.8% higher than that in 2013. In 2013, the rent for transfer-out cultivated land was 383 yuan per mu, and the rent for transfer-in cultivated land was 298 yuan per mu. In 2015, the rent for transfer-out cultivated land had increased to 425 yuan per mu and the rent for transfer-in cultivated land had increased to 443 yuan per mu. For transfer-out cultivated land, the average rent with the involvement of the village committee was 590 yuan per mu, while the average rent without the involvement of the village committee was 388 yuan per mu. For the transfer-in cultivated land, the average rent with the involvement of the village committee was 629 yuan per mu, while the average rent without the involvement of the village committee was 434 yuan per mu. Of rural households that had purchased houses in urban areas, 35.7% transferred out the cultivated land, which is 21% higher than those that had not purchased houses in urban areas.

3.1 Basic Situation of Agricultural Land

3.1.1 General Situation of Samples

The area of cultivated land contracted by rural households in the China Rural Panel Household Survey (CRHPS) of Zhejiang University is comparable with external data. *Communiqué on Land and Resources of China 2013* showed that the arable land in China totaled 2.03 billion mu among which rural households contracted cultivated land covered 1.33 billion mu. According to the 2015 CRHPS data, the area of cultivated land contracted by China's rural households was 1.29 billion mu (excluding Xinjiang, Tibet, Hong Kong, Macao and Taiwan). For Henan, Hunan, Shaanxi, Anhui, Sichuan and other provinces, the area of cultivated land contracted by rural households in the CRHPS was very close to external data (Fig. 3.1).

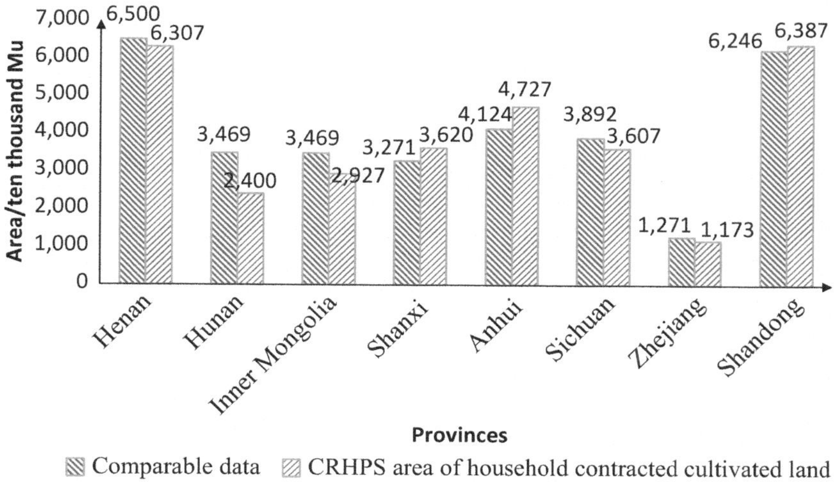

Fig. 3.1 Comparison between the area of cultivated land contracted by rural families in the 2015 CRHPS and external data, unit: 10,000 mu. Data source: work report and statistical yearbook of provincial governments

Table 3.1 Proportion of households with various types of land management right certificates

Category	*Cultivated land (%)*	*Woodland (%)*	*Grassland (%)*	*Garden (%)*
National	42.2	51.9	43.4	34.5
Agricultural family	42.0	51.2	47.9	34.7
Non-agricultural family	43.1	56.0	21.3	32.6
Eastern	40.4	29.8	17.7	33.7
Central	31.2	47.8	28.2	29.7
Western	57.8	61.5	48.1	40.8

3.1.2 Confirmation and Issuance of Certificates of Land

The confirmation and issuance of land certificates are the bases of regulating the circulation of agricultural land. Table 3.1 shows the proportion of the various types of certificates of land management rights owned by rural families. Nationwide, rural families with the certificate of woodland management rights account for the highest (51.9%) followed by grassland (43.4%), cultivated land (42.2%) and garden plot (34.5%), which indicates that our work on the confirmation and issuance of land certificates has not yet been universalized and perfected. Compared with non-agricultural households, agricultural families have a higher proportion of grassland management certificate, reaching 47.9%, but its ownership rate of woodland management certificate, which is 51.2%, is rather low. From the perspective of regional differences, the proportion of rural families in the eastern and central regions of China that owns various kinds of land right certificates is below the national average, while the implementation of the confirmation and issuance of certificates of land management in the western region is rather well, with the proportion of rural families with various kinds of land management right certificates higher than the national average.

To some extent, the views of rural families on the confirmation and issuance of land certificates reflect the effects of the implementation of this measure. A vast majority (94.8%) of Chinese rural households think that the confirmation and issuance of land certificates have brought benefits to farmers, and among them, agricultural families have a comparatively higher approval rate of this measure, reaching 95.4%. The approval rates of rural households in the eastern and central regions are similar and the rate in the western region is higher than 95% (Table 3.2).

Among those in the rural households who believe that the confirmation and issuance of certificates of land are not able to bring benefits, 31.8% consider that the "no increase or reduction of land by population" rule is unfair to a portion of agricultural households. Among them, 14% consider that the confirmation and issuance of land certificates are not good for land consolidation, and 13.2% consider that it is because farmers' awareness of land rights protection has grown, and the agricultural land circulation has become slow (Table 3.3).

Table 3.2 Proportion of rural families that consider the confirmation and issuance of land certificates can bring benefits

Category	*Recognition ratio (%)*
National	94.8
Agricultural family	95.4
Non-agricultural family	92.9
Eastern	94.4
Central	94.7
Western	95.3

Table 3.3 Proportion of reasons why the confirmation and issuance of land certificates cannot bring benefits

	Proportion (%)
"No increase or reduction of land by population" rule is unfair to part of agricultural households	31.8
Farmers' awareness of land rights protection grows and the circulation of agricultural land is slow	13.2
Not good for land consolidation	14.0
Other	41.1

3.2 Circulation of Cultivated Land

3.2.1 General Situation of the Circulation of Cultivated Land

3.2.1.1 Common Agricultural Households Are the Main Participants of Transfer-In and Transfer-Out of Cultivated Land

In the circulation of agricultural land, families either transfer in or transfer out their cultivated land, but rarely do both. In 2013, about 24.1% of agricultural households participated in the circulation of cultivated land. Among them, about 12.7% transferred out their cultivated land, and about 11% transferred in cultivated land. Only 0.4% of them did both. In 2015, about 32.9% of rural households participated in cultivated land circulation. Among them, about 18.9% transferred out their cultivated land, and about 13.7% transferred in cultivated land, while only 0.3% did both (Table 3.4).

In the circulation of agricultural land, although the proportion of transfer-out households is larger than that of transfer-in households, the average circulation area of transfer-out households is smaller than that of transfer-in households. Among the sample households, transfer-out households account for 19.2%, which is higher than transfer-in households, whose proportion is 14.1%. However, the average circulation area of transfer-in households is 4.7 mu, which is less than the average circulation area of transfer-in households of 13.6 mu. The circulation in different regions has similar characteristics, but that of the northeast region is an exception (Table 3.5).

Common agricultural households are the main participants in both transfer-in and transfer-out of cultivated land. The rural households that participated in the circulation of cultivated land are divided into common

Table 3.4 Agricultural households' participation in circulation

	2013		*2015*	
	Sample number	*Proportion (%)*	*Sample number*	*Proportion (%)*
Agricultural households involved in the circulation of agricultural land	2759	24.1	5392	32.9
Agricultural households that transferred out agricultural land only	1457	12.7	3088	18.9
Agricultural households that transferred in agricultural land only	1257	11.0	2244	13.7
Agricultural households involved in both	45	0.4	60	0.3
Agricultural households not involved in the circulation of cultivated land	8702	75.9	10,981	67.1
Total samples	11,461	100	16,373	100

agricultural households, enterprises, farmers' cooperative, family farms as well as large and specialized agricultural family operation. The characteristics of production and operation of the latter groups are obviously different from that of common agricultural households. Therefore, these groups are collectively referred to as other business entities. In the transfer-in and transfer-out of cultivated land, common agricultural households accounted for the vast majority of the proportion. In 2013, common agricultural households accounted for 82.6% and 97.1%, respectively, in transferring in and transferring out their cultivated land, and in 2015, the proportions are 82.2% and 86.8%, respectively (Table 3.6).

3.2.1.2 Circulation of Agricultural Land Is Mainly for Agricultural Use

The use of cultivated land circulation is still dominated by agricultural use. In 2013, cultivated land transferred out for planting and animal farming accounted for 91.4% and 3.98%, respectively, and those transferred in for planting and animal farming accounted for 95.9% and 3.14%, respectively. In 2015, the proportion of cultivated land transferred out and in for planting increased to 94.8% and 97.2%, respectively, and the proportion of that transferred for animal farming decreased to 2.2% and 2.0%, respectively (Table 3.7).

Table 3.5 Transfer-out and transfer-in of cultivated land by agricultural households in 2015

	Proportion of transfer-out agricultural households (%)	*The average circulation area of transfer-out agricultural households (mu)*		*Transfer-in agricultural household Proportion (%)*	*The average circulation area of transfer-in agricultural households (mu)*	
		Mean	*Median*		*Mean*	*Median*
National agricultural households	19.2	4.7	3.0	14.1	13.6	3.7
Agricultural households in the eastern region	21.1	3.9	2.5	11.3	12.2	3.0
Agricultural households in the central region	19.0	3.7	3.0	13.9	8.9	4.0
Agricultural households in the western region	17.1	4.7	2.5	16.1	9.5	2.5
Agricultural households in the northeast region	19.4	12.3	10.0	21.2	42.3	25.0

3.2.1.3 Paid Agricultural Land Transfer Is at a Relatively Low Level

The proportion of paid agricultural land transfer is comparatively small. In 2013, the proportion of paid transfer was 75%. In 2015, the proportion was 53.4%. In the paid cultivated land transfer, the rent is paid mainly in cash. In 2015, the proportion of fixed cash rent was about 73.4% and the proportion of rent-in-kind (including the conversion to cash and agricultural products according to the grain price of the year) was about 22%. In addition, dividend on shares and rent by regular negotiation started to be popular in some areas, accounting for about 4% (Table 3.8).

The rent level of cultivated land circulation is low. In the cultivated land circulation for agricultural use, the rent for transfer-out cultivated land was 383 yuan per mu and the rent for transfer-in cultivated land was 298 yuan

Table 3.6 Entities engaged in circulation

	2013				2015			
	Transfer-out		*Transfer-in*		*Transfer-out*		*Transfer-in*	
	Sample number	*Proportion (%)*	*Sample number*	*Proportion (%)*	*Sample number*	*Proportion (%)*	*Sample number*	*Proportion (%)*
Common agricultural households	1223	82.6	1259	97.1	2510	82.2	1968	86.8
Other business entities	257	17.4	38	2.9	545	17.8	300	13.2
Overall	1480	100	1297	100.00	3055	100	2266	100

Table 3.7 Use of circulated agricultural land

		2013				*2015*			
		Transfer-out		*Transfer-in*		*Transfer-out*		*Transfer-in*	
		Sample number	*Proportion (%)*	*Sample number*	*Proportion (%)*	*Sample number*	*Proportion (%)*	*Sample number*	*Proportion (%)*
Agricultural use	Planting	1332	91.4	1251	95.9	2884	94.8	2198	97.2
	Animal farming	58	4.0	41	3.1	66	2.2	45	2.0
Non-agricultural	Service management	13	0.9	5	0.4	23	0.8	6	0.3
	Building factory	35	2.4	8	0.6	36	1.2	1	0.1
	Other	20	1.3	0	0.0	34	1.0	11	0.4
Overall		1458	100	1305	100	3044	100	2261	100

Table 3.8 Proportion of paid agricultural land transfer

	2013		*2015*	
	Sample number	*Proportion (%)*	*Sample number*	*Proportion (%)*
Paid circulation	2070	75.0	2857	53.4
Free circulation	689	25.0	2496	46.6
Overall	2759	100.00	5353	100.00

Table 3.9 Rents for agricultural land circulation

		Agricultural use		*Non-agricultural use*	
		Mean (yuan/mu)	*Median (yuan/mu)*	*Mean (yuan/mu)*	*Median (yuan/mu)*
2013	Transfer-out	383	200	1693	1000
	Transfer-in	298	150	997	600
2015	Transfer-out	425	333	2927	1200
	Transfer-in	443	300	1495	12

per mu in 2013. In 2015, the land transfer rent for agricultural use increased slightly, reaching 425 yuan and 443 yuan per mu for transfer-out and transfer-in cultivated land, respectively. Land transfer rents for non-agricultural use are significantly higher than those for agricultural use. The former is more than twice times the latter. Nevertheless, the overall rent level of cultivated land circulation is still low because it's mainly for agricultural use (Table 3.9).

The rent to income ratio of the circulation of cultivated land, which is the rent for cultivated land circulation per mu divided by agricultural net income per mu, is also relatively low. In 2015, the rent-income ratio of the circulation of cultivated land in China was about 17.1%. The difference of the rent-income ratio in different regions was obvious. The highest is in the northeast region with about 28.2%; the lowest is in the central region with less than 10% (Fig. 3.2).

The rents for cultivated land circulation with the involvement of village committees are generally higher than those without the involvement of village committees. For transfer-out cultivated land, the average rent with the involvement of village committees is 590 yuan per mu, while the

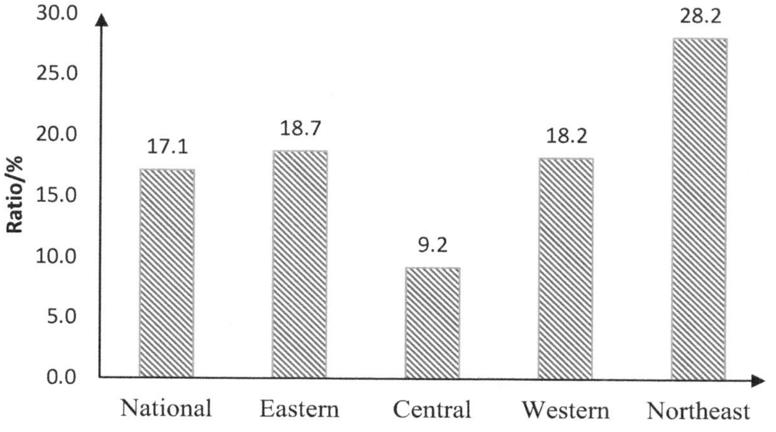

Fig. 3.2 Proportion of rent in agricultural income in different regions in 2015, unit: %

Table 3.10 Village committee intervention and circulation rent in 2015

	With village committee intervention		*Without village committee intervention*	
	Transfer-out (yuan/mu)	*Transfer-in (yuan/mu)*	*Transfer-out (yuan/mu)*	*Transfer-in (yuan/mu)*
National	590	629	388	434
Eastern	623	650	454	511
Central	382	207	249	322
Western	645	1117	356	352
Northeast	715	375	486	567

average rent without the involvement of village committees is 388 yuan per mu. For transfer-in cultivated land, the average rent with the involvement of village committees is 629 yuan per mu, while the average rent without the involvement of village committees is 434 yuan per mu. The relationship between circulation rents and the involvement of village committees is widespread in all regions, except for the transfer-in of cultivated land in the central and northeastern regions (Table 3.10).

3.2.1.4 The Degree of Agricultural Land Circulation Is Relatively Low

The proportion of irregular circulation of agricultural land is relatively high. In 2013, the proportion of irregular transfer in the transfer-out of agricultural land was 35.3% and the proportion of irregular transfer in the transfer-in of agricultural land was 36.3%. In 2015, irregular circulation accounted for 51.7% and 43.8% in transfer-out cultivated land and transfer-in cultivated land, respectively (Table 3.11).

The time limit for the circulation of agricultural land is relatively short. Although the time limit for cultivated land circulation for non-agricultural use is more than 10 years, the time limit for cultivated land circulation, which is more common, is only half of the former. In 2013, agricultural land for agricultural use was transferred out with an average time limit of 5.1 years and was transferred in with an average time limit of 4.5 years. In 2015, agricultural land for agricultural use was transferred out with an average time limit of 6.1 years and was transferred in with an average time limit of 5.5 years (Table 3.12).

There is a great difference in the time limit for cultivated land circulation among the regions. The time limit is the shortest in northeast China: merely 1.1 years on average for transfer-out cultivated land and 3 years for

Table 3.11 Regular circulation and irregular circulation of agricultural land

		Regular		*Irregular*	
		Sample size	*Proportion (%)*	*Sample size*	*Proportion (%)*
2013	Transfer-out	972	64.7	530	35.3
	Transfer-in	830	63.7	472	36.3
2015	Transfer-out	1486	48.3	1587	51.7
	Transfer-in	1276	56.2	994	43.8

Table 3.12 Time limit for agricultural land circulation

		Agricultural use		*Non-agricultural use*	
		Mean (year)	*Median (year)*	*Mean (year)*	*Median (year)*
2013	Transfer-out	5.1	1.0	13.2	11.0
	Transfer-in	4.5	1.0	18.5	15.0
2015	Transfer-out	6.1	3.0	12.1	10.0
	Transfer-in	5.5	2.0	21.9	20.0

Table 3.13 Time limit for cultivated land transfer for agricultural use in 2015

Location	*Transfer-out*		*Transfer-in*	
	Mean (year)	*Median (year)*	*Mean (year)*	*Median (year)*
National	6.3	5.0	5.5	2.0
Eastern	4.0	4.0	6.9	3.0
Central	9.2	5.0	7.1	3.0
Western	12.7	10.0	4.4	2.0
Northeast	1.1	1.0	3.0	1.0

transfer-in cultivated land. The western region has the longest time limit for transfer-out land: 12.7 years on average, while the time limit for transfer-in cultivated land in the central region is the longest, being 7.1 years on average (Table 3.13).

The time limit for cultivated land circulation is longer when involved with village committees. The average time limit for cultivated land transfer-out with village committees' intervention was 9.3 years, while the average time limit for cultivated land transfer-out without village committees' intervention was only 5.2 years. The average time limit for cultivated land transfer-in with village committees' intervention was 6.1 years, while the average time limit for cultivated land transfer-in without village committees' intervention was only 5.5 years. The relationship between the time limit for circulation and whether village committees are involved in circulation is prevalent in all regions, except for the transfer-in of cultivated land in the eastern region (Table 3.14).

3.2.1.5 Disputes Over the Circulation of Agricultural Land

The circulation of agricultural land involves the benefits of the transfer-in party and the transfer-out party and thus disputes over the circulation arise. There are 3.1% of rural families in China who have encountered land disputes, and non-agricultural families account for a higher proportion in encountering disputes than agricultural families. The proportion of land disputes shows a significant difference in different regions, among which the western region is the highest (3.7%), followed by the central region (3.2%), and then the eastern region (2.7%) (Table 3.15).

In the causes of land disputes, non-contractual disputes account for the largest proportion, exceeding 50%; the proportion of disputes arising from

Table 3.14 Time limit for cultivated land transfer and village committees' intervention in 2015

Location	*With village committees' intervention*		*Without village committees' intervention*	
	Transfer-out (year)	*Transfer-in (year)*	*Transfer-out (year)*	*Transfer-in (year)*
National	9.3	6.1	5.2	5.5
Eastern	8.4	6.1	4.7	7.0
Central	7.6	7.8	5.4	7.1
Western	12.3	5.5	7.9	4.4
Northeast	7.7	4.1	2.0	3.0

Table 3.15 Proportions of families that have encountered land disputes

Category	*Proportion (%)*
National	3.1
Agricultural families	3.0
Non-agricultural families	3.5
Eastern	2.7
Central	3.2
Western	3.7

subsidies is 20.1%, and the disputes arising from contracts account for a relatively small proportion: 16.0%. Therefore, it is effective to reduce agricultural disputes by formulating and strictly implementing scientific and reasonable subsidy standards as well as regulating related non-contractual circulation affairs (Table 3.16).

Cultivated land circulation rent can be paid using different methods. Nationwide, rural families that chose the payment of fixed amount account for the most (51.1%), and non-agricultural households prefer the conversion of rent-in-kind at market prices. Comparing to the eastern and central regions, rural households in the western region have a larger proportion of other ways of payment except for conversion of in-kind rents at the market price, fixed rent and conversion into shares (Table 3.17).

Besides land rent, there are trading information fee, intermediary fee and other types of expenses in the circulation of agricultural land. Figure 3.3 reflects the costs other than rent. The rural households across the country spent an average of 165.1 yuan, in which agricultural house-

Table 3.16 Causes of land disputes

Causes of disputes	*Proportion (%)*
Contractual disputes	16.0
Non-contractual disputes	52.9
Subsidy disputes	20.1
Other	11.0

Table 3.17 Proportion of households using different payment methods in the rent of agricultural land transfer

	National (%)	*Agricultural family (%)*	*Non-agricultural family (%)*	*Eastern (%)*	*Central (%)*	*Western (%)*
Rent in-kind at market price	14.0	12.6	17.8	15.3	14.5	11.9
Fixed rent	51.1	53.4	45.2	62.3	52.7	35.8
Conversion into shares, dividend by shares	0.3	0.3	0.0	0.2	0.5	0.1
Other	34.6	33.7	37.0	22.2	32.3	52.2

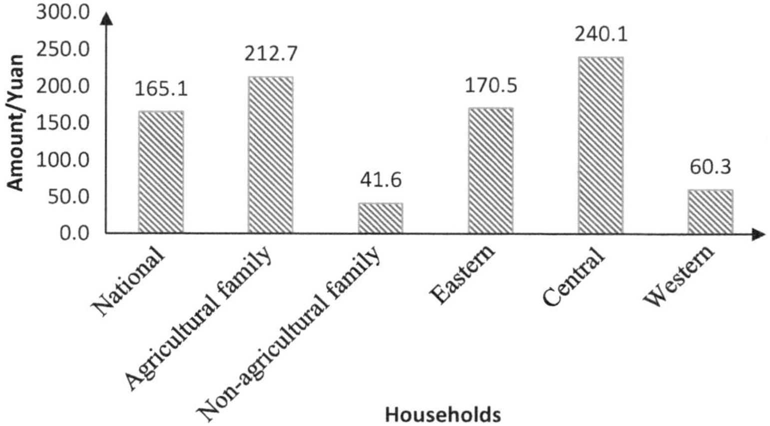

Fig. 3.3 Costs other than rent

holds and non-agricultural households had a huge difference. The agricultural households spent an average of 212.7 yuan and non-agricultural households spent only 41.6 yuan. From a regional perspective, rural households in the central region had the most additional expense (240.1 yuan), followed by the eastern region (170.5 yuan) and then the western region, at 60.3 yuan. The expenditures of the different regions vary significantly.

3.2.1.6 Services in the Circulation of Agricultural Land

Different types of services for rural families provided a lot of convenience for agricultural land circulation. About 81.4% of rural households thought that they don't need any services, but 10.6% of rural households urgently needed new services of agricultural circulation. Among rural households, 9.1% needed services to coordinate and standardize the contract signing and 8.8% of rural households needed services that offer publicity and interpretation of the agricultural circulation policy. In addition, 8.5% of rural households needed rent assessment of farmland circulation and 5–7% of rural households needed services that offer land dispute meditation, legal consulting and circulation supervision, and so on (Table 3.18).

Although rural households have different types of requirements for services, the proportion of which that had obtained any kinds of services in agricultural land circulation is very small, with only 7%. Nationwide, only 3.1% of rural households had received services of coordinating and standardizing contract signing. Only 2.7% of rural households had received

Table 3.18 Proportion of households in need of different types of services in agricultural land transfer

Type of service	*National (%)*
Provide information on agricultural land transfer	10.6
Provide information and interpretation of the agricultural land transfer policy	8.8
Provide an assessment of the rent of agricultural land transfer	8.5
Provide legal consulting service	6.6
Coordinate and regulate contract signing	9.1
Supervising the circulation behavior	5.9
Meditation of land disputes	6.8
No service needed	81.4

Table 3.19 Proportion of households that received different types of services in agricultural land transfer

Type of service	*National (%)*
Provide information on agricultural land transfer	2.7
Provide information and interpretation of agricultural land transfer policy	1.8
Provide an assessment of the rent of agricultural land transfer	1.5
Provide legal consulting service	1.0
Coordinate and regulate contract signing	3.1
Supervising the circulation behavior	1.1
Meditation of land disputes	1.5
No service received	93.0

services of agricultural land circulation information, and other types of services are all below 2%. These figures reflect that the related services of agricultural land circulation cannot meet the needs, and that the construction of relevant service organizations and institutions shall be strengthened, and all services shall be improved to meet the needs of rural households (Table 3.19).

Organizations which provide various services played a huge role in the process of agricultural land circulation, 68.8% of rural households across the country have received services from village committees, mutual help between villagers accounted for 26.6%, government-led transaction service center for 6.8%, while rural households that received services from rural cooperatives and agricultural land circulation intermediary for 3.5% and 2.5%, respectively. Therefore, on the one hand, continuing to improve the service level of village committees and government-led trading centers is needed, while on the other hand, the rural cooperatives, agricultural land circulation intermediary, Internet platform and other types of organizations shall be strengthened (Table 3.20).

3.2.2 Effects of Cultivated Land Circulation

Compared with the agricultural households that are not circulating land, the agricultural households circulating land have a larger agricultural land operating area. However, the efficiency of agricultural production does not increase in general. Compared with the farmers who contracted farmland and transferred in agricultural land, agricultural households with no contracted cultivated land but have transferred-in agricultural land have

Table 3.20 Proportion of households that received services from various organizations in agricultural land transfer

Organization	*National (%)*
Government-led trading service center	6.8
Agricultural land circulation intermediary	2.5
Village committee	68.8
Farming cooperative	3.5
Agricultural enterprise	0.7
Other villagers	26.6
Internet platform	0.0
Traditional media	0.8
Other	5.0

more "understanding" of agricultural management. The latter not only invest more costs per mu but also create more output value per mu, which leads to a higher revenue per mu.

3.2.2.1 Agricultural Land Circulation and Scale of Farming

The operation scale of the farmlands of agricultural households that transferred-in cultivated land is significantly larger. The area of agricultural land management is the area of the family-contracted cultivated land minus the transfer-in area, and plus the transfer-out area. Households can be divided into five categories according to the situation of whether they contract or transfer cultivated land. In 2013, the "contract but not transfer" households had an average management area of 6.3 mu, while the "contract and transfer in" households had 26.5 mu of land on average, and the "not contract but transfer in" households had 40.7 mu. This difference still existed in 2015 when the "contract but not transfer" households had an average management area of 6.7 mu of cultivated land, while the "contract and transfer" households managed 24 mu, and the "not contract but transfer in" households managed 17 mu (Table 3.21).

The average cultivated land area of the labor force of households that transferred in cultivated land is also significantly large. In 2013, the "contract but not transfer" households had an average agricultural land area per worker of 2.6 mu, the "contract and transfer in" had 10.2 mu and the "not contract but transfer in" had 12.1 mu. In 2015, the "contract but not transfer" households had an average agricultural land area per worker of 2.8 mu, the "contract and transfer in" had 10.2 mu and the "not contract but transfer in" had 6.7 mu (Table 3.22).

Table 3.21 Land management area per household

Type of agricultural household	*2013*		*2015*	
	Mean (mu)	*Median (mu)*	*Mean (mu)*	*Median (mu)*
Contract but not transfer	6.3	3.5	6.7	4.0
Contract and transfer in	26.5	11.0	24.0	9.0
Contract and transfer out	1.6	0.0	1.2	0.0
Both transfer in and transfer out	42.5	10.0	51.1	5.0
Not contract but transfer in	40.7	5.0	17.0	2.0
Total samples	8.3	3.0	8.1	3.1

Table 3.22 Average land management area of labor force

Type of agricultural household	*2013*		*2015*	
	Mean (mu)	*Median (mu)*	*Mean (mu)*	*Median (mu)*
Contract but not transfer	2.6	1.3	2.8	1.5
Contract and transfer-in	10.2	4.0	10.2	3.5
Contract and transfer-out	0.6	0.0	0.5	0.0
Both transfer in and transfer-out	15.3	2.6	17.8	2.0
Not contract but transfer in	12.1	2.0	6.7	1.0
Total samples	3.3	1.3	3.5	1.3

3.2.2.2 Agricultural Land Circulation and Agricultural Management

The agricultural production output value, cost and income of various kinds of households are different. The "Not contract but transfer" households show the highest agricultural productivity. Not only do they have the most average input cost, reaching 2782 yuan per mu, but they also create the highest average agricultural output of 6729 yuan per mu, and have the highest average agricultural income of 4068 yuan per mu. By contrast, the "contract and transfer in" households show rather low agricultural productivity. They have the lowest average input cost in the agricultural production of 939 yuan per mu, the lowest average agricultural output of 2354 yuan per mu, as well as a lower average agricultural income of 1457 yuan per mu (Table 3.23).

Table 3.23 Agricultural land transfer and the agricultural households' input and output in 2015

		Mean (yuan)	*Median (yuan)*
Contract but not transfer	Output value per mu	3532	1500
	Cost per mu	1353	603
	Income per mu	2238	888
Contract and transfer-in	Output value per mu	2354	1130
	Cost per mu	939	498
	Income per mu	1457	563
Contract and transfer-out	Output value per mu	3856	1667
	Cost per mu	1616	853
	Income per mu	2460	920
Both transfer in and transfer-out	Output value per mu	2476	1667
	Cost per mu	1312	694
	Income per mu	1205	548
Not contract but transfer-in	Output value per mu	6729	5000
	Cost per mu	2782	2750
	Income per mu	4068	3496
Total samples	Output value per mu	3352	1429
	Cost per mu	1300	593
	Income per mu	2115	827

3.2.3 *Factors Influencing Agricultural Household Circulation Behavior*

The behavior of agricultural households' circulation is influenced by many factors. The size and quality of the household labor force, the structure of employment, the family burden structure, the state of the family economy, and the quality and quantity of land are all closely related to the behavior of circulation.

3.2.3.1 Family Labor Force Characteristics and the Circulation of Agricultural Land

The size of the family labor force is closely related to the households' willingness of cultivated land circulation. First, the family population size is negatively correlated with the willingness of transferring out cultivated land and positively correlated with the willingness of transferring in cultivated land. For families with only one to two members, 22.1% of households transfer out their cultivated land, while 12.4% of families transfer in cultivated land. The greater the number of families, the smaller the

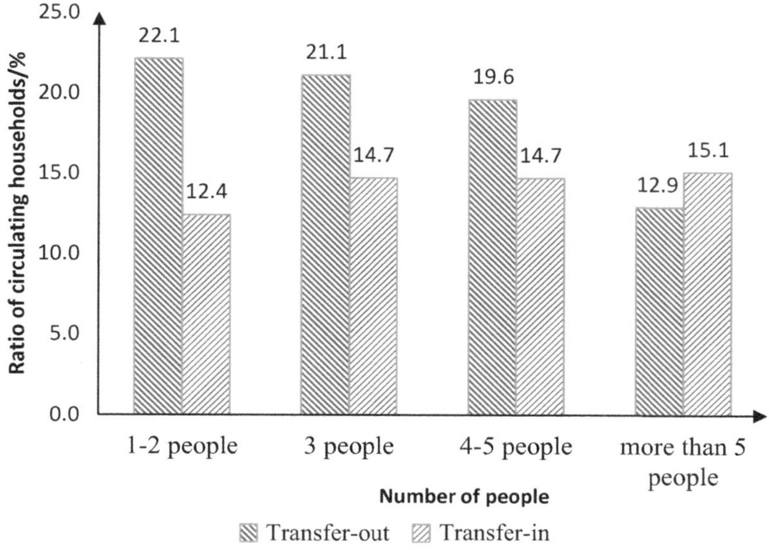

Fig. 3.4 Family scale and circulation of cultivated land, unit: %

proportion of households that transfer out cultivated land and the larger the proportion of households that transfer in their cultivated land. For families with more than five members, 12.9% of the households transfer out their cultivated land, while 15.1% of the households transfer in cultivated land (Fig. 3.4).

In addition, the size of the family labor force and the willingness of households to circulate their cultivated land have similar characteristics. For families without any labor force, 30.6% of households transfer out their cultivated land and 7.7% of households transfer in their cultivated land. As the size of the family labor force increases, the proportion of the families who transfer out land decrease, and the proportion of the families that transfer in their cultivated land increase. For families with five workers, 13.6% of households transfer out their cultivated land, while 18.4% of households transfer in cultivated land (Fig. 3.5).

The quality of the family labor force is closely related to the agricultural households' willingness to transfer agricultural land. First of all, the proportion of the labor force being male has a "U" relationship with the transfer-out cultivated land, and an inverted "U" relationship with the

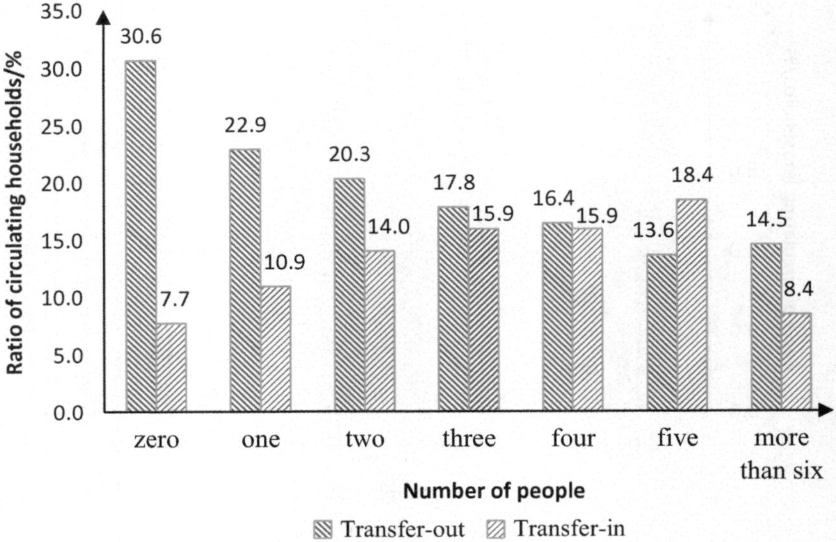

Fig. 3.5 Size of the family labor force and circulation of cultivated land, unit: %

transfer-in cultivated land. For families with a male labor force of less than 20%, 24.3% of those transferred out cultivated land and only 12.4% of those transferred in cultivated land. For families with a male labor force of about 50%, the proportion of families that transferred out cultivated land fell to 18.7%, while the proportion of those that transferred in cultivated land rose to 14.8%. For families with a male labor force of more than 80%, the proportion of families that transferred out cultivated land rose to 20.5% and 9.8% of those transferred in their cultivated land (Fig. 3.6).

Second, the average education years of the family labor force showed monotonically increasing or decreasing relationship with the households' willingness of cultivated land circulation. The higher the education of the household labor force, the higher the proportion of households that transfer out cultivated land, and the smaller the proportion of households that transfer in cultivated land. For households with an average education of less than six years, 14% transferred out farmland, while 16.8% of households transferred in their cultivated land. As the average education years of the labor force increased, more and more families transferred out their cultivated land, while fewer and fewer families transferred in their cultivated

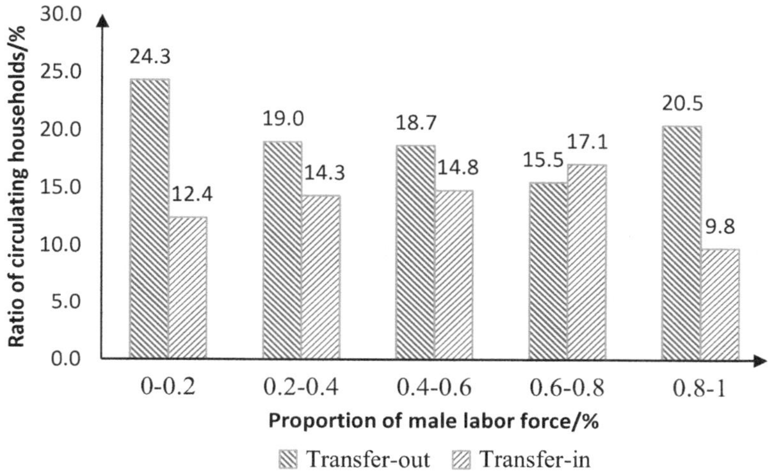

Fig. 3.6 Family male labor force ratio and circulation of cultivated land, unit: %

land. For families with average education years of more than 12 years, 27.6% of the households transferred out cultivated land, while only 8.7% of households transferred in cultivated land (Fig. 3.7).

The employment structure of the family labor force is also closely related to the households' willingness for agricultural land circulation. In general, the larger the proportion of non-agricultural employment in the household, the higher the proportion of households that transferred out to the cultivated land, and the lower the proportion of the households that transferred in cultivated land. For households with less than 20% non-agricultural employment, 13.9% of the households transferred out their cultivated land and 17.9% transferred in their cultivated land. For households with more than 80% non-agricultural employment, 34.4% of households transferred out cultivated land, compared with 4.9% for households that transferred in cultivated land (Fig. 3.8).

3.2.3.2 Family Burden Structure and Circulation of Agricultural Land

The more minors that the family raises, the more likely the family tends to transfer in cultivated land, and the less inclined it is to transfer out cultivated land. For families that raise no minors, 20.4% of them transferred

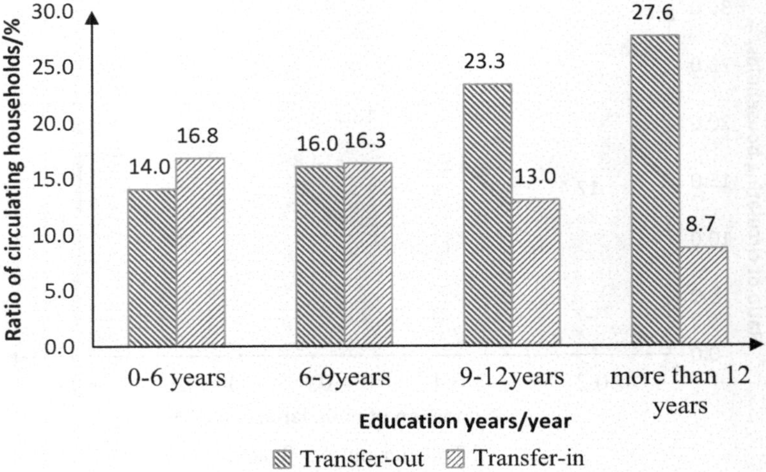

Fig. 3.7 The average number of the years of education and circulation of cultivated land, unit: %

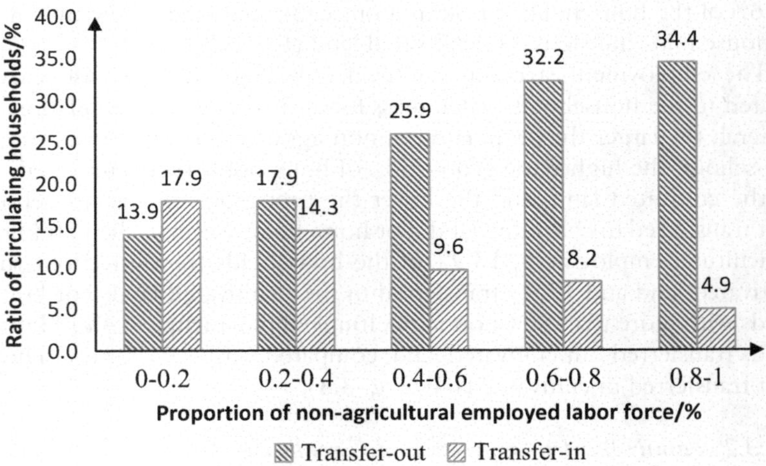

Fig. 3.8 Proportion of non-agricultural employed labor force and circulation of cultivated land, unit: %

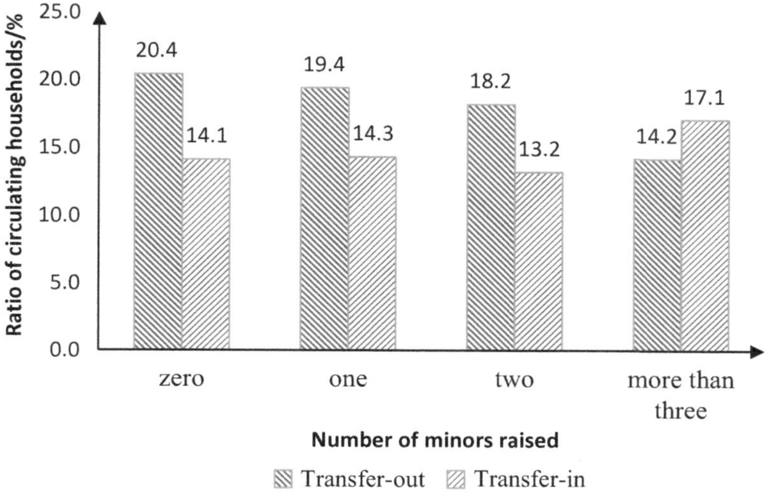

Fig. 3.9 Number of minors raised and the circulation of cultivated land, unit: %

out their cultivated land and 14.1% of them transferred in cultivated land. For families with more than three minors, the proportion of the households that transferred out cultivated land fell to 14.2%, while the proportion of households that transferred in cultivated land rose to 17.1% (Fig. 3.9).

Whether the family is hollow or not is also closely related to the agricultural households' willingness to cultivated land circulation. We define the hollow family as a family that does not have a male family member of 16–65 years. According to this definition, the proportion of hollow households in rural China is 14%. Hollow families are more likely to transfer out cultivated land than non-hollow families, and less likely to transfer in cultivated land. The proportion of hollow households that transferred out their cultivated land was 28.6%, significantly higher than the 18.4% of non-hollow households. In contrast, the proportion of hollow households that transferred in their cultivated land was 3.0%, significantly lower than the 7.2% of non-hollow households. In addition, the proportion of paid transfer-out of hollow households is higher than that of non-hollow households, and the proportion of paid transfer-in of hollow households is lower than that of non-hollow households (Table 3.24).

Table 3.24 Family structure and circulation of agricultural land

Family structure	*Transfer-out (%)*	*Paid transfer-out (%)*	*Transfer-in (%)*	*Paid transfer-in (%)*
Hollow family	28.6	14.9	3.0	1.1
Non-hollow family	18.4	9.8	7.2	4.0

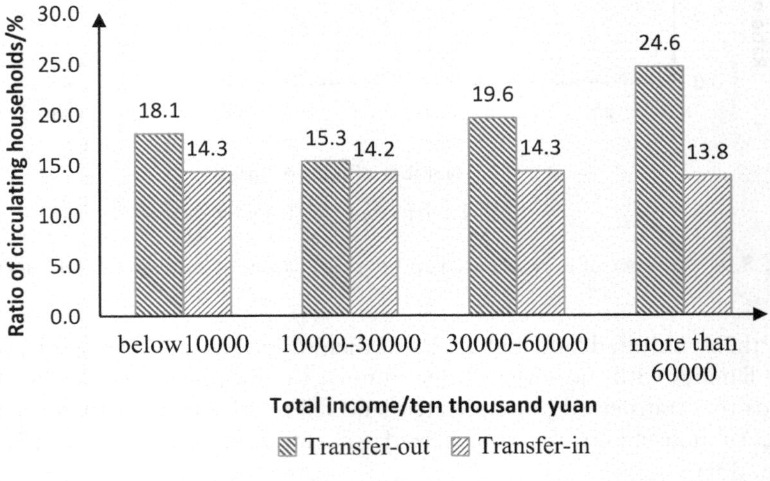

Fig. 3.10 Total household income and circulation of cultivated land, unit: %

3.2.3.3 *Family Economic Situation and Circulation of Agricultural Land*

The family economic situation is closely related to the household's willingness to transfer cultivated land. Family income has a "U" type relationship with the transfer-out cultivated land. However, it has little impact on transfer-in cultivated land. The proportion of households with a total income of less than 10,000 yuan that transferred out their cultivated land was 18.1%. The proportion of households with a total income of between 10,000 and 30,000 yuan that transferred out cultivated land fell to 15.3%. Subsequently, the higher the income, the greater the proportion of the families that transferred out cultivated land. In households with an income of more than 60,000, 24.6% of them transferred out cultivated land. The proportion of households that transferred in cultivated land remained at around 14%, without obvious change as the income increased (Fig. 3.10).

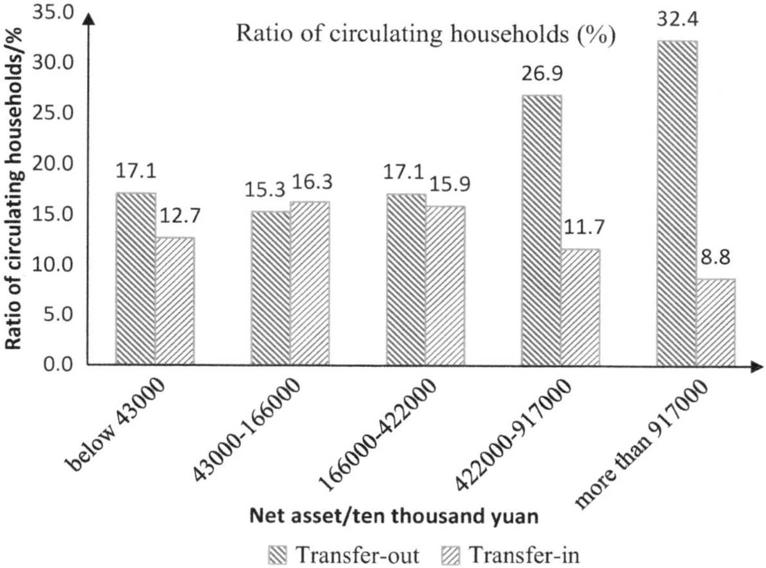

Fig. 3.11 Household net asset and circulation of cultivated land, unit: %

Families with a higher net worth are more inclined to transfer out cultivated land and less likely to transfer in cultivated land. For families with a net asset of less than 43,000 yuan, 17.1% of them transferred out their cultivated land, while 12.7% of them transferred in their cultivated land. For households with net worth of more than 917,000 yuan, 32.4% of them transferred out cultivated land, while 8.8% of them transferred in their cultivated land (Fig. 3.11).

The agricultural households' willingness to transfer cultivated land and whether they have purchased houses in urban areas are clearly related. For families that have bought homes in urban areas, 35.7% of the households transferred out their cultivated land, while 7.3% of the households transferred in cultivated land, which shows a huge difference between the two. For families that did not buy homes in urban areas, 14.7% of them transferred out their cultivated land, while 16.3% transferred in cultivated land, which shows little difference between the two (Fig. 3.12).

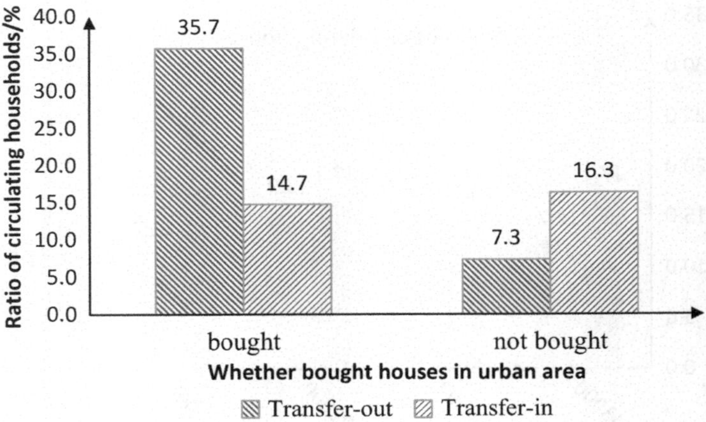

Fig. 3.12 Whether the urban area has housing and circulation of cultivated land, unit: %

3.2.3.4 Land Characteristics and Circulation of Agricultural Land

The more abundant the land is, the more likely the family inclines to transfer in cultivated land. For families with a land per capita of less than half a mu, only 8.6% of households transferred out their cultivated land. However, for families with a land per capita of more than 5 mu, 16.8% of households transferred in cultivated land. The tendency of transferring out their cultivated land of the household has no significant relationship with the land area per capita of the family (Fig. 3.13).

3.3 Confirmation of Rural Land Right and Circulation of Agricultural Land

In recent years, the implementation of rural land confirmation and certification across the country has greatly influenced the circulation of rural land. In the following, an analysis of the related situation of cultivated agricultural land will be conducted.

3.3.1 Confirmation of Rural Land Right and the Transfer-Out of Cultivated Land

Confirmation and issuance of certificates of land confirm the farmers' land rights. From the view of cultivated lands (Table 3.25), among rural households that have completed confirmation and certification across the nation,

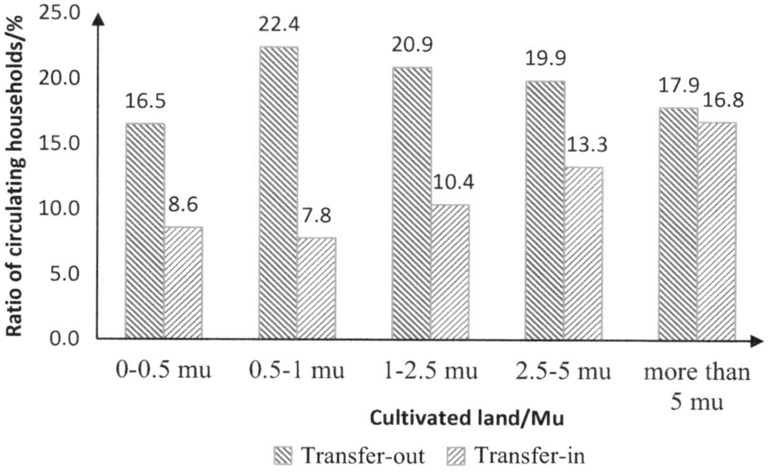

Fig. 3.13 Contracted cultivated land per capita and circulation of cultivated land, unit: %

Table 3.25 Confirmation of the rural families' land rights and the transfer-out of cultivated land

Confirmation of rights	*Transfer-out*		*Not transfer-out*	
	Number of households (household)	*Proportion (%)*	*Number of households (household)*	*Proportion (%)*
Confirmed	553	13.80	3454	86.20
Not confirmed	648	11.84	4827	88.16

families that have transferred their land right to other persons or institutions accounted for 13.8% and households that have not transferred the right of cultivated land accounted for 86.2%. Among rural families that have not completed confirmation and certification, only 11.84% transferred out their cultivated land and 88.16% of them did not transfer out their cultivated land. Thus, the rural families that have completed land confirmation and certification are more inclined to transfer out cultivated land than those that have not completed the process.

Table 3.26 Confirmation of the rural families' land rights and the time limit for the transfer-out of cultivated land

Confirmation of rights	*Percentage of transfer-out families (%)*				*Transfer-out time limit (year)*
	0–1 year(s)	*1–5 year(s)*	*5–15 years*	*15–100 years*	*Mean*
Confirmed	0.75	42.18	22.78	34.29	24.67
Not confirmed	1.33	47.35	27.01	24.30	19.66

3.3.2 *Confirmation of Rural Land Right and the Time Limit for Transferring Out of Cultivated Land*

The rural land confirmation and issuance of certificates do not only affect the transfer-out of cultivated land, but also relate to the time limit for land transfer-out. Table 3.26 reflects the situation of land confirmation and certification of rural families and the time limit for land transfer-out. The table shows that among rural families that have completed land confirmation and certification, the time limit for cultivated land is 24.67 years on average. Among these families, 42.93% of them have a transfer-out time limit of below 5 years, while more than 50% of them have a limit of more than 5 years, reaching 57.07%. By contrast, for rural families that have not completed land confirmation and certification, the time limit for the transfer-out of cultivated land is only 19.66 years on average, of which the proportion of transfer-out time limit below 5 years is 48.68%, which is 5.75 percentage points higher than those that have completed the process. It can be seen that the agricultural households that have not completed confirmation usually set a short time limit for the cultivated land due to the consideration of risks, while the rural land confirmation and issuance of certificates have promoted the extension of the time limit of land to a certain extent.

3.3.3 *The Confirmation of Rural Land Right and the Transfer-In of Cultivated Land*

The confirmation and issuance of the certificates of rural land have promoted more agricultural households to transfer out their cultivated land and have also affected their transfer-in of cultivated land. According to Table 3.27, among rural families that have completed confirmation and

Table 3.27 Confirmation of the rural families' land right and the transfer-in of cultivated land

Confirmation of rights	*Transfer-in*		*Not transfer*	
	Number of households (household)	*Proportion (%)*	*Number of households (household)*	*Proportion (%)*
Confirmed	696	17.37	3312	82.63
Not confirmed	852	15.55	4627	84.45

certification across the country, 17.37% of them have transferred in cultivated land management right and 82.63% have not yet transferred in cultivated land. As for the unconfirmed and unissued rural families, only 15.55% of them have transferred in cultivated land, which is 1.81% lower than those that have completed the process. Thus, it can be seen that more rural families that have completed the land confirmation and issuance of certificates chose to transfer in cultivated land than families that have not completed the process.

3.4 Land Expropriation

Since 2000, the land of rural families has encountered varying degrees of expropriation. Rural households across the country have experienced an average of 0.8 times of land expropriation, and the difference between agricultural and non-agricultural households is small. However, the number of times that the rural households in different regions have encountered expropriation varies significantly. The frequency of expropriation among rural households in the central region is 0.1 times, while that of the western region is as high as 2.6 times, which shows that the expropriation and utilization in the western rural areas are more frequent than the other regions in China since 2000 (Fig. 3.14).

The frequency of land expropriation among rural families varies, and Fig. 3.15 shows the statistical data of the number of expropriated households in different years according to the most recent time of land expropriation among rural families. The figure shows that since 2000, the number of land expropriation among rural households in our country took on a fluctuation change trend. Before 2015, the number of expropriated rural households in China has generally increased with fluctuation.

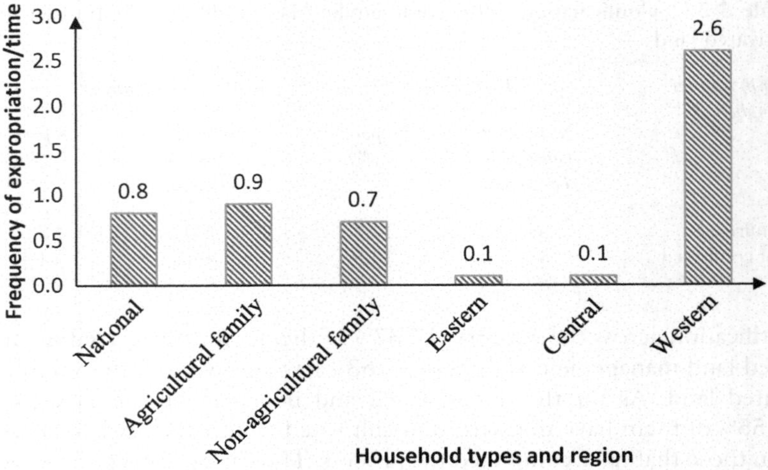

Fig. 3.14 Frequency of land expropriation since 2000, unit: time

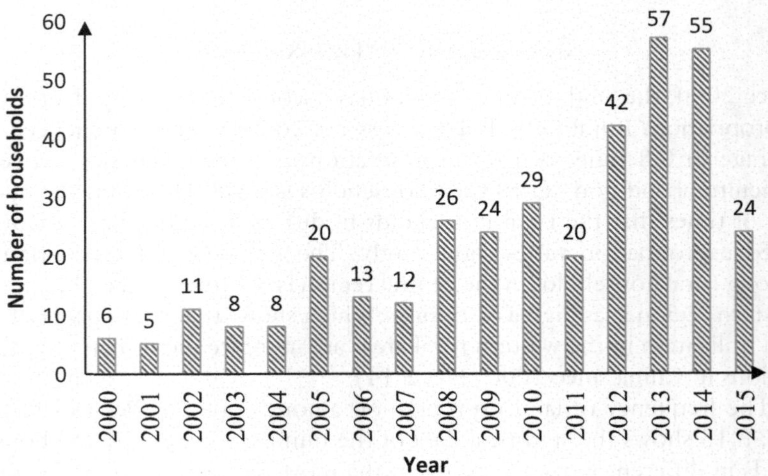

Fig. 3.15 Number of expropriated households in different years (the last time of expropriation), unit: household

Before 2005, the number of expropriated households was relatively small; between 2005 and 2012, the number of expropriated rural households increased with fluctuation; in 2013 and 2014, the number of expropriated rural households reached the peak, reaching 57 and 55 households, respectively. In 2015, the number significantly reduced to 24 households.

The average expropriated area of rural families across the country is 6.1 mu, and the average expropriated area of agricultural families is 7.0 mu, but the median is only 1.0, which shows that the expropriated area of different agricultural households varies greatly. The average expropriated area of non-agricultural households is 4.6 mu. From a geographical view, the average expropriated area of rural families in the western region is the largest, reaching 8.8 mu, followed by the eastern region (5.8 mu), while the central region is the smallest with 3.4 mu. The gap of the expropriated land area between different rural families in the central and western regions is huge (Fig. 3.16).

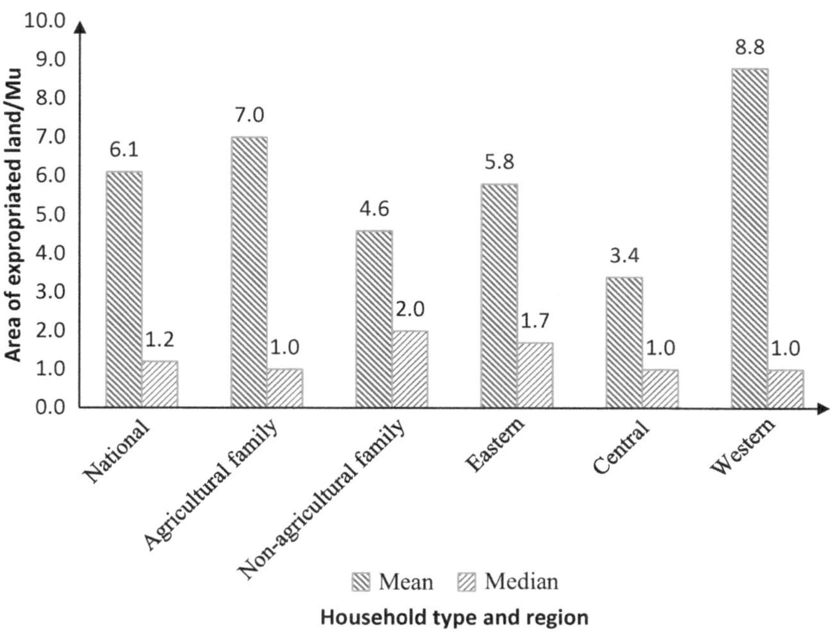

Fig. 3.16 Area of expropriated land, unit: mu

Land expropriation generally has two kinds of compensation methods: monetary compensation and non-monetary compensation. Of the rural households across the country, 76.8% have obtained monetary compensation, 3.9% of the rural households have obtained non-monetary compensation and households with both kinds account for 1%. There are still 17.3% of rural households that did not receive compensation during the land expropriation process (Table 3.28).

Figure 3.17 reflects the amount of monetary compensation for land expropriation. On average, rural households across the country receive

Table 3.28 Proportion of households with different forms of compensation for land expropriation

Compensation method	*National (%)*
Monetary compensation	76.8
Non-monetary compensation	3.9
Both	1.0
No compensation	17.3
Other	0.9

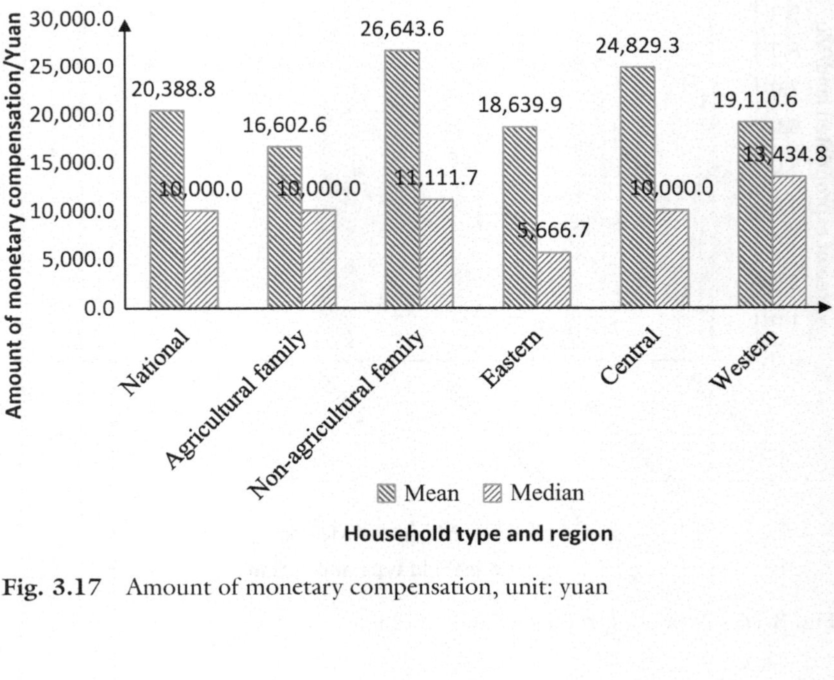

Fig. 3.17 Amount of monetary compensation, unit: yuan

Table 3.29 Proportion of families receiving different types of non-monetary compensation

Non-monetary compensation	*National (%)*
Pension insurance	1.8
Medical insurance	0.0
Grain compensation	18.5
Land compensation	59.8
Other	20.0

20,388.8 yuan per mu, and non-agricultural households receive 26,643.6 yuan, which is much higher than that of agricultural households (16,602.6 yuan). In terms of regional differences, rural households in the central region receive an average of 24,829.3 yuan, followed by the western region with 19,110.6 yuan and then the eastern region with 18,639.9 yuan, which shows that the amount of monetary compensation differs sharply among different regions.

Non-monetary compensation is another form of effective compensation. Table 3.29 reflects the proportion of rural households receiving various types of non-monetary compensation. Land compensation and grain compensation are the main methods of non-monetary compensation, with land compensation accounting for the highest proportion (59.8%), while 18.5% of rural households receive grain compensation. Fewer rural households receive pension insurance compensation, but the medical insurance and other methods of compensation have not yet been used. Rural families receiving other kinds of compensation account for 20.0%.

CHAPTER 4

Migration of Rural Households and Citizenization of Migrant Workers

This chapter uses the samples of "rural families living in rural areas" and "rural families living in urban areas (migrant workers' families)" from the China Rural Household Panel Survey (CRHPS) by Zhejiang University to analyze the migration of rural families and citizenization of migrant workers. This study found that the average age of migrant workers is 37.7 years, and the average schooling year is 9.4 years. On average, the working time of migrant workers is 9.1 hours per day and 25 days per month, which is generally higher than the regulations set by the Labor Law. The overall education level of migrant workers is not high, but we can see an obvious improvement in the level among the new generation of migrant workers: previously, the illiterate migrant workers accounted for 11.0% of the population, workers with primary school education accounted for 22.4% and workers with junior secondary education accounted for 35.8%. From the old generation to the post-1980s and then to the post-1990s, there is a very clear improvement in the level of education. The proportion of migrant workers with a primary or lower education has dropped, from 47.8% of the older generation to 8.3% of the post-1980s and then to 3.9% of the post-1990s; meanwhile, people with a high school degree or above among migrant workers have markedly increased, from 15.6% of the old generation to 51.4% of the post-1980s and then to 69.8% of the post-1990s.[1] The urban hukou, or household registration, became less appealing

[1] Corresponding to "the Post 80s and the Post 90s", "the old generation of migrant workers" refers to the migrant workers who were born in or before 1979.

© Zhejiang University Press 2020

W. Qian et al., *The Economy of Chinese Rural Households*,
https://doi.org/10.1007/978-981-13-8591-9_4

to migrant workers that only 17.0% of migrant workers were willing to obtain a non-agricultural hukou. The citizenization of migrant workers has not been marked chiefly by whether they have obtained or been willing to obtain urban hukou. Migrant workers are more or less related to agriculture, but there is a clear trend: in 2015, 27.8% of migrant workers in China engaged in agricultural production and management; however, compared with that in 2013 and 2011, the relationship between migrant workers and agriculture has obviously weakened. The proportion of migrant workers participating in agricultural production and management has dropped from 31.7% in 2010 to 30.4% in 2012 and then to 27.8% in 2014. The number of months which migrant workers are involved in agricultural production has fallen from 6.76 to 6.26 months, and then to 6.15 months. Migrant workers' families have a tendency to rapidly rent out agricultural land: since 2011, migrant workers' families have rented out agricultural land faster and shows a trend of continuously renting out land. According to a survey conducted in 2011, the proportion of migrant workers' families having rented out agricultural land was 12.9%, which was higher than that of rural families (6.0%) by 6.9 percentage points. In 2013, that of migrant workers' families became 16.4%, which was higher than that of rural families (10%) by 6.4 percentage points. By 2015, 30.9% of migrant workers' families had rent out agricultural land, which was higher than the 11.3% of rural families by 19.6 percentage points. By 2015, migrant worker families who have rent out agricultural land have, on average, rent out 5.1 mu per household, which is 15.9% higher than the 4.4 mu of rural households. Migrant workers' families generally have higher expectations of their children's education than rural families. The more highly educated migrant workers are, the higher annual income they could get. But no matter what academic background female migrant workers have, their income was significantly lower than that of men. The overall social security level of migrant workers is low: 39.8% of migrant workers do not have any pension insurance, and 57.1% of migrant workers are supported by social endowment insurance. Among various social endowment insurances, the new rural social old-age insurance plays a major role, accounting for 66.9%. The coverage rate of medical insurance for migrant workers is 85.2%, but it is still mainly based on the New Rural Cooperative Medical System (NRCMS), accounting for 76.5%. Only 10.7% of migrant workers have registered for the Urban Employee Basic Medical Insurance (UEBMI).

4.1 Population Migration of Rural Residents

This section provides a simple statistical analysis of the population migration targeting rural families living in rural areas.

4.1.1 *Overview of Population Migration*

Table 4.1 shows the rate at which rural residents in China leave the place in which they registered their *hukou* to work elsewhere. From the national perspective, 13.9% of farmers have gone to work elsewhere. From the regional perspective, the proportion of the central region was the highest, followed by that of the western region, and then the eastern region, at 19.8%, 16.5% and 5.9%, respectively.

4.1.2 *Composition of Migrant Workers' Jobs*

As seen in Table 4.2, migrant workers who are mainly engaged in temporary work accounts for 78.4%. Migrant workers employed by others are the second largest group, accounting for 15.6%. There are also a small number of migrant workers who are sole traders, are in private enterprises or are self-employed, accounting for 4.1%. Overall, migrant workers always have lower-level jobs.

Table 4.1 Rural population migration rate, unit: %

National	*Eastern*	*Central*	*Western*
13.9	5.9	19.8	16.5

Table 4.2 Nature of migrant workers' jobs, unit: %

Nature of job	*National*	*Eastern*	*Central*	*Western*
Employed by others or companies	15.6	20.0	16.6	12.5
Temporary job	78.4	65.8	78.1	83.9
Sole trader or private enterprises, self-employment, online shop	4.1	9.2	3.8	2.4
Others	1.9	5.0	1.5	1.2

Table 4.3 Willingness for urban hukou, unit: %

Are you willing to get a non-agricultural account	*National*	*Eastern*	*Central*	*Western*
Yes	21.0	21.0	21.1	20.9
No	79.0	79.0	78.9	79.1

4.1.3 Willingness for Urban Hukou

From the national perspective, as shown in Table 4.3, rural residents show little incentive to obtain urban hukou with only 21% of rural residents wanting to get the non-agricultural hukou. This figure is not quite different in the eastern, central and western regions, with 21.0%, 21.1% and 20.9%, respectively.

4.2 The Citizenization of Migrant Workers

4.2.1 Sample Characteristics

The samples used in this section are different from the other chapters in this book, so a brief description of the sample characteristics is given. This section makes a statistical analysis on the "rural families living in cities (i.e. migrant workers' families)" sample from the CRHPS by Zhejiang University. Compared with other domestic migrant worker databases, this sample has the following characteristics:

4.2.1.1 Sampling from Cities Inhabited by Migrant Workers

The survey of migrant workers can be targeted at rural households where relevant information on migrant workers can be obtained by interviewing the heads of households in rural families or family members who are well aware of the situation. An example of this type of survey can be seen in the survey and analysis data as shown in Sect. 4.1 of this chapter. This type of survey can accurately reflect the total number of migrant workers, the rate of migration and other relevant information. However, two problems exist in this kind of survey: first, since the interviewers are not migrant workers, mistakes may be made on the reflection of the outside work and life of migrant workers; and second, as migrant workers who moved their family away from home can hardly be included in the sample, it is difficult to obtain accurate information. The sample of migrant workers' families in the CRHPS was obtained by stratified sampling in cities. The definition of migrant workers is: people who live in the city with agricultural hukous, or people who now reside in the city with unified household registrations[2] and prior to obtaining this, had agricultural hukous. Among the samples, the first category includes 31,947 people from 10,515 households, and the second category includes 766 people from 366 households.

4.2.1.2 Only Investigate Migrant Workers Residing in Residential Buildings in Urban Areas

Generally speaking, the overall sampling scheme of CRHPS is based on the stratified sampling, three-stage sampling and probability proportionate to size (PPS) sampling (see Chap. 2). At the time of ultimate sampling, the map and address are used for field sampling. On the basis of drawing the residential distribution map and making the list of households, it uses the "Residential Distribution Geographic Information" as a sampling frame for ultimate sampling. During the household survey, it starts with the following question for screening: "Does this house belong to residential buildings? (including commercial and residential houses)". If the answer is "yes", the questionnaire survey could be continued, or be exited and targeted at another family.

According to the "2015 Migrant Workers Monitoring Survey Report" by the National Bureau of Statistics (NBS), migrant workers living in the staff quarters accounted for 28.7%, in temporary sheds at construction sites accounted for 11.1%, and in the places of production and operation occupied 4.8%. About 14% of migrant workers work outside their hometown but live at home. About 41.4% of migrant workers live in urban residential housing, who are relatively advanced in citizenization.

4.2.1.3 Only Investigate "Permanent Residents"[2] Who Have Resided in the City for More Than 6 Months

The survey used the following question for screening: "Last year, did anyone in your family reside in this city/county for more than 6 months"? If the answer is "yes", the questionnaire survey could be continued, or be exited and targeted at another family. This step ensures that the migrant workers in the sample are permanent residents of the city, and excludes the floating population.

[2] Unified Household Registration means that some places, after the reform on the hukou system, no longer distinguish between agricultural and non-agricultural accounts, but implement the unified household registration.

4.2.1.4 Only Investigate Migrant Workers' Families Whose Main Activities (Consumptions) Are in the City

In the actual survey, we continued to use the following question for screening: "Does your main economic activities (consumptions) take place here"? If the answer is "yes", the questionnaire survey could be continued, or else it would be exited and targeted at another family.

Through the above samplings and screenings, it can be concluded that the CRHPS' sample of migrant workers' families is a group of migrant workers who have relatively stable jobs and lives in the city, or to some extent, could even be considered as "urban citizens", except that they do not have urban hukou.

In addition, it is necessary to state that the eastern, central and western regions in this section are divided according to the location of the rural migrant workers, rather than according to the source of migrant workers.

4.2.2 *Basic Structure*

4.2.2.1 Source Structure

Here we focus on distinguishing between local migrant workers and foreign migrant workers. Local migrant workers refer to migrant workers who are employed within the town area of the household register, and foreign migrant workers refer to migrant workers who are employed outside the town area of the household register. The actual composition of migrant workers is as follows (Table 4.4).

From Table 4.4, we can see that the local migrant workers accounted for 56.1% of the CRHPS' sample of migrant workers, which is 16.9 percentage points higher than the 39.2% published by the NBS. This difference is related to the characteristics of the CRHPS sample of which the

Table 4.4 Source structure of migrant workers

		National	*Eastern*	*Central*	*Western*
Local migrant workers	Number	18,367	10,818	3507	4153
	Percentage (%)	56.1	61.0	50.8	51.3
Foreign migrant workers	Number	14,356	6901	3395	3949
	Percentage (%)	43.9	39.0	49.2	48.7
Total	Number	32,723	17,719	6902	8102
	Percentage (%)	100	100	100	100

Table 4.5 Age and gender structure of migrant workers

Project	*Average (year old)*	*Median (year old)*	*Percentage of gender (%)*			
Total population	*37.7*	*37*	*National*	*Eastern*	*Central*	*Western*
Male	36.5	36	49.5	49.6	48.9	49.7
Female	38.8	38	50.5	50.4	51.1	50.3
Gender ratio	–	–	98.0	98.4	95.7	98.8

local migrant workers are mostly in accordance with conditions (2), (3) and (4) summarized in Sect. 4.2.1, while most of the foreign migrant workers who do not meet the above conditions are excluded from CRHPS samples.

4.2.2.2 Age and Gender Structure

The basic structure of the age and gender of migrant workers shown in Table 4.5 shows that the gender ratio of migrant workers is basically equal. The national average gender ratio is 98:100. There is little difference in terms of the gender ratio regionally, with the exception of the central region being relatively low at 95.7:100, while that of the other regions are around 98:100.

4.2.2.3 Years of Schooling and Academic Structure

Looking at the genders and their respective figures, the migrant workers' mean years of schooling are generally low. The eastern region is slightly higher than that of the central and western regions, and the mean years of schooling of males are generally more than that of females in various regions (Table 4.6).

Table 4.7 shows the academic structure of migrant workers. It can be seen from the table that, in the survey samples, the number of illiterate persons is 12,685, which accounts for 11.0% of the total migrant worker population, and the number of primary school graduates is 23,831, accounting for 22.3%; that of middle school graduates is 34,112, accounting for 35.8%; that of high school graduates is 15,726, accounting for 13.8%; that of the secondary or vocational school graduates is 6471, accounting for 5.3%; that of college or technical secondary school graduates, accounting for 6.5%; that of university graduates is 10,150, accounting for 5.1%; and that of people with master's degree or above is 1007, accounting for 0.2%.

Table 4.6 Genders of the working-age population and their average years of schooling, unit: year

	Male	*Female*
Eastern	9.4	8.2
Central	9.3	8.2
Western	8.9	7.8
National	9.3	8.2

Table 4.7 Academic structure of migrant workers, unit: %

Education background	*National*	*Eastern*	*Central*	*Western*
Illiteracy	11.0	10.8	11.1	11.5
Primary school	22.3	21.6	19.6	26.8
Middle school	35.8	35.3	38.5	34.0
High school	13.8	13.4	15.1	13.1
Secondary or vocational school	5.3	5.8	4.7	4.8
College or technical secondary school	6.5	7.4	5.5	5.6
Bachelor's degree	5.1	5.5	5.0	4.1
Master's degree	0.2	0.2	0.5	0.1
Doctor's degree	0.0	0.0	0.0	0.0

Next, we will further analyze the changes in the education of the old generation and the new generation (the post-1980s and the post-1990s) of migrant workers (Table 4.8).

From Table 4.8, there is a very clear upward trend in the education of migrant workers from the old generation to the post-1980s and then to the post-1990s. The proportion of people with primary school education or below has declined significantly, from 47.5% of the old generation to 8.2% of the post-1980s, and then to 3.8% of the post-1990s. The proportion of people with high school education and above has obviously improved, from 15.5% of the old generation, to 51.5% of the post-1980s, and then to 69.9% of the post-1990s. Moreover, we could see an upward trend in the number and proportion of high school graduates, secondary or vocational school graduates, undergraduates and masters.

4.2.2.4 Household Registration (Hukou)

As shown in Table 4.9, the vast majority of migrant workers surveyed still have agricultural hukous, the proportion of which is as high as 97.7%. The proportion of migrant workers in the survey who have a unified hukou is only 2.3%. From the regional perspective, the proportion of migrant work-

Table 4.8 Comparison of the academic structure between the new and the old generation of migrant workers, unit: %

Education background	*National*			*Eastern*			*Central*			*Western*		
	Old generation	*The post-1980s*	*The post-1990s*	*Old generation*	*The post-1980s*	*The post-1990s*	*Old generation*	*The post-1980s*	*The post-1990s*	*Old generation*	*The post-1980s*	*The post-1990s*
Illiteracy	15.6	0.7	0.4	15.7	0.6	0.5	15.1	0.4	0.2	15.8	1.3	0.4
Primary school	31.9	7.5	3.4	31.8	6.4	3.1	27.7	6.5	3.4	36.5	11.6	4.3
Middle school	37.0	40.3	26.3	36.7	38.9	25.1	39.9	43.9	29.7	34.8	40.1	25.5
High school	10.7	15.0	26.6	10.5	15.4	24.3	12.8	15.5	26.5	9.2	13.4	31.5
Secondary or vocational school	2.0	10.7	11.7	2.2	11.5	12.3	1.9	8.6	11.9	1.7	10.8	10.2
College or technical secondary school	1.9	14.4	15.3	2.0	15.9	17.7	2.1	12.0	11.3	1.5	13.0	14.3
Undergraduate	0.9	10.7	15.5	1.1	10.6	16.7	0.5	12.1	15.2	0.5	9.6	13.6
Master	0.0	0.6	0.8	0.0	0.6	0.3	0.0	0.9	1.8	0.0	0.2	0.2
Doctor	0.0	0.1	–	0.0	0.1	–	0.0	0.1	–	0.0	0.0	–

Table 4.9 Household registration of migrant workers, unit: %

Type of household registration	*National*	*Eastern*	*Central*	*Western*
Agricultural household registration	97.7	96.9	98.9	98.0
Unified household registration	2.3	3.1	1.1	2.0
Total	100.0	100.0	100.0	100.0

ers in the eastern region with a unified household registration is the highest, reaching 3.1%, which is in line with the highest urbanization rate of the east. The second highest was the western region with a proportion of 2.0%, while the migrant workers in the central region of traditional rural areas have the lowest proportion in having non-agricultural accounts, at only 1.1%.

4.2.2.5 *Family Migration Rate*

Table 4.10 shows the migration of migrant worker families. "Family migration rate" here refers to the percentage of family members living together after the migration in the total family population. Living together here means staying at home for at least 6 months, and still living here now. People who go to work or school on weekdays but come back home on weekends are also taken into account. Moreover, the data include babies of less than 6 months old and people who have been married for less than 6 months.

From Table 4.10, it can be seen that the family migration rate of migrant workers is very high, with the national average reaching 89.65%. The family migration rate of migrant workers in the eastern region reached to about 90.79%, followed by that of the central region, at 88.61%. The western region had the lowest rate, reaching 87.06%. Such a high rate of family migration is of course related to the characteristics of the CRHPS sample of migrant worker families. More specifically, the vast majority of migrant workers in line with the four conditions of migrant workers' families summarized in Sect. 4.2.1 have migrated with their family. In fact, the proportion of individual migration (i.e. the number of family members living together with respondents is 0) is very low (see Table 4.11).

It can be seen from Table 4.11 that no person migrated and lived together with the respondents, that is, the average rate of individual migration is only 6.78%, and that of local migrant workers is only 5.27%. Now let's take a look at the number of migrant workers' family members who don't live together (Table 4.12).

It is clear from Table 4.12 that the number of family members who do not live with the respondents is 0, that is, the migrant workers who migrated with their family accounts for 79.76%.

Table 4.10 Family migration rate of migrant workers

	National			*Eastern*			*Central*			*Western*		
	Average	*Local*	*Non-local*	*Average*	*Local*	*Non-local*	*Average*	*Local*	*Non-local*	*Average*	*Local*	*Non-local*
Number of family members	3.96	4.18	3.75	3.91	4.1	3.74	4.04	4.43	3.74	4.02	4.31	3.73
Number of family members living together except for the respondent	2.55	2.72	2.40	2.55	2.72	2.40	2.58	2.82	2.40	2.50	2.66	2.34
Number of family members not living together	0.41	0.46	0.35	0.36	0.38	0.34	0.46	0.61	0.34	0.52	0.65	0.39
Family migration rate (%)	89.65	89.00	90.67	90.79	90.73	90.91	88.61	86.23	90.91	87.06	84.92	89.54

Note: For local migrant workers, referring to it as "migration" may not be accurate, but it can also be understood as moving from the countryside to the urban areas, so it is also meaningful to consider about the "family migration rate"

Table 4.11 Number of family members of migrant workers living together, unit: %

Number of family members living together except for the respondent	*National*			*Eastern*			*Central*			*Western*		
	Average	*Local*	*Non-local*	*Average*	*Local*	*Non-local*	*Average*	*Local*	*Non-local*	*Average*	*Local*	*Non-local*
0	6.78	5.27	8.33	6.91	5.37	8.63	5.35	3.50	6.84	7.63	6.38	8.91
1	22.34	21.99	22.69	22.49	22.02	23.01	22.38	22.28	22.46	21.76	21.66	21.87
2	21.83	21.23	22.44	21.88	21.13	22.72	19.74	18.86	20.46	23.59	23.59	23.59
3	21.91	18.65	25.29	20.94	18.61	23.53	25.48	19.76	30.09	22.01	17.87	26.22
4	17.18	19.37	14.91	17.71	20.02	15.17	19.01	21.69	16.85	13.56	15.07	12.02
5	6.77	8.51	4.97	6.43	7.46	5.28	5.80	10.05	2.36	8.91	11.13	6.65
6	2.06	3.40	0.66	2.46	3.89	0.88	1.06	2.06	0.26	1.57	2.74	0.37
7	0.84	1.13	0.54	0.85	1.11	0.55	0.95	1.27	0.68	0.74	1.10	0.37
8	0.20	0.25	0.14	0.21	0.19	0.23	0.24	0.54	0.00	0.12	0.23	0.00
9	0.09	0.17	0.00	0.11	0.20	0.00	0.00	0.00	0.00	0.10	0.20	0.00
Number of samples	16,349	10,429	5920	10,259	6428	3831	2699	1711	988	3391	2290	1101

Table 4.12 Number of family members of migrant workers not living with the respondents (%)

Number of family members of migrant workers not living with the respondents	*National*			*Eastern*			*Central*			*Western*		
	Average	*Local*	*Non-local*	*Average*	*Local*	*Non-local*	*Average*	*Local*	*Non-local*	*Average*	*Local*	*Non-local*
0	79.76	77.39	82.23	81.94	80.76	83.25	77.41	72.99	80.99	74.27	68.58	80.07
1	8.78	10.07	7.43	8.44	9.65	7.10	8.34	8.65	8.08	10.38	12.82	7.89
2	5.90	6.23	5.56	4.61	4.77	4.44	8.53	8.87	8.25	7.99	9.42	6.54
3	3.55	3.57	3.53	2.93	2.23	3.71	3.57	5.80	1.76	5.75	6.70	4.78
4	1.07	1.44	0.69	1.17	1.48	0.83	0.92	1.49	0.46	0.84	1.22	0.45
5	0.70	1.04	0.35	0.70	0.99	0.36	1.12	1.94	0.46	0.35	0.48	0.21
6	0.13	0.07	0.19	0.17	0.05	0.30	0.12	0.28	0.00	0.00	0.00	0.00
7	0.06	0.11	0.01	0.00	0.00	0.00	0.00	0.00	0.00	0.33	0.58	0.07
12	0.05	0.08	0.01	0.04	0.07	0.01	0.00	0.00	0.00	0.10	0.19	0.00
Number of samples	16,344	10,429	5915	10,255	6428	3827	2698	1711	987	3391	2290	1101

Table 4.13 Migrant workers' willingness to obtain an urban hukou

Are you willing to obtain a non-agricultural hukou	*National*	*Eastern*	*Central*	*Western*
Yes	17.0	16.5	16.9	18.3
No	83.0	83.5	83.1	81.7

4.2.2.6 Willingness to Obtain an Urban Hukou

It is clear from Table 4.13 that even for migrant workers' families living relatively a stable life in a city, they still do not have a strong will to get an urban hukou. On average, migrant workers who are willing to get non-agricultural accounts in the whole country only accounts for 17.0%, which is even lower than the21.0% of "rural residents living in rural areas" (see Table 4.3). These rural migrant workers who live in towns and cities should be more aware of the difference between urban and rural hukou than the farmers who live in the countryside, so we believe that the attractiveness of urban hukou to migrant workers has been greatly reduced, and whether or not to obtain or be willing to obtain urban hukou is no longer the main indicator of the citizenization of migrant workers. The more developed the area in the eastern region is, the lower the willingness of migrant workers to obtain non-agricultural hukous.

4.2.3 Household Income and Expenditure

Table 4.14 shows that average household income of migrant workers' families in 2014 was 66,628 yuan, the per capita income was 16,825 yuan. The ratio of agricultural income was very low, accounting for only 8.15%, and non-agricultural income accounting for 91.85%. The main part of non-agricultural income was from wage, accounting for 48.31%, followed by the income ofindustrial and commercial management, which accounted for 27.55%.

Table 4.15 shows the expenditure of migrant workers' families and the structure of non-productive expenditure. In 2014, the average household non-productive expenditure of migrant workers' families was 47,239 yuan. Among them, food expenditure accounted for 39.8%, living and residing expenses for 17.7% and health care expenditure for 13.5%, while the proportion of education and entertainment expenditure was low, accounting for only 9.8%.

Table 4.14 Structure of household income of migrant workers' families

	Total income	*Agricultural net income*	*Non-agricultural income*				
			Subtotal	*Wage income*	*Income of industrial and commercial operating*	*Property income*	*Transfer income*
Average income per household (yuan)	66,628	5429	61,199	32,185	18,353	7837	2824
Per capita income (yuan)	16,825	1371	15,454	8128	4635	1979	713
Ratio (%)	100	8.15	91.85	48.31	27.55	11.76	4.23

Table 4.15 Expenditure structure of migrant workers' families

	Per household	*Per capita*
Total expenditure (yuan)	51,183	12,925
Non-productive expenditure (yuan)	47,239	11,929
Food expenditure (%)	39.8	39.8
Clothing expenditure (%)	5.4	5.4
Living and residing expenditure (%)	17.7	17.7
Expenditure of daily necessities and durable goods (%)	6.5	6.5
Health care expenditure (%)	13.5	13.5
Traffic and communication expenditure (%)	7	7
Education and entertainment expenditure (%)	9.8	9.8
Other expenditure (%)	0.3	0.3
Transfer expenditure (yuan)	3196	807
Expenditure of agricultural production (yuan)	748	189

4.2.4 Connection with Agriculture

4.2.4.1 Connection Between Migrant Workers and Agriculture

As seen in Table 4.16, there is a certain degree of connection between migrant workers and agriculture. About 27.8% of migrant workers in China were engaged in agricultural production and operation in 2015, 25.8% for eastern China and 29.8% for both the central and western

Table 4.16 Migrant workers' participation in agricultural production and management, unit: %

		National	*Eastern*	*Central*	*Western*
2015	Ratio of migrant workers who engaged in agricultural production and management (%)	27.8	25.8	29.8	29.8
	Duration of participation in agricultural production and management (month)	6.15	6.03	5.33	7.24
	Number of family members who engaged in agricultural production and management (person)	1.94	1.93	1.93	1.97
2013	Ratio of migrant workers who engaged in agricultural production and management (%)	30.4	24.1	37.8	34.0
	Duration of participation in agricultural production and management (month)	6.26	6.07	5.35	7.25
	Number of family members who engaged in agricultural production and management (person)	1.94	1.92	1.98	1.93
2011	Ratio of migrant workers who engaged in agricultural production and management (%)	31.7	24.2	41.3	68.2
	Duration of participation in agricultural production and management (month)	6.76	6.61	6.14	8.79
	Number of family members who engaged in agricultural production and management (person)	1.89	1.82	1.94	2.00

China. In 2015, each migrant worker's family in various regions had basically two family members who have previously engaged in agricultural production and management. However, when comparing the situation of 2013 with that of 2011, the degree of connection between migrant workers and agriculture has significantly reduced. The ratio of migrant workers who engaged in agricultural production and management fell from 31.7% in 2011 to 30.4% in 2013 and then down to 27.8% in 2015. The duration of participation in agricultural production and management fell from 6.76 to 6.26 months, and then to 6.15 months.

Table 4.17 A comparison of agricultural land ownership between migrant workers' families and rural families

Sample	*National*	*Eastern*	*Central*	*Western*
Ratio of agricultural land ownership in rural families (%)	89.9	84.7	93.5	91.3
Ratio of agricultural land ownership in migrant workers' families (%)	60.1	55.1	64.1	66.8

4.2.4.2 *Agricultural Land[3] Ownership*

From Table 4.17 we can see that the ratio of migrant workers' families that own agricultural land is 60.1%; the ratio for eastern China is 55.1%, 64.1% for central China and 66.8% for western China. From the table we can also see that migrant workers' families own agricultural land with a far lower ratio than rural families, indicating that much more migrant workers' families are landless farmers.

Table 4.18 reflects the agricultural land area owned by rural families and migrant workers' families and self-use ratio of agricultural land.[4]

Table 4.18 shows that the national average agricultural land owned by migrant workers' families is 6.4 mu, 9.9 mu in western region, 6.7 mu in central region and 4.7 mu at least in eastern region, but it is obviously lower than that owned by rural families.

4.2.4.3 *The Transfer-Out of Agricultural Land*

The transfer-out of agricultural land refers to the transfer of agricultural land with contracting rights to others, including subcontracting, land shares, exchange, cooperation, hosting and free of charge to others. We define the transfer-out ratio as the share of migrant workers' families that transfer agricultural land in all migrant workers' families or the share of rural families that transfer agricultural land in all rural families. Transfer-out area is calculated according to families that have transferred land. In

[3] The agricultural land here refers to the land used for agricultural production, including cultivated land, garden, woodland, pasture and so on. "Owning" refers to the right to contract with agricultural land; owned contract area includes: land assigned to their own to contract, cultivated land that is paid to or freely given to friends and families, big household, cooperatives, companies or village committee; The following land is not "owned": land that has been levied, used for greenland, recovered and transferred by village committee.

[4] The area of self-use is used for production of agriculture, forestry, animal husbandry and fishery.

Table 4.18 Agricultural land area owned by rural families and migrant workers' families and self-use ratio of agricultural land

Location	*Total area of agricultural land (mu)*	
	Rural families	*Migrant workers' families*
National	7.9	6.4
Eastern	5.4	4.7
Central	6.1	6.7
Western	15.7	9.9

Table 4.19 A comparison of agricultural land transfer-out between migrant workers' families and rural families (Statistics in 2015)

Location	*Type of family*	*Transfer-out ratio (%)*	*Transfer-out area (mu)*	
			Mean	*Median*
National	Rural families	11.3	4.4	3
	Migrant workers' families	30.9	5.1	3
Eastern	Rural families	14.1	3.6	2
	Migrant workers' families	29.0	5.0	3
Central	Rural families	10.4	5.4	3.5
	Migrant workers' families	37.2	5.7	3.3
Western	Rural families	9.6	4.4	2
	Migrant workers' families	28.0	4.6	2.5

the following contents, we will analyze the trend of transfer-out of agricultural land in migrant workers' families based on statistics in 2011, 2013 and 2015, and compare them with families that live in rural areas (Tables 4.19, 4.20, and 4.21).

From Tables 4.19, 4.20, and 4.21, we can see that migrant workers' families have been transferring out agricultural land at a fast speed since 2011 and that there is a tendency to acceleration. From the statistics in 2011, the ratio of migrant workers' families that have transferred land was 12.9%, 6.9 % higher than the 6.0% of rural families. In 2013, the ratio was 16.4%, 6.4 % higher than the 10% of rural families. By 2015, however, the ratio in migrant workers' families rose to 30.9%, outnumbering rural families by 19.6 %. By 2015, the average area of agricultural land transferred by migrant workers' families was 5.1 mu, 15.9% higher than the

Table 4.20 Comparison of agricultural land transfer-out between migrant workers' families and rural families (statistics in 2013)

Location	*Type of families*	*Transfer-out ratio (%)*	*Transfer-out area (mu)*	
			Mean	*Median*
National	Rural families	10.0	5.3	3
	Migrant workers' families	16.4	5.7	3
Eastern	Rural families	10.4	2.5	2
	Migrant workers' families	16.5	3.4	2.25
Central	Rural families	9.9	6.5	4
	Migrant workers' families	19.1	8.7	4
Western	Rural families	9.7	6.4	3
	Migrant workers' families	14.1	5.9	2.5

Table 4.21 A comparison of agricultural land transfer-out between migrant workers' families and rural families (statistics in 2011)

Location	*Type of families*	*Transfer-out ratio (%)*	*Transfer-out area (mu)*	
			Mean	*Median*
National	Rural families	6.0	5.1	1.8
	Migrant workers' families	12.9	4.8	3
Eastern	Rural families	8.6	1.8	1.4
	Migrant workers' families	13.7	5.5	4
Central	Rural families	5.1	10.3	4
	Migrant workers' families	12.4	4.0	3
Western	Rural families	3.9	1.7	1.2
	Migrant workers' families	9.4	2.3	1

4.4 mu of rural families. From the ratio of land-transfer-out families and the average area of transferred land, central China hit the highest, followed by eastern China, and then western China.

In the following, further information will be given to analyze the reasons for migrant workers' families to transfer land (Table 4.22).

It can be seen in Table 4.22 that the main reason for both migrant workers' families and rural families to transfer land is quitting agricultural production, followed by "residence change" of migrant workers' families and "income factors" of rural families.

Table 4.22 Reasons for migrant workers' families and rural families to transfer land, unit: %

Reason	*National*		*Eastern*		*Central*		*Western*	
	Rural families	*Migrant workers' families*	*Rural families*	*Migrant workers' families*	*Rural families*	*Migrant workers' families*	*Rural families*	*Migrant workers' families*
Income factors	9.3	4.8	9.5	5.6	6.9	3.8	12.4	4.7
Residence change	3.2	13.5	3.0	13.1	3.6	18.0	3.1	8.2
Motivation by other villagers	4.3	1.6	4.4	2.3	4.0	1.6	4.6	0.1
Motivation by village collective	10.9	9.1	14.3	13.9	5.4	2.2	13.2	9.5
Families that don't involve in agricultural production	57.5	66.7	58.6	61.7	65.0	70.1	45.8	71.4
Others	14.8	4.3	10.2	3.4	15.1	4.3	20.9	6.1

4.2.4.4 Agricultural Land Renting

If a migrant workers' family rents agricultural land from others and rent for the purpose of agricultural production or aquaculture, this family is defined as the leased family. We further define the leasing proportion as the share of migrant workers' families that renting land from others in all migrant workers' families. The rented area is calculated on the basis of families that rent land from others. Table 4.23 indicates that nationally the proportion of migrant workers' families that rent land is 4.7%. The number is highest in western region, at 7.1%. In eastern and central China, it is 3.4 and 5.2%, respectively. We now further analyze the area of rented land in those families. As shown in Table 4.23, the average area is 15.9 mu, the median is 3.0 mu. Viewed from different areas, the average area in central region is 20.2 mu, the median is 7.0 mu; in western region, the numbers are 14.7 and 2.2; in eastern region, 14.1 and 3.0. It is easy to find out that the rented area of agricultural land in central region is significantly larger than that of the east and west. From Table 4.23, we can also see that the migrant workers' families have a much smaller ratio of rented land than rural families, but a larger average area, by 29.27%.

Table 4.23 A comparison of rented agricultural land between migrant workers' families and rural families

Location	*Type of family*	*Renting ratio (%)*	*Rented area (mu)*	
			Mean	*Median*
National	Rural families	15.0	12.3	4
	Migrant workers' families	4.7	15.9	3
Eastern	Rural families	12.0	11.4	3
	Migrant workers' families	3.4	14.1	3
Central	Rural families	16.8	16.7	6.5
	Migrant workers' families	5.2	20.2	7
Western	Rural families	16.3	7.4	3
	Migrant workers' families	7.1	14.7	2.2

Table 4.24 Source of rented agricultural land in migrant workers' families, unit: %

Source	*National*	*Eastern*	*Central*	*Western*
Common agricultural household	87.3	80.2	93.0	91.2
Large and specialized agricultural family operation	3.9	2.8	3.1	5.7
Family farm	0.0	0.0	0.0	0.0
Cooperative	0.1	0.0	0.0	0.2
Village collective	0.8	1.0	0.9	0.1
Companies or enterprises	6.7	15.1	1.2	1.8
Agents	0.3	0.0	0.5	0.5
Other sources	0.9	0.9	1.3	0.5

Table 4.24 shows the distribution of source of rented agricultural land in migrant workers' families. It can be seen that 88.30% of families rented land from common agricultural households; only 3.92 and 6.72% of families from large and specialized agricultural family operation and companies or enterprises. It indicates that migrant workers' families currently rent agricultural land mainly from common agricultural households.

4.2.5 Employment and Income

4.2.5.1 Working Hours of Migrant Workers

Table 4.25 shows the working hours of migrant workers. In terms of the annual employment time, migrant workers are fully employed with the average period of 10.6 months. In terms of different regions, migrant

Table 4.25 Working hours of migrant workers

	National	*Eastern*	*Central*	*Western*
Annual employment time (month)	10.6	10.8	10.5	10.1
Monthly employment time (day)	25.0	25.2	25.6	24.1
Working hours in weekdays (hour)	9.1	9.0	9.1	9.3

workers in the eastern region have the longest average employment time, which reaches 10.8 months per year; 10.5 months in central region and 10.1 months at least in western region. In terms of monthly employment time, the national average level is 25 days. Migrant workers in central region have the longest monthly employment time, which reaches 25.6 days; followed by the east with 25.2 days and the west with 24.1 days. In terms of daily working hours, migrant workers have generally a long time of labor with average of 9.1 hours per day, which excesses the national legal standard. Migrant workers in the western region work for the longest time, which reaches 9.3 hours; 9.1 hours for central China, and migrant workers in the eastern region work for 9.0 hours every day.

In the following, we will compare the difference of working hours between the post-1990s' generation, post-1980s' generation and migrant workers of elder generation (Table 4.26).

As can be seen in Table 4.26, the monthly working hours and daily working hours are decreasing in migrant workers of the elder generation to the post-1980s and to the post-1990s. From monthly working days, the elder generation work 25.3 days per month, followed by post-1980s' generation of 24.7 days and then the post-1990s of 24.0 days. From daily working hours, the elder generation work 9.2 hours per day, the post-1980s' work 9.0 hours and the post-1990s work 8.6 hours. This may be an indication that migrant workers of the younger generation are getting increasingly better knowledge of how to protect themselves with working hours more and more close to the standard of labor law.

Statistics in 2011 and 2013 are as followed (Tables 4.27 and 4.28).

There is no obvious change in working hours from the evidence shown in statistics above. However, daily working hours of the elder generation has decreased by 4.17%, from 9.6 hours in 2011 to 9.2 hours in 2015.

4.2.5.2 Employment Distribution of Migrant Workers

From the table of employment structure, we can see that various types of employment differ from employment ratio: migrant workers that work temporarily hit the highest, accounting for 33.1%, followed by migrant

Table 4.26 Migrant workers' working hours between different generations in 2015, unit: %

Working hours	*National*			*Eastern*			*Central*			*Western*		
	Elder generation	*The post-1980s*	*The post-1990s*	*Elder generation*	*The post-1980s*	*The post-1990s*	*Elder generation*	*The post-1980s*	*The post-1990s*	*Elder generation*	*The post-1980s*	*The post-1990s*
Annual employment time (month)	10.4	11.0	10.4	10.7	11.1	10.3	10.2	11.0	10.9	9.8	10.7	9.9
Monthly employment time (day)	25.3	24.7	24.0	25.5	24.9	23.6	25.8	25.1	25.1	24.2	23.8	23.9
Working hours in weekdays (hour)	9.2	9.0	8.6	9.1	8.9	8.5	9.2	9.0	8.9	9.5	9.1	8.8

Table 4.27 Migrant workers' working hours between different generations in 2013, unit: %

Working hours	*National*			*Eastern*			*Central*			*Western*		
	Elder generation	*The post-1980s*	*The post-1990s*	*Elder generation*	*The post-1980s*	*The post-1990s*	*Elder generation*	*The post-1980s*	*The post-1990s*	*Elder generation*	*The post-1980s*	*The post-1990s*
Annual employment time (month)	9.5	9.5	7.3	9.7	9.9	7.5	9.2	9.0	7.0	9.3	9.2	6.9
Monthly employment time (day)	6.0	5.7	5.8	6.0	5.7	5.8	5.9	5.9	5.5	5.8	5.5	5.7
Working hours in weekdays (hour)	9.1	8.8	8.4	9.2	8.7	8.4	9.2	9.1	8.6	9.1	8.6	8.4

Table 4.28 Migrant workers' working hours between different generations in 2011, unit: %

Working hours	*National*			*Eastern*			*Central*			*Western*		
	Elder generation	*The post-1980s*	*The post-1990s*	*Elder generation*	*The post-1980s*	*The post-1990s*	*Elder generation*	*The post-1980s*	*The post-1990s*	*Elder generation*	*The post-1980s*	*The post-1990s*
Annual employment time (month)	9.8	9.9	7.7	10.1	10.0	8.1	9.1	9.9	5.2	8.2	8.2	–
Monthly employment time (day)	6.0	6.0	–	6.0	6.1	–	5.8	5.6	–	6.1	5.3	–
Working hours in weekdays (hour)	9.6	8.8	–	9.6	8.7	–	9.4	8.9	–	9.8	8.7	–

Table 4.29 Employment structure of migrant workers, unit: %

	National	*Eastern*	*Central*	*Western*
Being employed by others	28.2	33.1	24.1	21.5
Temporary employment	33.1	30.1	36.5	36.4
Farming	15.9	14.2	15.9	19.4
Self-employment	20.4	20.4	20.9	19.8
Freelancers	2.0	1.7	2.1	2.5
Other	0.4	0.5	0.5	0.4

workers employed by others for 28.2%; migrant workers of self-employment for 20.4%, 15.9% for farmers, 2.0% for freelancers and 0.5% for other migrant workers (Table 4.29).

Next we analyze the differences of working hours in 2015, 2013 and 2011 between the post-1990s' generation, the post-1980s' generation and the elder generation (Tables 4.30, 4.31, and 4.32).

From the tables above, significant difference of employment structure arises between different generations. Especially, the ratio of migrant workers in the younger generation who engaged in farm work has dramatically decreased: the elder generation, the post-1980s' and the post-1990s' generations account respectively for 23.7%, 4.5% and 4.0%. At the same time, even the proportion of old generation engaging in agriculture is declining, with a 5.7 percentage points fall from 2011 to 2015.

In the following contents, we will present a further analysis of different industries engaged by migrant workers and the distribution of it.

Table 4.33 gives the distribution of employment industries engaged by migrant workers. We can know that the largest parts are manufacturing industry, construction industry and citizen services, repair and other services, accounting for respectively 24.1%, 15.8% and 10.6%. The ratio of tourism, online wholesale and retail, social work and social organization are comparatively smaller, accounting for 0.2%, 0.5% and 0.7%.

Table 4.34 shows the distribution of migrant workers in various sectors. We can see that nationally the ratio of migrant workers working in enterprise is the highest, accounting for about 67.8%; it is followed by self-employed workers of about 21.6%. The number of other migrant workers working in public institutions accounted for about 6.1%, migrant workers in government departments for 3.8%, and non-profit non-governmental organizations for 0.5%.

Table 4.30 Employment structure of migrant workers between different generations in 2015, unit: %

Employment structure	*National*			*Eastern*			*Central*			*Western*		
	Elder generation	*The post-1980s*	*The post-1990s*	*Elder generation*	*The post-1980s*	*The post-1990s*	*Elder generation*	*The post-1980s*	*The post-1990s*	*Elder generation*	*The post-1980s*	*The post-1990s*
Being employed by others	18.3	43.4	41.6	22.6	47.6	48.0	15.5	39.9	32.1	12.5	35.6	38.7
Temporary employment	34.0	28.4	39.3	32.4	24.3	33.2	35.9	32.8	46.6	35.4	34.9	43.9
Farming	23.7	4.5	4.0	22.1	3.5	3.3	22.5	6.0	4.8	27.9	5.5	4.6
Self-employment	21.7	21.2	11.9	20.9	22.0	13.1	23.6	18.9	12.9	21.5	21.3	8.5
Freelancers	2.0	2.2	1.5	1.6	2.2	0.7	2.0	2.3	2.3	2.6	2.3	2.3
Other	0.3	0.3	1.7	0.4	0.4	1.7	0.5	0.1	1.3	0.1	0.4	2.0

Table 4.31 Employment structure of migrant workers between different generations in 2013, unit: %

Employment structure	*National*			*Eastern*			*Central*			*Western*		
	Elder generation	*The post-1980s*	*The post-1990s*	*Elder generation*	*The post-1980s*	*The post-1990s*	*Elder generation*	*The post-1980s*	*The post-1990s*	*Elder generation*	*The post-1980s*	*The post-1990s*
Being employed by others	35.0	57.8	81.4	41.5	61.9	81.8	26.6	50.1	87.6	31.7	55.4	76.4
Self-employment or private enterprises	21.8	29.4	15.9	22.5	26.8	14.7	23.2	37.4	11.4	19.2	28.2	21.6
Farming	33.9	6.7	1.1	26.5	5.1	1.4	41.0	7.8	0.0	39.9	9.2	1.0
Re-employment	0.0	0.0	0.0	0.0	0.0	0.0	0.0	0.0	0.0	0.0	0.0	0.0
Freelancers	7.9	5.6	1.1	7.9	5.9	1.1	7.5	4.0	1.0	8.4	6.5	1.0
Other types	0.3	0.1	0.0	0.4	0.1	0.0	0.3	0.0	0.0	0.2	0.2	0.0
Seasonal work	1.1	0.4	0.5	1.2	0.2	1.0	1.4	0.7	0.0	0.6	0.5	0.0

Table 4.32 Employment structure of migrant workers between different generations in 2011, unit: %

Employment structure	*National*			*Eastern*			*Central*			*Western*		
	Elder generation	*The post-1980s*	*The post-1990s*	*Elder generation*	*The post-1980s*	*The post-1990s*	*Elder generation*	*The post-1980s*	*The post-1990s*	*Elder generation*	*The post-1980s*	*The post-1990s*
Being employed by others	40.1	70.1	80.5	44.2	71.7	74.8	34.6	65.2	92.5	25.4	67.8	74.2
Temporary employment	20.9	19.2	12.1	22.5	20.2	17.6	21.3	18.0	3.1	7.5	11.0	4.6
Farming	29.4	4.3	2.0	21.5	0.7	0.1	37.8	12.8	3.9	63.9	18.5	11.0
Self-employment	0.0	0.1	0.0	0.0	0.1	0.0	0.0	0.0	0.0	0.0	0.0	0.0
Freelancers	9.0	6.3	5.4	11.2	7.3	7.5	5.7	4.0	0.5	2.4	2.3	10.2
Other types	0.6	0.0	0.0	0.6	0.0	0.0	0.6	0.0	0.0	0.8	0.4	0.0

Table 4.33 Distribution of employment industries, unit: %

Industry	*National*	*Eastern*	*Central*	*Western*
Agriculture, forestry, animal husbandry and fishery	1.2	1.2	1.0	1.7
Mining	0.8	0.5	0.6	1.8
Manufacturing	24.1	31.1	18.6	11.8
Electricity, heat, gas and water production and supply	3.3	3.5	4.0	1.9
Construction industry	15.8	12.9	17.9	21.0
Online wholesale and retail	0.5	0.5	0.7	0.4
Off-line wholesale and retail	6.9	6.5	8.4	6.3
Transportation	5.1	4.5	4.5	7.2
Warehousing, logistics and postal services	1.8	1.7	2.4	1.5
Accommodation and catering	6.3	5.3	7.4	7.5
Information transmission, software and information technology services	2.2	2.7	1.6	1.6
Financial industry	2.5	2.3	2.7	3.0
Real estate	1.2	1.1	0.8	1.7
Leasing and business services	1.5	0.8	2.2	2.8
Scientific research and education	3.0	3.2	3.1	2.7
Water, Environment and Public Facilities Management	0.8	0.9	0.5	0.6
Residents services, repairs and other services	10.6	9.3	11.7	12.9
Tourism	0.2	0.2	0.0	0.3
Health care	2.2	1.4	3.3	3.1
Culture, media, sports and entertainment	1.0	1.0	1.1	0.7
Public management and social security	3.2	3.7	1.9	3.4
Social work and social organization	0.7	0.7	0.8	0.5
International organizations	0.0	0.0	0.0	0.0
Other industries	5.1	5.0	4.8	5.6

Table 4.34 Distribution of employment sectors, unit: %

Sector	*National*	*Eastern*	*Central*	*Western*
Government departments	3.8	3.9	2.7	4.4
Public institutions	6.1	5.7	5.6	7.5
Enterprises	67.8	67.7	66.8	69.2
Non-profit non-governmental organizations	0.5	0.7	0.3	0.3
Army	0.2	0.1	0.4	0.2
Self-employment	21.6	21.9	24.1	18.3

Table 4.35 Distribution of the nature of enterprises that migrant workers work in, unit: %

Nature of enterprise	*National*	*Eastern*	*Central*	*Western*
State-owned enterprise	11.1	10.6	14.1	9.4
Collective enterprise	2.9	3.7	2.0	1.7
Private enterprise	79.9	77.4	80.0	86.2
Foreign-funded enterprise	6.1	8.3	3.9	2.7

Table 4.35 shows the distribution of the nature of enterprises that migrant workers work in. On the national level, most migrant workers work in private enterprises, accounting for 79.9%; followed by state-owned enterprises accounting for 11.1%, foreign-funded enterprises for 6.1% and collective enterprises for 2.9%. Private enterprises took the largest part through the eastern, central and western China, followed by state-owned enterprises, foreign-funded enterprises and collective enterprises.

4.2.5.3 Years of Education and Employment

The years of education for migrant workers in different industries are quite different across the country. It means that degree of education has a significant impact on employment of farmers. From Table 4.36, it can be seen that the top five industries that highly educated migrant workers work in are medical research and education, information transmission, software and information technology services, finance, health care and real estate, with years of education for 13.5, 13.4, 12.7 and 12.3 years. For less-educated industries like mining industry, agriculture, forestry, animal husbandry, fishery, lodging and catering industry, construction industry, residents service, repair service and other services, the years of education were 8.3, 8.5, 8.7, 8.9 and 9.0 years. The years of education in other industries are ranging from 9 to 12 years.

Table 4.37 shows the years of education of migrant workers in different sectors. The Army was the main sector that high-educated migrant workers are employed in, with the average years of education for 13.2 years; followed by 12.4 years for public institutions, 11.9 years for state-owned enterprises, 11.5 years for foreign-funded enterprises and collective enterprises, 11.3 years for government departments, 10.1 years for private enterprises and 8.9 years for private enterprises and 9.8 years for non-profit non-governmental organizations.

Table 4.36 Years of education for migrant workers in different industries, unit: year

Industry	*National*	*Eastern*	*Central*	*Western*
Agriculture, forestry, animal husbandry and fishery	8.4	8.7	7.8	8.2
Mining	8.3	8.9	9.5	7.5
Manufacturing	9.6	9.5	10.2	9.5
Electricity, heat, gas and water production and supply	11.0	10.8	11.8	10.3
Construction industry	8.9	8.7	9.5	8.7
Online wholesale and retail	11.7	13.2	8.7	12.0
Off-line wholesale and retail	10.8	11.0	10.3	10.8
Transportation	9.3	9.3	9.6	8.9
Warehousing, logistics and postal services	10.2	10.4	10.9	8.6
Accommodation and catering	8.7	9.0	8.7	8.3
Information transmission, software and information technology services	13.4	13.8	13.6	11.6
Financial industry	13.2	14.3	11.7	12.5
Real estate	12.3	11.4	12.7	13.6
Leasing and business services	10.2	11.5	8.9	10.5
Scientific research and education	13.5	13.6	12.7	14.1
Water, Environment and Public Facilities Management	9.1	9.9	7.4	7.4
Residents services, repairs and other services	9.0	8.9	9.0	9.0
Tourism	9.4	8.9	–	10.3
Health care	12.7	12.9	12.6	12.6
Culture, media, sports and entertainment	11.6	10.9	13.0	12.0
Public management and social security	11.5	11.9	10.3	11.3
Social work and social organization	11.6	12.0	9.9	12.9

Table 4.37 Years of education for migrant workers in different sectors, unit: year

Sector	*National*	*Eastern*	*Central*	*Western*
Government departments	11.3	11.5	11.7	10.6
Public institutions	12.4	12.5	12.2	12.5
State-owned enterprises	11.9	11.8	11.7	12.2
Collective enterprises	11.5	11.6	11.1	11.2
Private enterprises	10.1	10.2	10.3	9.9
Foreign-funded enterprises	11.5	11.0	12.2	14.0
Non-profit non-governmental organizations	9.8	10.0	9.6	9.0
The Army	13.2	11.0	14.0	14.1
Private enterprises	8.9	8.7	9.6	8.6

4.2.5.4 Industries of Employment and Income

Table 4.38 shows that annual income of information transmission, software and information technology services were the highest with 62,696 yuan per year; followed by culture, media, sports and entertainment industries with 59,069 yuan; industries that could provide over 40,000 yuan also including real estate, financial industry, social work and social organization, as well as health care, with annual income of 46,994, 46,973, 46,147 and 42,655 yuan. The five industries with the least income are agriculture, forestry, animal husbandry and fishery, resident services, accommodation and catering, leasing and business services, with an income of 23,742, 24,246, 26,418, 26,723 and 28,404 yuan.

Table 4.38 Income and employment industries, unit: yuan per year

Industry	*National*	*Eastern*	*Central*	*Western*
Agriculture, forestry, animal husbandry and fishery	23,742	25,991	21,041	21,424
Mining	30,508	38,557	22,012	30,569
Manufacturing	36,462	38,169	32,472	31,109
Electricity, heat, gas and water production and supply	38,204	38,146	39,155	36,529
Construction industry	37,171	41,049	35,334	32,832
Online wholesale and retail	31,277	51,606	11,569	22,410
Off-line wholesale and retail	33,518	35,011	31,013	33,383
Transportation	38,986	42,994	37,433	34,072
Warehousing, logistics and postal services	33,917	41,431	21,378	33,014
Accommodation and catering	26,723	30,243	22,729	24,652
Information transmission, software and information technology services	62,696	71,555	32,755	62,218
Financial industry	46,973	48,199	47,345	44,271
Real estate	46,994	50,248	64,046	34,879
Leasing and business services	28,404	38,458	12,462	35,120
Scientific research and education	38,283	43,028	26,694	38,000
Water, Environment and Public Facilities Management	26,418	33,137	7533	16,389
Resident services, repairs and other services	24,246	26,350	23,249	21,411
Tourism	30,501	37,658	–	14,782
Health care	42,655	46,522	37,888	43,589
Culture, media, sports and entertainment	59,069	56,400	88,273	26,446
Public management and social security	30,699	33,926	16,086	31,534
Social work and social organization	46,147	58,897	24,410	32,103

Table 4.39 Academic background and income, unit: yuan per year

Academic background	*National*	*Male*	*Female*
Illiterate	20,373	21,099	19,681
Primary school	24,497	28,480	19,417
Secondary school	31,403	35,803	23,388
High school	35,005	38,851	27,763
Technical secondary school or secondary vocational school	37,190	44,168	30,490
Junior colleges or higher vocational college	40,038	45,111	34,395
Bachelor's degree	50,400	56,422	43,636
Master's degree	63,976	77,142	42,298
Doctor's degree	103,630	200,000	68,846

4.2.5.5 Academic Background and Income

Table 4.39 shows that migrant workers' academic background is positively corresponded with their average income per year. The income of the illiterate is 20,373 yuan per year, 24,497 yuan for the primary school graduated, 31,403 yuan for the secondary school graduated, 35,005 yuan for the high school graduated, and 37,190 yuan for the technical secondary educated or secondary vocational technical school educated. Migrant workers graduated from junior colleges or higher vocational colleges can earn 40,038 yuan per year, workers with bachelor degree can earn 50,400 yuan, workers with master degree can earn 63,976 yuan and workers with doctor degree can earn 103,630 per year. It is worth noticing that male migrant workers earn more than female regardless of education levels.

4.2.6 *Education for Children*

4.2.6.1 Expectation for Children's Education

In Table 4.40 we can see the difference of children education between migrant workers' families and rural families. Children education expectations from migrant workers' families are mainly bachelor degree or doctor degree, with ratio of 54.1% and 21.4% nationally. In eastern region, 55.2% of migrant workers' families expect their children to get a bachelor degree and 17.9% for a doctor degree; in central region that is 57.0% for bachelor degree and 17.7% for doctor degree; in western region that is 48.9% and 32.3%. The difference between migrant workers' families and rural families are that: expectations from migrant workers are generally higher than

Table 4.40 Expectation for children education in migrant workers' families and rural families, unit: %

Expectation of education	*National*		*Eastern*		*Central*		*Western*	
	Migrant workers	*Rural citizens*	*Migrant workers*	*Rural citizens*	*Migrant workers*	*Rural citizens*	*Migrant workers*	*Rural citizens*
Primary school	0.2	0.5	0.2	0.4	0.3	0.4	0.2	0.8
Middle school	0.7	2.7	1.0	1.6	0.3	3.1	0.7	3.1
High school (including technical secondary school and secondary vocational school)	3.6	4.8	3.8	5.3	4.5	4.1	2.3	5.1
Junior college	2.2	2.7	2.7	3.5	1.4	1.8	1.9	3.2
Bachelor's degree	54.1	54.1	55.2	54.6	57.0	54	48.9	53.7
Master's degree	6.4	3.5	6.4	4.3	6.7	3.1	6.0	3.5
Doctor's degree	21.4	18.2	17.9	16.8	17.7	19	32.3	18.3
No expectation	11.4	13.5	12.8	13.5	12.1	14.5	7.7	12.3

rural citizens. More migrant workers' families expect their children to get a bachelor degree or master degree or doctor degree; however, more rural citizens expect their children to get other five levels of education.

4.2.6.2 Children's Education Obtained

Table 4.41 shows the nature of schools that migrant workers' and rural citizens' children are studying in. There is no big difference between them. Both migrant workers' and rural citizens' children are studying mainly in public schools that not special for migrant workers' children.

Taking families whose children study in public schools as examples, Table 4.42 shows the different levels of public schools. Children from migrant workers' families generally have a better choice of schools than

Table 4.41 Nature of schools that migrant workers' and rural citizens' children are studying in, unit: %

Nature of schools	*National*		*Eastern*		*Central*		*Western*	
	Rural families	*Migrant workers' families*	*Rural families*	*Migrant workers' families*	*Rural families*	*Migrant workers' families*	*Rural families*	*Migrant workers' families*
Public schools for all children	89.1	89.1	89.6	87.0	85.8	91.4	92.8	90.6
Public schools for migrant workers children	1.8	2.1	0.8	2.3	1.9	1.0	2.6	3.0
Private schools for all children	8.4	7.2	8.5	8.7	11.7	6.1	4.1	5.5
Private schools for migrant workers children	0.5	0.7	0.6	0.8	0.4	0.4	0.4	0.7
International schools	0.0	0.1	0.0	0.2	0.0	0.0	0.0	0.1
Other schools	0.2	0.8	0.5	1.0	0.2	1.0	0.1	0.1

Table 4.42 Levels of public school children of migrant workers' families and rural families go to, unit: %

Levels of public school	*National*		*Eastern*		*Central*		*Western*	
	Rural families	*Migrant workers' families*	*Rural families*	*Migrant workers' families*	*Rural families*	*Migrant workers' families*	*Rural families*	*Migrant workers' families*
National key school	0.4	0.3	0.4	0.2	0.3	0.2	0.4	0.4
Provincial key school	1.1	2.2	1.2	2.0	1.5	3.1	0.5	1.5
City key school	5.3	10.4	8.5	12.4	4.9	9.8	3.4	7.5
County key school	19.0	27.5	17.0	25.9	20.1	32.3	19.5	25.3
Non-key school	74.2	59.6	72.9	59.5	73.2	54.6	76.2	65.3

those from rural families. Nationally speaking, 27.5% of migrant workers' families and 19.0% of rural families send their children to county key schools; 10.4% of migrant workers' families and 5.3% of rural families send their children to city key schools. Very few children from those two types of families go to provincial and national key schools. Meanwhile, 59.6% and 74.2% of children in the two families are in non-key schools.

Table 4.43 shows the natures of schools of migrant workers' children living in different areas study in. Nationally speaking, there is no big difference, most of them study in schools that are not special for migrant workers' children: the average is 89.1%; 89.3% for migrant workers' children living in small cities and towns, a little higher than the average; 88.3% and 86.7% for those living in urban cities and suburban areas.

Table 4.44 shows the levels of public schools that migrant workers' children living in different areas study in. 30.9% of migrant workers' children living in urban cities study in county key schools and 14.3% study in city key schools. The table also shows that 24.7% of migrant workers' children living in suburban areas study in county key schools and 8.2% study in city key schools. It also reveals 36.1% of migrant workers' children living in small towns study in county key schools and 9.0% study in city key schools. Only a small part of these two groups goes to provincial key schools and national key schools. Generally speaking, migrant workers living in suburban areas have a worse choice of education for their children.

Table 4.43 Nature of school migrant workers' children living in different areas study in, unit: %

Living area	*Location*	*Nature of schools*					
		Public schools for all children	*Public schools for migrant workers children*	*Private schools for all children*	*Private schools for migrant workers children*	*International school*	*Other schools*
Average	National	89.1	2.1	7.2	0.1	0.7	0.8
	Eastern	87.0	2.3	8.7	0.8	0.2	1.0
	Central	91.4	1.0	6.1	0.4	0.0	1.1
	Western	90.6	3.0	5.5	0.7	0.1	0.1
Urban cities	National	88.3	2.6	7.8	0.5	0.0	0.8
	Eastern	86.2	2.6	9.3	1.0	0.0	0.9
	Central	90.5	1.4	6.8	0.0	0.0	1.3
	Western	89.3	4.1	6.3	0.3	0.0	0.0
Suburb areas	National	86.7	1.9	9.1	1.8	0.5	0.0
	Eastern	83.9	2.4	11.3	1.5	0.9	0.0
	Central	86.0	1.2	10.6	2.2	0.0	0.0
	Western	93.2	2.0	2.6	1.7	0.0	0.5
Small towns	National	89.3	2.9	3.6	0.3	0.0	3.9
	Eastern	76.3	8.4	7.0	0.2	0.0	8.1
	Central	94.1	0.5	1.9	0.0	0.0	3.5
	Western	95.8	0.8	2.6	0.8	0.0	0.0

Table 4.44 Levels of public school migrant workers' children living in different areas study in, unit: %

Living area	*Location*	*Level of public schools*				
		National key school	*Provincial key school*	*City key school*	*County key school*	*Non-key school*
Urban cities	National	0.2	3.5	14.3	30.9	51.1
	Eastern	0.4	2.9	17.6	35.7	43.4
	Central	0.0	5.4	14.2	33.6	46.8
	Western	0.0	2.3	8.6	18.9	70.2
Suburban areas	National	0.0	2.3	10.1	23.2	64.4
	Eastern	0.1	1.7	8.2	24.7	65.3
	Central	0.0	2.0	15.3	26.0	56.7
	Western	0.0	3.8	8.3	17.5	70.4
Small towns	National	0.0	1.2	9.0	36.1	56.7
	Eastern	0.0	3.0	15.0	28.0	54.0
	Central	0.0	0.3	4.9	41.2	53.6
	Western	0.0	0.8	8.9	36.8	53.5

Table 4.45 Long-distance education about migrant workers' and rural citizens' children, unit: %

Long-distance education or not	*National*		*Eastern*		*Central*		*Western*	
	Rural families	*Migrant workers' families*	*Rural families*	*Migrant workers' families*	*Rural families*	*Migrant workers' families*	*Rural families*	*Migrant workers' families*
Yes	7.0	13.4	7.8	14.7	7.0	12.0	6.2	12.5
No	93.0	86.6	92.2	85.3	93.0	88.0	93.8	87.5

Table 4.46 Long-distance education about migrant workers' and rural citizens' children living in different areas, unit: %

Living area	*Location*	*Long-distance education or not*	
		Yes	*No*
Urban cities	`lational	20.6	79.4
	Eastern	23.4	76.6
	Central	17.4	82.6
	Western	19.4	80.6
Suburb districts	National	17.6	82.4
	Eastern	20.0	80.0
	Central	13.6	86.4
	Western	17.4	82.6
Small towns	National	12.4	87.6
	Eastern	22.9	77.1
	Central	9.4	90.6
	Western	6.1	93.9

Table 4.45 shows the long-distance education about migrant workers' and rural citizens' children. In national average level, 13.4% of migrant workers' families and 7.0% of rural families send their children away for school. The ratios are not too high but ratios of migrant workers' families are higher than that of rural families. This may be related to migrant workers' sample and their family moves.

Table 4.46 shows long-distance education about migrant workers' and rural citizens' children living in different areas. We can see that nationally speaking, the ratio of long-distance education of migrant workers' children living in urban cities is the highest, which is 20.6%, followed by those live living in suburban areas and in small cities and towns, which are respectively 17.6% and 12.4%.

Table 4.47 Education fees for children in migrant workers' families and rural families, unit: %

Education fee (yuan)	*National*		*Eastern*		*Central*		*Western*	
	Rural families	*Migrant workers' families*	*Rural families*	*Migrant workers' families*	*Rural families*	*Migrant workers' families*	*Rural families*	*Migrant workers' families*
<100	19.0	17.7	22.6	19.2	14.1	17.0	22.3	16.9
100–1000	36.9	38.2	34.3	35.2	35.7	39.4	40.4	42.5
1000–2000	12.8	12.6	13.2	13.0	12.5	13.7	12.7	10.3
2000–3000	7.7	7.1	6.4	6.5	9.6	5.3	6.3	10.1
3000–5000	8.8	10.4	8.3	10.7	10.1	10.0	7.7	10.0
5000–10,000	9.7	8.3	8.5	9.0	12.6	8.6	7.0	6.5
>10,000	5.1	5.7	6.7	6.4	5.4	6.0	3.6	3.7

Table 4.47 shows the education fees for children in migrant workers' families and rural families. In 2015, 38.2% of migrant workers paid 100–1000 yuan for children's education fee, 17.7% was below 100 yuan; 12.6% paid 1000–2000 yuan; 10.4% paid 3000–5000 yuan; 8.3% paid for 5000–10,000 yuan; 7.1% for 2000–3000 yuan and 5.7% was above 10,000 yuan. There is no significant difference between migrant workers' families and rural families, 55% of which paid less than 1000 yuan for children's education every year.

4.2.7 *Housing Situation*

4.2.7.1 Homeownership Rate

As is shown in Table 4.48, the homeownership rate of migrant workers, among the samples of CRHPS, is relatively higher. The average figure across the country is 74.4%. The figure in the eastern region of China is 75.4%, 75% in the central region, and 71.1% in the western region.

Table 4.49 illustrates the proportion of the migrant workers' families that own different number of houses. As we can see, the proportion of migrant workers' families owning one house is the highest, which is 80.5%.

4.2.7.2 The Current Housing Situation

Table 4.50 illustrates the nature of houses occupied currently by migrant workers' family. From this table, we can see that 74.4% of the houses are possessed only by family members. From regional perspective, self-owned

Table 4.48 Situation of migrant workers' homeownership, unit: %

	National	*Eastern*	*Central*	*Western*
Ownership rate	74.4	75.4	75.0	71.7

Table 4.49 Proportion of different numbers of houses possessed by family, unit: %

Number of houses possessed by family	*National*	*Eastern*	*Central*	*Western*
One	80.5	77.7	84.3	82.7
Two	16.8	18.5	14.0	15.8
Three or more	2.7	3.8	1.7	1.5

Table 4.50 Nature of houses occupied currently by migrant workers, unit: %

Type of urban area	*Location*	*Situation of current housing*		
		Owned by family	*Renting*	*Free accommodation*
Average	National	74.4	22.8	2.8
	Eastern	75.4	22.0	2.6
	Central	75.0	22.0	3.0
	Western	71.6	25.4	3.0
Urban area	National	58.7	37.5	3.8
	Eastern	57.1	38.8	4.1
	Central	62.9	35	2.1
	Western	57.1	37.6	5.3
Suburban area	National	62.2	34.7	3.1
	Eastern	60.6	36.5	2.9
	Central	69.9	24.9	5.2
	Western	57.8	40.7	1.5
Small cities and towns	National	76.5	21	2.5
	Eastern	85.8	11.9	2.3
	Central	73.7	22.8	3.5
	Western	68.3	30.6	1.1

house rate of the eastern region ranks the highest, which is 75.4%. The figures in the central and western regions are 75.0% and 71.6%, respectively. In terms of the types of urban area, the rate of small cities and towns ranks the highest, which is 76.5%. The figures of urban and suburban areas are 62.2% and 58.7%, respectively. Three reasons may explain why the self-owned house rate here is distinctly higher than that in other researches of the same kind: the first is that only migrant workers who reside in urban residential houses are surveyed in the samples. In contrast, according to the Migrant Workers Monitoring Survey Report in 2015 released by the NBS, only around 41.4% of migrant workers who work in urban areas live in urban residential houses, while others reside in accommodations provided by employers, temporary sheds in construction, sites for production and operation, and so on. Second, the samples here only concern those migrant workers' families who have been in a specific city or town for more than six months and mainly lead their activities consumptions in that area. These families enjoy higher stability and self-owned house rate. The third reason is that the samples here include a higher proportion of local migrant workers. In recent years, local governments have helped many farmers to migrate by means of village reforms, transforming homestead for other uses, land demolition and other policies. As a result, the self-owned house rate of these people is relatively higher.

We will now analyze the nature of the current housing occupied by local and non-local migrant workers (Tables 4.51 and 4.52).

From Tables 4.51 and 4.52, we can see that the average self-owned house rate currently occupied by local migrant workers is 76.6%, which is

Table 4.51 Nature of the current housing of local migrant workers, unit: %

Type of urban area	*Location*	*Situation of the current housing of local migrant workers*		
		Owned by family	*Renting*	*Free accommodation*
Average	National	76.6	19.7	3.7
	Eastern	80.0	16.1	3.9
	Central	76.5	21.7	1.8
	Western	69.7	24.2	6.1
Urban area	National	76.6	19.7	3.7
	Eastern	80.0	16.1	3.9
	Central	76.5	21.7	1.8
	Western	69.8	24.2	6.0
Suburban area	National	79.4	17.7	2.9
	Eastern	79.3	17.8	2.9
	Central	84.8	13.0	2.2
	Western	71.0	25.3	3.7
Small cities and towns	National	82.4	15.5	2.1
	Eastern	90.2	6.6	3.2
	Central	85.2	12.8	2.0
	Western	66.3	33.6	0.1

Table 4.52 Nature of the current housing of non-local migrant workers, unit: %

Type of urban area	*Location*	*Situation of the current housing of non-local migrant workers*		
		Owned by family	*Renting*	*Free accommodation*
Average	National	55.6	40.6	3.8
	Eastern	51.4	45.3	3.3
	Central	61.0	34.9	4.1
	Western	58.0	38.0	4.0
Urban area	National	52.4	43.7	3.9
	Eastern	49.3	46.5	4.2
	Central	57.5	40.4	2.1
	Western	53.0	41.9	5.1
Suburban area	National	50.3	46.4	3.3
	Eastern	46.9	50.3	2.8
	Central	57.5	34.9	7.6
	Western	51.6	47.9	0.5
Small cities and towns	National	68.7	28.2	3.1
	Eastern	76.3	23.0	0.7
	Central	63.1	31.9	5.0
	Western	70.8	27.0	2.2

21% points higher than that of non-local migrant workers, which is 55.6%. Among the local migrant workers, the rate of small cities and towns ranks the highest at 82.4%, and particularly in the eastern region, where the figure has reached to 90.2%.

Table 4.53 illustrates the house decoration of migrant workers. From this table, we can see that most people prefer simple decoration. On average, only 7.6% of houses are finely decorated. Except that the rate in small cities and towns in the eastern region reaches 24.2%, that in other regions is below 10%.

Table 4.54 illustrates the forms of house leasing of migrant workers. For people who mainly move into urban areas with their families, renting a whole house is the mainstream. Only 10.7% of people share a house with others and this rate in the western urban area ranks the highest at 17.5% and ranks the lowest in small cities and towns in this region, which is 5.7%.

Table 4.55 further analyzes the shared housing situation of migrant workers. From this table, we can see that even though migrant workers live in shared houses, the actual usable area of the house is not small, and on average, it reaches 64.4 square meters. Among them, the figure can

Table 4.53 House decoration of migrant workers

Type of urban area	*Location*	*Situation of house decoration*		
		Rough house	*Simple decoration*	*Refined decoration*
The average	National	18.3	74.1	7.6
	Eastern	15.8	75.2	9.0
	Central	18.7	73.4	7.9
	Western	22.8	72.9	4.3
Urban area	National	16.4	75.7	7.9
	Eastern	12.4	78.7	8.9
	Central	21.5	70.8	7.7
	Western	19.2	74.6	6.2
Suburban area	National	18.1	74.6	7.3
	Eastern	16.7	73.7	9.6
	Central	8.2	83.1	8.7
	Western	30.2	69.8	0.0
Small cities and towns	National	22.0	68.4	9.6
	Eastern	18.4	57.4	24.2
	Central	15.1	77.2	7.7
	Western	32.3	64.5	3.2

Table 4.54 Forms of house leasing of migrant workers, unit: %

Type of urban area	*Location*	*Forms of house leasing*		
		Sharing	*Whole leasing*	*Others*
Average	National	10.7	88.6	0.7
	Eastern	10.4	89.3	0.3
	Central	12.7	85.3	2.0
	Western	9.3	90.2	0.5
Urban area	National	11.9	87.9	0.2
	Eastern	11.4	88.5	0.1
	Central	13.3	86.7	0.0
	Western	17.5	81.8	0.7
Suburban area	National	9.0	90.8	0.2
	Eastern	8.0	92.0	0.0
	Central	11.2	88.8	0.0
	Western	10.2	89.4	0.4
Small cities and towns	National	11.1	83.9	5.0
	Eastern	9.1	90.9	0.0
	Central	17.1	70.9	12.0
	Western	5.7	94.3	0.0

Table 4.55 The shared housing situation of the migrant workers' family

Type of urban area	*Location*	*Situation of the occupation of rental house*		
		Number of families sharing a house	*Actual area occupied (square meter)*	*Rent (yuan/ month)*
The average	National	4.49	64.4	1042
	Eastern	4.21	62.6	1264
	Central	5.43	64.5	812
	Western	3.90	67.6	830
Urban area	National	3.28	60.2	1237
	Eastern	3.65	56.9	1578
	Central	2.65	61.9	890
	Western	3.31	64.7	918
Suburban area	National	5.72	60.3	929
	Eastern	5.62	62.0	1023
	Central	6.14	52.5	722
	Western	5.60	62.5	844
Small cities and Towns	National	10.35	81.0	567
	Eastern	6.71	92.6	1096
	Central	13.01	81.5	503
	Western	4.75	73.9	372

Table 4.56 Situation of migrant workers owning houses with limited property rights, unit: %

	National	*Eastern*	*Central*	*Western*
Proportion of ownership	3.7	4.5	2.3	2.5

reach 92.6 square meters for those in small cities and towns in the eastern region, where the average area is the largest. The smallest, which is in suburban areas in the central region, also reaches 52.5 square meters.

4.2.7.3 Owning House with Limited Property Rights

As Table 4.56 shows, the proportion of migrant workers who own houses with limited property rights is quite low, which is about 3.7% around China, while the rate in the eastern region is 7.5%, 2.3% in the central region and 2.5% in the western region.

4.2.7.4 Willingness to Purchase or Build a House

As Table 4.57 shows, the overall migrant workers' willingness to purchase a new house is relatively low, at merely 17.9%. However, migrant workers

Table 4.57 Plan of migrant workers to purchase (build) a house, unit: %

Plan to purchase or to build a new house or neither	*National*	*Eastern*	*Central*	*Western*
Plan to purchase	17.9	18.3	19.3	15.7
Plan to build	8.9	7.6	9.4	10.8
Purchase as well as build	1.2	1.6	0.3	1.3
Neither	72.0	72.5	71.0	72.2

Table 4.58 Plan of migrant workers living in different types of cities and towns to purchase (build) a house, unit: %

Type of urban area	*Location*	*Plan to purchase or build a new house*			
		Plan to purchase	*Plan to build*	*Purchase as well as build*	*No plan*
Urban area	National	27.8	5.7	1.4	65.1
	Eastern	29.5	5.8	2.1	62.6
	Central	30.0	4.5	0.3	65.2
	Western	22.4	6.9	1.3	69.4
Suburban area	National	18.6	9.7	0.6	71.1
	Eastern	16.0	9.4	0.8	73.8
	Central	23.6	11.6	0.7	64.1
	Western	19.9	8.4	0.0	71.7
Small cities and towns	National	12.7	9.3	0.8	77.2
	Eastern	16.8	6.5	1.5	75.2
	Central	12.2	12.1	0.5	75.2
	Western	9.1	8.5	0.5	81.9

in the central region are more willing to purchase house so this figure reaches to 19.3%. The eastern region comes in second place, where the figure is 18.3%; whereas only 15.7% of migrant workers in the western region are willing to purchase a house. The average proportion of migrant workers who plan to build a new house is 8.9%, with the western region ranking the highest at 10.8% and the eastern region ranking the lowest at 7.6%.

Next, the willingness to of migrant workers living in different types of cities and towns to purchase and build houses will be analyzed. From Table 4.58, we can see that the willingness of migrant workers' families living in small cities and towns in the central region is the strongest which is 12.1%; while the least lies in those living in the urban areas in the central region, which is 4.5%.

Table 4.59 Time planned by migrant workers to purchase a house, unit: %

When to purchase a house	*National*	*Eastern*	*Central*	*Western*
Within a year	9.1	5.8	14.4	10.3
One to two years	22.8	22.7	22.2	23.8
Two to five years	34.0	39.7	25.5	31.4
Five years later	34.1	31.8	37.9	34.5

Table 4.60 Time planned to purchase a house of migrant workers living in different types of cities and towns, unit: %

Type of urban area	*Location*	*When to purchase a house*			
		Within a year	*One to two years*	*Two to five years*	*Five years later*
Urban area	National	9.9	21.2	35.3	33.6
	Eastern	7.3	19.4	43.3	30.0
	Central	9.9	28.1	20.6	41.4
	Western	15.8	16.4	35.0	32.8
Suburban area	National	2.9	30.2	31.9	35.0
	Eastern	0.7	39.0	32.6	27.7
	Central	1.8	15.1	32.7	50.4
	Western	9.7	32.7	29.2	28.4
Small cities and towns	National	16.1	24.3	33.4	26.2
	Eastern	2.4	20.6	42.2	34.8
	Central	34.4	16.1	31.5	18.0
	Western	5.7	48.7	19.6	26.0

As Table 4.59 shows, in terms of the purchasing time, fewer migrant workers planned to purchase a house within a year and most people said that they would purchase a house two years later, which take up 68%. Compared to this, only 32% of migrant workers planned to purchase a house within two years. It can therefore be seen that migrant workers do have wishes to settle down in urban areas to some degree, but their dream may be less likely to come true in the short term.

Next, we will analyze the time planned by the migrant workers' families living in different types of cities and towns to purchase a house. From Table 4.60, we can see that the proportion of these families that are planning to purchase a house within a year reaches to 16.1%, which is much higher than the average figure of 9.1%. This may indicate that these families have relatively strong purchasing power.

4.2.7.5 Housing Vacancy Rate

As Table 4.61 shows, the migrant workers' housing vacancy rate is 38.8% on average across the country. In comparison, the eastern region is the lowest with 36.9%; the central region is 39.3%; while in the western region is the highest with 45.0%. The one-house vacancy rate across the country is 13.9% on average, whereas that of many houses is distinctly higher, which is 24.9%.

Next, the housing vacancy rate of migrant workers who own different number of houses will be further analyzed. Table 4.62 shows the housing vacancy proportion of migrant workers who own different number of houses. The housing vacancy rate of one house across the country is 29.8%, with the highest in the western region, which is 46.2%, 34.3% in the central region and 19.2% in the east. These figures indicate that these families live in urban areas by renting, whereas their own house is vacant. The vacancy rate of families with two houses is 45.1% on average across the nation, with 47.8% in the west, 44.8% in the eastern region and 43.8% in the central region; the housing vacancy rate of families with three houses is 32.3% on average across the nation, with 33.3% in the western region, 32.4% in the central region and the lowest 22.2% in the eastern region.

Table 4.63 illustrates the housing vacancy situation of migrant workers in different regions. In general, the rate in small cities and towns is the highest, which is 47.0%, and the lowest is in villages and towns, which is 28.8%.

Table 4.61 Housing vacancy rate of migrant workers

Location	*Vacancy rate*	*From one house owner*	*From more house owners*
National	38.8	13.9	24.9
Eastern	36.9	8.1	28.8
Central	39.3	18.0	21.3
Western	45.0	26.6	18.4

Table 4.62 Housing vacancy rate of migrant workers owning different number of houses, unit: %

	National	*Eastern*	*Central*	*Western*
Family owning one house	29.8	19.2	34.3	46.2
Family owning two houses	45.1	44.8	43.8	47.8
Family owning three or more houses	32.3	33.3	32.4	22.2

Table 4.63 Housing vacancy rate of migrant workers in different regions, unit: %

Location	*Location of housing*					
	Urban area	*Suburban area*	*Small cities and towns*	*Villages and towns*	*Rural area*	*On average*
National	45.1	39.5	47.0	28.8	38.1	38.8
Eastern	47.0	39.6	39.9	28.1	35.6	36.9
Central	41.6	54.5	32.9	28.1	39.3	39.3
Western	39.1	32.8	66.9	41.4	44.9	45.0

Table 4.64 Housing vacancy rate of local migrant workers in different areas, unit: %

Location	*Location of housing*					
	Urban area	*Suburban area*	*Small cities and towns*	*Villages and towns*	*Rural area*	*Average*
National	41.2	25.3	57.1	29.1	36.2	36.5
Eastern	42.7	24.4	47.6	28.2	34.3	34.0
Central	42.3	39.9	16.2	24.7	45.5	37.8
Western	32.0	20.5	86.3	49.3	37.1	47.3

Table 4.65 Housing vacancy rate of non-local migrant workers in different areas, unit: %

Location	*Location of housing*					
	Urban area	*Suburban area*	*Small cities and towns*	*Villages and towns*	*Rural area*	*Average*
National	47.7	51.6	33.1	27.6	38.3	40.3
Eastern	50.0	55.6	32.4	26.7	35.0	38.9
Central	41.1	63.4	50.0	33.2	36.9	40.3
Western	44.4	37.4	8.6	34.3	47.8	43.8

Next, we will analyze the housing vacancy situation of local and non-local migrant workers in different areas (Tables 4.64 and 4.65).

We can see from the comparisons in Tables 4.64 and 4.65 that the average housing vacancy rate of non-local migrant workers is 40.3%, which is 3.8 percentage points higher than that of local ones with a rate of 36.5% The housing vacancy rate of non-local migrant workers in rural areas

Table 4.66 The current vacancy period of the migrant workers' unoccupied housing, unit: %

Location		*Housing vacancy period*				
		Less than one month	*One to six months*	*Six to twelve months*	*One to two years*	*Two years or more*
National	Urban area	21.4	20.9	10.0	19.6	28.1
	Rural area	10.4	11.4	8.9	13.6	55.7
Eastern	Urban area	18.9	24.2	7.5	19.5	29.9
	Rural area	7.6	15.9	9.7	13.1	53.7
Central	Urban area	31.0	11.5	17.1	15.4	25.0
	Rural area	8.1	7.6	10.0	11.7	62.6

reaches 38.3%, which is 2.1 percentage points higher than that of the local ones with a rate of 36.2%. In addition, the housing vacancy rate of local migrant workers in small cities and towns is particularly high, reaching to 57.1%, whereas that of non-local ones in the suburban areas is relatively high, reaching to 51.6%.

Next, the current vacancy period of the migrant workers' unoccupied housing will be further analyzed (Table 4.66).

From Table 4.66, we can see that, among the vacant houses of migrant workers, those in rural areas have mostly been unoccupied over a long period of time. Houses which have been vacant for longer than one year take up 69.3%, and the rate of those being vacant for more than two years is 55.7%, whereas as for vacant houses in urban areas, more than half have been vacant just for a short term. More than half (52.3%) of them have been vacant for less than a year and 42.3% for less than six months, with 21.4% for less than a month. However, being vacant for more than two years only takes up 28.1%.

Next, the current housing vacancy period of the local migrant workers' unoccupied housing will be analyzed (Tables 4.67 and 4.68).

We can see from the comparisons in Tables 4.67 and 4.68 that the proportion of long-term house vacancy of non-local migrant workers is narrowly higher than that of the local ones. The houses being kept vacant more than one year take up 70.2%, higher than 67.5% of that of local ones

Table 4.67 The current housing vacancy period of the local migrant workers' self-owned housing, unit: %

Location		*Housing vacancy period*				
		Less than a month	*One to six months*	*Six to twelve months*	*One to two years*	*Two years or more*
National	Urban area	17.8	15.6	7.0	25.1	34.5
	Rural area	18.1	7.4	7.0	11.8	55.7
Eastern	Urban area	13.6	18.2	8.6	21.6	38.0
	Rural area	15.6	7.8	6.5	11.1	59.0
Central	Urban area	29.0	14.1	1.6	23.9	31.4
	Rural area	4.2	13.7	16.6	12.9	52.6
Western	Urban area	28.7	13.0	3.7	30.9	23.7
	Rural area	34.6	1.8	1.9	14.5	47.2

Table 4.68 The current vacancy period of the on-local migrant workers' self-owned housing, unit: %

Location		*Housing vacancy period*				
		Less than a month	*One to six months*	*Six to twelve months*	*One to two years*	*Two years or more*
National	Urban area	24.4	22.8	11.7	15.7	25.4
	Rural area	6.8	12.7	10.3	14.4	55.8
Eastern	Urban area	23.7	25.7	6.5	18.1	26.0
	Rural area	3.3	18.5	12.0	13.3	52.9
Central	Urban area	31.0	11.5	17.1	15.4	25.0
	Rural area	11.1	2.9	5.4	11.5	69.1
Western	Urban area	23.7	17.2	14.4	19.0	25.7
	Rural area	9.7	4.6	13.2	17.2	55.3

by 2.7%. Only 19.5% of houses have been vacant for less than six months, which is 6 percentage points lower than that of the local ones with a proportion of 25.5%. We can therefore see that the long-term vacancy rate of non-local migrant workers is higher because it is more difficult for these people to pay attention to their houses in the rural areas. The current vacancy period of the non-local migrant workers' unoccupied housing in the urban areas is relatively shorter. Houses which have been vacant for less than a year take up 68.9%, which is higher than the 40.4% of that of local migrant workers by 28.5 percentage points. As a result, although there is vacancy in the houses of the non-local migrant workers in urban areas, most of the houses are only kept vacant for a temporary period of time.

4.2.8 Healthcare and Social Security

4.2.8.1 Chronic Diseases

As Table 4.69 shows, on national level, 26.7% of migrant workers have chronic diseases. On regional level, 22.8% of migrant workers in the eastern region have chronic diseases, whereas as for those in the central and western regions, the proportion is higher, at 30.3% and 31.7%, respectively.

Table 4.70 illustrates the severity of chronic diseases assessed by migrant workers themselves compared with their peers. From it we can see that self-assessment of migrant workers is between "rather severe" and "generally severe".

As Table 4.71 shows that, at the national level, the chances of female migrant workers having chronic diseases are higher than that of male migrant workers. Among the rates of having chronic diseases, the male proportion is 24.9% and while the female proportion is 28.3% across the country.

Table 4.69 Situation of migrant workers having chronic diseases, unit: %

Suffer from chronic diseases	*National*	*Eastern*	*Central*	*Western*
Yes	26.7	22.8	30.3	31.7
No	73.3	77.2	69.7	68.3

Table 4.70 Self-assessment of migrant workers over the severity of chronic diseases

National	*Eastern*	*Central*	*Western*
2.83	2.99	2.80	2.60

Note: "1" indicates the most severe; "2" indicates rather severe; "3" indicates generally severe; "4" indicates not too severe; "5" indicates not severe

Table 4.71 Gender differences of migrant workers having chronic diseases, unit: %

Gender	*National*	*Eastern*	*Central*	*Western*
Male	24.9	21.1	28.1	30.4
Female	28.3	24.4	32.2	32.9

Table 4.72 Age differences of migrant workers having chronic diseases, unit: %

Age	*National*	*Eastern*	*Central*	*Western*
<30	5.3	4.0	6.7	6.9
31–40	13.8	9.8	18.7	18.4
41–50	26.7	19.5	30.3	36.4
51–60	42.8	37.8	50.5	46.8
>60	58.4	54.0	62.0	65.1

From Table 4.72, we can see that the rate of migrant workers beyond 60 years ranks the highest. Meanwhile, as people get older, the figure gets bigger. At the national level, 58.4% of migrant workers over 60 years suffer from chronic diseases.

4.2.8.2 Coverage of Pension

Table 4.73 illustrates the distribution of Chinese migrant workers and rural residents over ways of living their retirement life. On the national level, 39.8% of migrant workers have no old-age security of any form. The table shows that 57.1% of migrant workers depend on social endowment insurance to live their retirement life. Only 2.1% of migrant workers depend on their pension. On the regional level, migrant workers without any social security in the western region account for the most, taking up 45.8% of the population, and the rate in the eastern region is the least, which is 36.6%. Among migrant workers receiving pension, the central region takes up the most, which is 2.5%, followed by the eastern region with 2.1%. The western region takes the least, which is only 1.5% and below the average. There is room for improvement on the coverage of pension. From the comparison with rural residents in rural areas, only 59.3% of migrant workers have social security, which is 7 percentage points lower than that of rural residents with 66.3%. We can therefore see that the situation of the migrant workers' social security is not optimistic.

Table 4.74 illustrates the comparison between migrant workers and rural residents over the distribution of the types of social endowment insurance. Whether it is the migrant workers or rural residents, the New Rural Social Endowment Insurance is the most favored among all the social endowment insurances. Although there is a much fewer proportion of migrant workers who have the New Rural Social Endowment Insurance than that of rural residents, the figure is still as large as 66.9%. Ranking in

Table 4.73 Distribution of migrant workers and rural residents over ways of living retirement life, unit: %

Ways of living retirement life	*National*	*Eastern*	*Central*	*Western*	*National*	*Eastern*	*Central*	*Western*
	Rural residents	*Migrant worker*	*Rural residents*	*Migrant worker*	*Rural residents*	*Migrant worker*	*Rural residents*	*Migrant worker*
No social security	33.4	39.8	32.8	36.6	30.3	41.1	37.7	45.8
Have social security	66.3	59.3	66.2	63.0	69.1	58.4	61.8	53.7
Social insurance	64.9	57.1	64.5	59.9	67.7	55.9	60.7	52.2
Retirement pay	1.4	2.1	1.5	2.1	1.4	2.5	1.1	1.5
Others	0.3	0.9	1.0	0.4	0.6	0.5	0.5	0.5

Table 4.74 The comparison between migrant workers and rural residents over distribution of types of social endowment insurance, unit: %

Types of social endowment insurance	*National*	*Eastern*	*Central*	*Western*	*National*	*Eastern*	*Central*	*Western*
	Rural residents	*Migrant workers*	*Rural residents*	*Migrant workers*	*Rural residents*	*Migrant workers*	*Rural residents*	*Migrant workers*
Basic endowment insurance for urban employees	5.4	22.8	8.4	29.2	2.6	16.3	5.8	13.6
New rural social endowment insurance	90.7	66.9	87.7	59.2	94.4	74.6	89.2	77.6
Social endowment insurance for urban residents	1.7	6.5	1.6	6.8	1.2	7.0	2.7	5.4
Rural-urban unification social endowment insurance	2.2	3.8	2.3	4.8	1.8	2.1	2.3	3.4

second place is the Basic Endowment Insurance for Urban Employees, followed by the Endowment Insurance for Urban Employees, and in the last place, the Rural-Urban Unification Social Endowment Insurance. As for the New Rural Social Endowment Insurance, people in the western region have the highest proportion of 77.6%, whereas the eastern region has the lowest proportion of 59.2%.

Next, we will analyze the differences between the new generation of migrant workers (the post-1980s and the post-1990s) and the old generation of migrant workers over the distribution of the types of social endowment insurances. From Table 4.75, we can learn that the rates of the new generation of migrant workers (the post-1980s and the post-1990s) over having the basic pension for urban employees are 42.3% and 42.8%, respectively, both of which are much higher than that of the old generation, which is 15.1%. However, the proportions of having the new rural social endowment insurance are 47.3% and 51.8%, respectively, which are distinctly lower than that of the old generation, which is 74.2%.

4.2.8.3 The Insurance Premium of the Social Endowment Insurance and Income

Table 4.76 illustrates the personal payment of migrant workers for social endowment insurance and income. The average payment is 2490.0 yuan per year and the annual income is 6889.2 yuan. On the regional level, people in the eastern region pay the most, which is 3271.2 yuan/year. This is followed by the western region, which is 1696.8 yuan per year. People in the central region pay the least, which is 1472.4 yuan per year. The income is in accordance with the tendency of payment. The highest income lies in the eastern region, which is 7954.8 yuan per year, followed by the central region with 5875.2 yuan per year. The least is in the western region, which is only 5186.4 yuan per year.

4.2.8.4 Implementation of the Pension System Unification

Table 4.77 illustrates the implementation of the Pension System Unification of companies which migrant workers work in. The table shows that 26.7% of companies have carried out the policy. On the regional level, the implementation works best in the central region, where the rate amounts to 43.0%, and the performance in the western region is the worst, where the rate is only 19.2%.

Table 4.75 Distribution of the types of social endowment insurance of migrant workers of different ages, unit: %

Types of social endowment insurance	*National*	*Eastern*	*Central*	*Western*	*National*	*Eastern*	*Central*	*Western*	*National*	*Eastern*	*Central*	*Western*
	Post-1990s	*Post-1980s*	*Old generation*	*Post-1990s*	*Post-1980s*	*Old generation*	*Post-1990s*	*Post-1980s*	*Old generation*	*Post-1990s*	*Post-1980s*	*Old generation*
Basic endowment insurance for urban employees	42.8	42.3	15.1	20.9	48.6	20.9	34.9	34.9	9.0	29.3	29.3	7.9
New rural social endowment insurance	51.8	47.3	74.2	67.1	39.7	67.1	58.5	58.5	81.0	60.3	60.3	83.1
Social endowment insurance for urban residents	2.8	6.5	6.8	6.9	7.1	6.9	4.9	4.9	7.7	6.4	6.4	5.5
Rural-urban unification social endowment insurance	2.6	3.9	3.9	5.1	4.5	5.1	1.7	1.7	2.3	4.0	4.0	3.5

Table 4.76 Comparison between personal payment on social endowment insurance and income of migrant workers

Item for comparison	*National*	*Eastern*	*Central*	*Western*
Payment (yuan/year)	2490.0	3271.2	1472.4	1696.8
Income (yuan/year)	6889.2	7954.8	5875.2	5186.4

Table 4.77 Implementation of the pension system unification in the migrant workers' company, unit: %

Implemented or not	*National*	*Eastern*	*Central*	*Western*
Implemented	26.7	23.2	43.0	19.2
Not implemented	73.3	76.8	57.0	80.8

Table 4.78 Medicare coverage of migrant workers, unit: %

Have Medicare or not	*National*	*Eastern*	*Central*	*Western*
Have	85.2	82.8	87.3	88.4
Not	14.8	17.2	12.6	11.6

Table 4.79 Medicare coverage of migrant workers at different ages, unit: %

Have Medicare or not	*National*			*Eastern*			*Central*			*Western*		
	≤30	*31–50*	*>50*	*≤30*	*31–50*	*>50*	*≤30*	*31–50*	*>50*	*≤30*	*31–50*	*>50*
Have	80.0	87.6	89.9	76.2	85.9	88.3	82.0	89.3	93.3	86.2	89.4	91.3
Not have	20.0	12.4	10.1	23.8	14.1	11.7	18.0	10.7	6.7	13.8	10.6	9.7

4.2.8.5 Social Medical Insurance Coverage

Table 4.78 illustrates the medical insurance coverage of migrant workers. From it, we can see that national average medical insurance coverage of migrant workers is 85.2%. On the regional level, the western region ranks the highest with 88.4%. The eastern region is the least with 82.8%. The rate in the western region is narrowly higher than that in the central region.

Table 4.79 analyzes the social Medicare coverage of migrant workers at different ages. Among the migrant workers over 50 years of age, 89.9% have basic medical insurance across the country, while this proportion is

Table 4.80 Differences in the Medicare coverage of migrant workers of different genders, unit: %

Have Medicare or not	*National*		*Eastern*		*Central*		*Western*	
	Male	*Female*	*Male*	*Female*	*Male*	*Female*	*Male*	*Female*
Have	84.9	85.5	83.0	82.6	86.8	87.9	87.2	89.6
Not have	15.1	14.5	17.0	17.4	13.2	12.1	12.8	10.4

88.3% in the eastern region, 93.3% in the central region and 91.3% in the western region. Across the country, 87.6% of migrant workers aged between 31 and 50 have basic medical insurance, while this figure is 85.9% in the eastern region, 89.3% in the central region and 89.4% in the western region. Among the migrant workers aged 30 years or below, 80.0% have basic Medicare across the country, while this figure is 76.2% in the eastern region, 82.0% in the central region and 86.2% in the western region.

Table 4.80 analyzes the social Medicare coverage of migrant workers of different genders. In the western region, the Medicare coverage of the male population is the highest amongst all regions, which is 87.2%, while the same applies to the female population as well, which is 89.6%. In terms of the genders, the Medicare coverage of the female population is a little higher than that of the male population, with the exception of the eastern region where the coverage of males is narrowly higher.

From Table 4.81 we can learn about the types of medical insurance of Chinese migrant workers. Among those who have social medical insurances, 76.5% of them have the New Rural Cooperative Medical Insurance. On the regional level, the rate of having the New Rural Cooperative Medical Insurance in the western region is the highest, which is 85.3%. This is followed by the central region with a rate of 82.9. The figure in the eastern region is the lowest, which is only 69.0%.

From Table 4.82, we can see that, compared to the older generation, the proportion of young migrant workers having the New Rural Cooperative Medical Insurance is declining. The figure of the older generation is 79.7%, 23.9% for the post-1980s and 74.1% for the post-1990s. However, the proportion of having the basic medical insurance for urban employees is distinctly increasing. The figure of the older generation is 8.9%, 23.9% for the post-1980s and 10.9% for the post-1990s. Additionally, it is worth noticing that even though the proportion of the post-1990s who have the new rural cooperative insurance is smaller than that of the

Table 4.81 Distribution of the types of medical insurance of migrant workers, unit: %

Types	*National*	*Eastern*	*Central*	*Western*
Basic medical insurance for urban employees	10.7	14.9	7.1	5.8
Basic medical insurance for urban residents	5.6	6.6	5.5	3.7
New rural cooperative medical insurance	76.5	69.0	82.9	85.3
Basic medical insurance for rural and urban residents	2.1	2.8	1.0	2.0
Free Medicare service	0.4	0.5	0.3	0.3
Commercial medical insurance (at company's expense)	0.8	0.8	0.7	0.8
Commercial medical insurance (at personal expense)	1.7	2.1	1.3	1.2
Enterprise supplementary medical insurance	0.1	0.1	0.1	0.1
Medical overall plan for serious illness	1.0	1.7	0.7	0.1
Social mutual aid	0.1	0.1	0.1	0.1
Others	1.	1.4	0.3	0.6

older generation, it is higher than that of the post-1980s. This may be due to the fact that most of the post-1990s have just moved into cities, but changing their minds and the actual process in obtaining the Basic Medical Insurance for Urban Employees requires a certain period of time. As a result, there is a great proportion of people who have not yet to join the Basic Medical Insurance for Urban Employees.

4.2.8.6 *Overall Plan for Serious Illness*

Table 4.83 illustrates that the basic situation of the overall plan for serious illness of Chinese migrant workers is not so promising. On the national level, only 0.9% of migrant workers enjoy this policy. The rate in the eastern region is the highest, which is 1.4%. The next is that in the central region, which is 0.6%. That in the western region is the least, which is only 0.1%.

4.2.8.7 *Housing Fund*

As Table 4.84 shows, only 6.8% of migrant workers have the housing fund. The figure in the eastern region is 8.5%, 5.6% in the central region and 4.3% in the western region. About 96.2% of them are still paying it. The average payment for housing fund is 399.1 yuan per month in 2015. The figure in the eastern region is 398.6 yuan per month, 427.5 yuan per

Table 4.82 Distribution of the types of medical insurance of migrant workers at different ages, unit: %

Types	*National*	*Eastern*	*Central*	*Western*	*National*	*Eastern*	*Central*	*Western*	*National*	*Eastern*	*Central*	*Western*
	Post-1990s	*Post-1980s*	*Older generation*	*Post-1990s*	*Post-1980s*	*Older generation*	*Post-1990s*	*Post-1980s*	*Older generation*	*Post-1990s*	*Post-1980s*	*Older generation*
Basic medical insurance for urban employees	10.9	23.9	8.9	13.8	31.4	12.7	8.5	15.8	5.8	8.1	14.1	4.2
Basic medical insurance for urban residents	7.0	5.1	5.3	8.5	6.0	6.3	7.2	4.1	5.6	4.2	3.8	2.9
New rural cooperative medical insurance	74.1	64.5	79.7	66.2	54.5	72.7	80.0	75.1	84.9	81.6	77.6	89.0
Basic medical insurance for rural and urban residents	1.6	2.0	2.3	2.6	2.3	3.1	0.5	0.9	1.1	1.1	2.4	2.1
Free Medicare service	0.3	0.4	0.4	0.5	0.4	0.5	0.2	0.7	0.2	0.1	0.0	0.5
Commercial medical insurance (at company's expense)	1.8	1.0	0.4	1.5	1.3	0.4	1.6	0.8	0.4	2.5	0.6	0.1
Commercial medical insurance (at personal expense)	1.0	2.0	1.1	1.2	2.8	1.3	0.9	1.1	1.0	0.6	1.3	0.9
Enterprise supplementary medical insurance	0.2	0.1	0.1	0.0	0.1	0.1	0.1	0.2	0.0	0.8	0.1	0.0
Medical overall plan for serious illness	0.4	0.9	1.3	0.8	0.9	2.1	0.0	1.3	0.8	0.0	0.1	0.1
Social mutual aid	0.0	0.0	0.1	0.0	0.0	0.0	0.0	0.0	0.1	0.1	0.0	0.1
Other	2.7	0.1	0.4	4.9	0.3	0.8	1.0	0.0	0.1	0.9	0.0	0.1

Table 4.83 Basic situation of the overall plan for serious illness of migrant workers

Basic situation of overall plan for serious illness	*National*	*Eastern*	*Central*	*Western*
Proportion of having this plan	0.9	1.4	0.6	0.1

Table 4.84 Basic situation of housing fund of migrant workers

Basic situation of housing fund	*National*	*Eastern*	*Central*	*Western*
Proportion of having housing fund (%)	6.8	8.5	5.6	4.3
Proportion of continuous payment (%)	96.2	96.6	94.9	96.3
Period of accumulative paid fund (month)	54.9	58.6	43.1	54.4
The housing fund paid in 2015 (yuan/ month)	399.1	398.6	427.5	363.8
Balance of housing fund account	29,711.6	15,833.4	18,208.4	93,795.1
The proportion of housing fund use in 2015 (%)	11.8	12.3	6.2	16.8
The amount of housing fund withdraw (yuan)	20,332.0	19,254.2	44,269.9	13,040.4

month in the central region and 363.8 yuan per month in the western region. The average balance of housing fund accounts is 29,711.6 yuan. The figure in the eastern region is 15,833.4 yuan, 18,208.4 yuan in the central region and 93,795.1 yuan in the western region. Among migrant workers who have housing fund, 11.8% of them have used it, while the figure in the eastern region is 12.3%, with 6.2% in the central region, as well as 16.8% in the western region. In 2015, the average withdrawal of housing fund is 20,332.0 yuan. The figure in the eastern region is 19,254.2 yuan, with 44,269.9 yuan in the central region and 13,040.4 yuan in the western region.

As Table 4.85 illustrates, among all the reasons for withdrawing housing fund, purchasing a house is the one that most people choose. In the eastern region, this proportion is 26.9%, 80.0% in the central region, as well as 26.8% in the western region. On the regional level, the major reason is to purchase a house and pay back the principal and interest of the housing loan, from which we come to feel the migrant workers' heavy pressure in purchasing a house.

Table 4.85 Reasons for withdrawing the housing fund

Reasons	*National*	*Eastern*	*Central*	*Western*
Purchase a house	32.3	26.9	80.0	26.8
Build/repair/rebuild a house	5.0	5.0	0.0	7.1
Pay back the principal and interest of house loan	27.2	24.5	11.1	43.8
Pay the rent	8.8	13.0	0.0	0.0
Retire from office	1.3	1.2	4.7	0.0
Leave the office	4.9	2.1	0.0	16.4
Invest stock and others	1.1	1.6	0.0	0.0
Settle down in other countries	0.7	1.0	0.0	0.0
Others	18.7	24.7	4.2	5.9

Table 4.86 Coverage of migrant workers' unemployment, maternity and employment injury insurances

Coverage of the three insurances	*The whole country*	*The eastern region*	*The central region*	*The western region*
The unemployment insurance	18.3	23.4	13.5	11.4
The employment injury insurance	19.9	24.5	14.9	14.1
The maternity insurance	15.0	18.8	11.0	10.4

4.2.8.8 Unemployment Insurance, Maternity Insurance and Employment Injury Insurance

Table 4.86 shows the situation of unemployment insurance, maternity insurance and employment injury insurance of migrant workers is quite dim. The national average coverages are respectively only 18.3%, 19.9% and 15.0%.

As for regional differences, the situation in the eastern region is the best, followed by the central region and the western region.

4.2.8.9 Commercial Insurance

From Table 4.87, which illustrates the proportion of having a commercial insurance, we can learn that the proportion of migrant workers who have commercial insurance is relatively low, with 92.3% of migrant workers not having any commercial insurance. The table also shows that 3.6% of migrant workers have a commercial life insurance. The proportion of

Table 4.87 Proportion of migrant workers taking out commercial insurances, unit: %

Situation of commercial insurances	*National*	*Eastern*	*Central*	*Western*
Life insurance	3.6	4.0	4.0	2.5
Health insurance	2.4	2.8	2.7	1.4
Other insurances	1.7	1.9	1.2	1.6
None	92.3	91.3	92.1	94.5

migrant workers who take out health insurances accounts for 2.4%, as for other commercial insurances, the figure is 1.7%. On the regional level, the participation rates in commercial insurance in the eastern, central and western regions are quite close and all of them are not high. The proportions of migrant workers without any commercial insurance are 91.6%, 92.1% and 94.5%, respectively. In the eastern region, the proportion of migrant workers with commercial life insurance is 4.0%, which is the same as those in the central region and higher than those in the western region, which is 2.5%. Among the migrant workers in the eastern region, those who have a commercial health insurance take up 2.8%, and those who have other commercial insurances take up 1.9%. In the central region, 2.7% of migrant workers have commercial health insurances, while 1.2% of migrant workers apply for other types of insurances. In the western region, 1.4% of migrant workers have a commercial health insurance and there are 1.6% of migrant workers who have other commercial insurances.

CHAPTER 5

Financial Behavior of Rural Households

This chapter analyzes the financial behavior of rural households including the participation behavior of rural households in the financial market, agricultural production and management loans of rural households, private lending of rural households, and financial knowledge and behavior of rural households according to the databases of China Rural Household Panel Survey (CRHPS) by Zhejiang University and China Household Finance Survey (CHFS). The study found that the development of the current rural financial market was very backward, and the participation rate of rural households in risk markets such as stocks and funds was very low, accounting for only 2.4%, far behind the national overall level of 17.1%. The participation level of rural households in the formal credit market was also low, and the demand proportion of agricultural production and management loans in 2015 was only 12.7%, down by more than 50% compared with 2013. However, rural households actively participated in the private lending market, as there were over 28% of rural households with private loans, far higher than the national level. Private borrowing was mainly used for housing as well as production and management projects, which served as a good supplement to the insufficient formal borrowing. As for inclusive finance, the financial service infrastructure coverage of rural areas, bank account ownership and convenience of banking services still had a great room for improvement. Most agricultural households preferred informal financing channels, while only 22.4% of rural households preferred formal bank loans. The financial knowledge level of China's rural households was

© Zhejiang University Press 2020

W. Qian et al., *The Economy of Chinese Rural Households*,
https://doi.org/10.1007/978-981-13-8591-9_5

generally low, while financial knowledge has a significant impact on financial behavior. The higher the level of financial knowledge, the higher the proportion of households participating in financial markets, and these households also hold more risky assets. Among households with higher financial knowledge, the proportion of loans will be increased, while the proportion of participation in private finance will be reduced.

5.1 Basic Situation of Rural Households Participating in Financial Markets

5.1.1 Risk Markets

5.1.1.1 Overview of Households Participating in Risk Markets

CRHPS investigated the holdings of various types of risky assets in the households, including stocks, funds, bonds, financial products, financial derivatives, non-RMB assets, gold and so on. If one household holds any one or more of the above-mentioned risk assets, the household is considered to be involved in the risk markets.

As can be seen from Fig. 5.1, the proportion of households participating in risk markets in 2015 has increased significantly compared with that

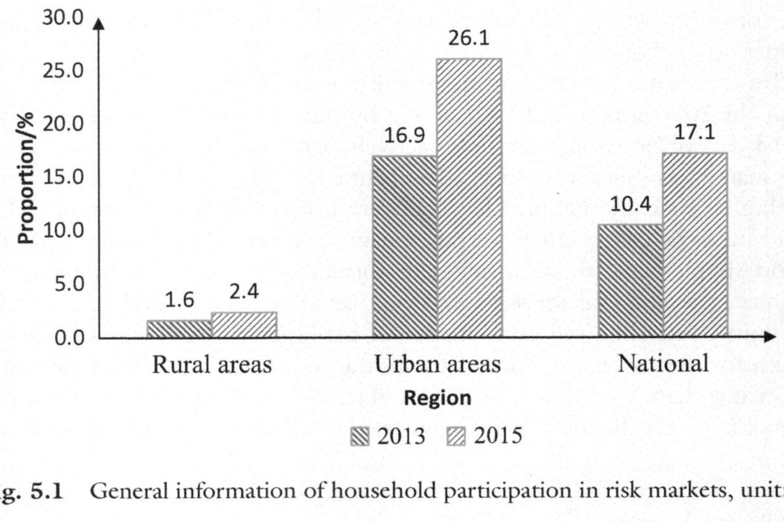

Fig. 5.1 General information of household participation in risk markets, unit: %

in 2013. The proportion of rural households participating in risk markets was much lower than that of the national average and urban households. In 2015, for example, the rural household participation rate was only 2.4%, the average level of the country was 17.1% and the urban household participation rate was up to 26.1%. The participation proportion of rural households was less than one-tenth of that of urban households.

5.1.1.2 *Comparison of Household Participation in Various Types of Risk Markets*

As of 2015, the participation rate of rural households in the stock market had risen from 0.4% in 2013 to 0.5%, far below the town level, indicating that the vast majority of rural households were still unfamiliar with the stock market, which may be the result of information asymmetry. The participation ratio of the financial planning product market had risen from 0.1% to 1.5%. Thus it can be seen that, in recent years, major domestic banks strongly promote financial planning products in rural areas, which has produced a positive effect. Non-RMB market and gold market participation ratios have declined slightly, mainly because the rural household funds are limited so that there are no surplus liquid funds invested in such risky assets (see Table 5.1).

In terms of urban and rural areas, the proportion of rural households participating in various risk markets was much lower than that of urban households. According to the data of 2015, the participation rate of rural

Table 5.1 Situation of household participation in all types of risk markets, unit: %

	2013			*2015*		
	Rural areas	*Urban areas*	*National*	*Rural areas*	*Urban areas*	*National*
Stock market	0.4	11.0	6.5	0.5	14.7	9.4
Fund market	0.4	5.2	3.1	0.4	5.0	3.3
Bond market	0.2	1.1	0.7	0.2	0.8	0.6
Financial derivative market	–	–	–	0.0	0.1	0.1
Financial product market	0.1	3.0	1.8	1.5	14.5	9.6
Non-RMB market	0.2	1.5	0.9	0.1	0.2	0.2
Gold market	0.4	1.3	0.9	0.2	0.7	0.5

households in various risk markets was not more than 1.5%, while the participation rate of urban households in various risk markets was much higher. In the stock market, for example, the rural household participation ratio was 0.5% and the participation rate of urban households in the stock market was higher than that of rural households by nearly 14 percentage points, which indicates that risk markets in rural areas are seriously lagging behind.

5.1.2 Credit Market

5.1.2.1 Overall Situation of Rural Households Participating in the Loan Market

In terms of time, compared with 2013, in 2015 the ratio of rural households with loans declined from 14.1% to 12.0% while the ratio of urban households with loans increased by 18.4 percentage points. The proportion of households with loans in the country has risen sharply. In terms of urban and rural areas, in 2015, the proportion of urban households with loans was about 2.9 times as much as that of rural households. The gap between urban and rural areas is widening (see Fig. 5.2).

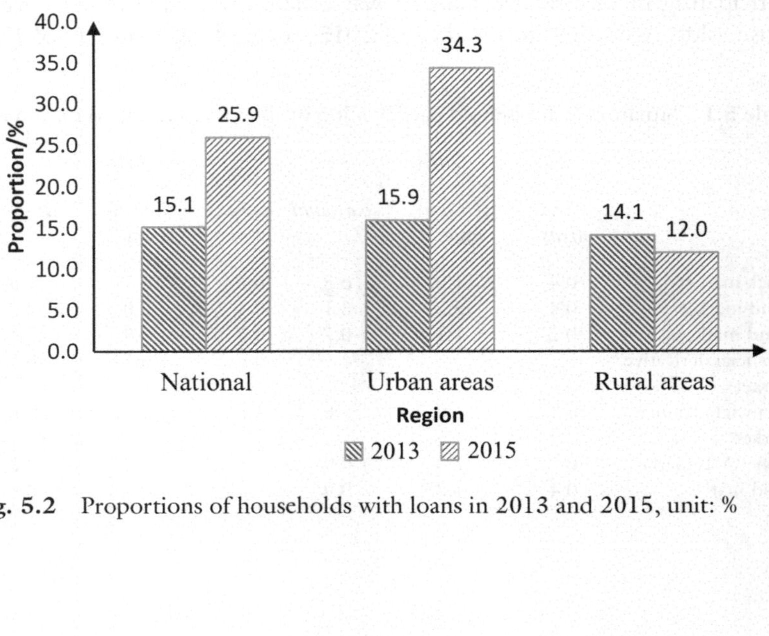

Fig. 5.2 Proportions of households with loans in 2013 and 2015, unit: %

5.1.2.2 Household Acquirement of Various Loans

According to the use of loans, loans can be divided into five categories, namely, production and management loans, housing loans, education loans and other loans. In terms of years, the proportions of both urban and rural households with various loans in 2013 and 2015 have changed. The participation rate of rural households in all kinds of loan markets has decreased significantly, especially the management loans, housing loans and education loans. The proportion of urban households in various types of loan markets has also changed. The participation rates of housing loans and car loans increased slightly, while those of education loans and other loans declined slightly. Aside from the rising trend of production and management loans, the participation rates of households in the country in other loan markets and those of urban households had the same change trend (see Table 5.2).

In terms of urban and rural areas, the proportions of rural households with production and management loans and education loans in 2015 were significantly higher than those of the national average and urban households; the proportion of rural households with housing loans was much lower than that of the national average and urban households; the proportion of rural households with car loans was also significantly lower than that of the national average and urban households.

In terms of the proportions of households with various loans in 2015, rural household loans were mainly used for production and management activities, with a ratio of 3.7% for such loans, followed by housing loans of 3.2%, and then education loans of 1.5%. Nationwide, household loans were mainly used for house purchases, with the proportion of households having housing loans at 9.5%, followed by loans used for production and management activities at 2.9% (see Fig. 5.3).

Table 5.2 The participation situation of households in loan markets, unit: %

	2013			*2015*		
	National	*Urban areas*	*Rural areas*	*National*	*Urban areas*	*Rural areas*
Production and management loans	4.0	2.4	6.2	2.9	2.4	3.7
Housing loans	8.8	11.7	4.9	9.5	13.4	3.2
Car loans	1.4	1.8	1.0	1.7	2.2	0.9
Education loans	1.8	1.1	2.9	0.9	0.6	1.5
Other loans	1.0	0.7	1.4	0.4	0.5	0.3

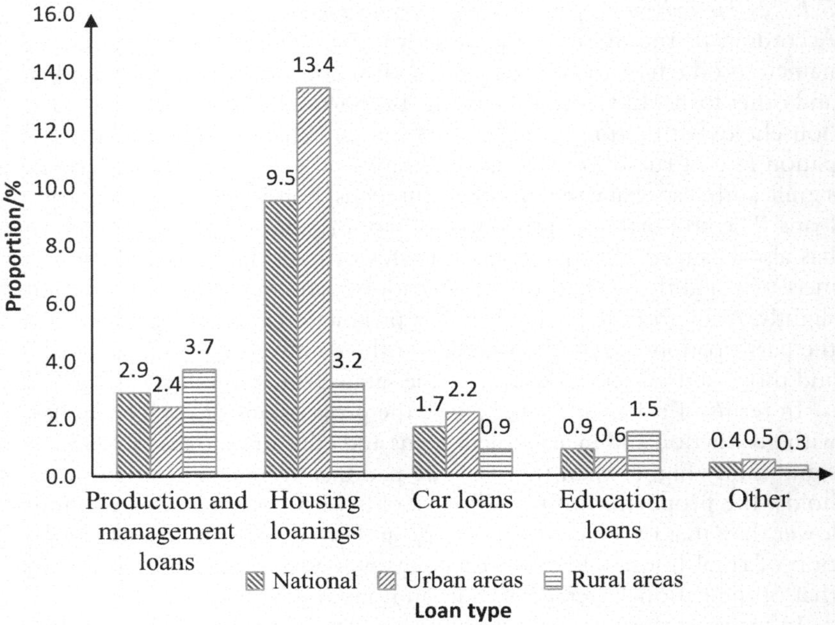

Fig. 5.3 Proportions of households with various loans in urban and rural areas in 2015, unit: %

5.1.2.3 The Mortgage of Household Loans

According to the security, loans can be roughly divided into four categories, namely, mortgage loans, pledge loans, guaranteed loans and credit loans. In the following passage, the security for household production and management loans in 2015 is to be analyzed. In accordance with the industry involved, the production and management loans are divided into two categories: agricultural loans, and industrial and commercial loans.

As to agricultural loans, households with credit loans accounted for the highest proportion (nearly 60%), followed by guaranteed loans (25.9%) and mortgage loans (16.1%), pledge loans the lowest (0.2%). As to industrial and commercial loans, households with credit loans also accounted for the highest proportion (47.6%) but the ratio was lower than that of agriculture; followed by guaranteed loans (31.7%), and then mortgage loans (20.8%). There were no pledge loans in households of industrial and commercial production and management (see Fig. 5.4).

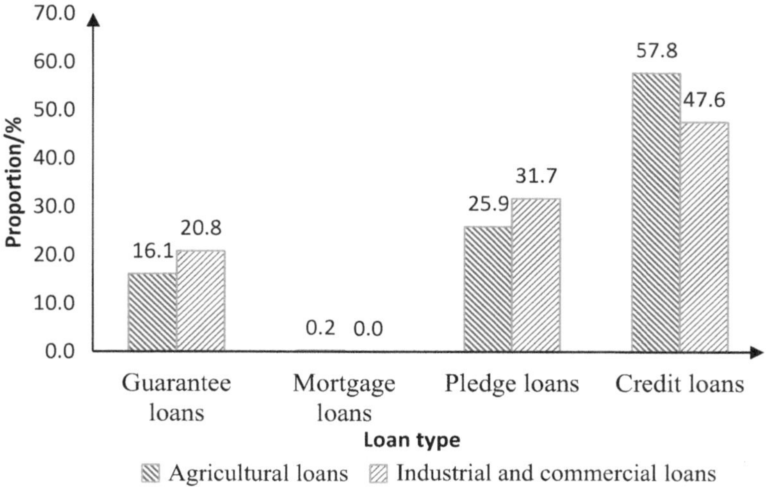

Fig. 5.4 The mortgage of household loans in different industries in 2015, unit: %

5.1.2.4 Private Lending Market

Figure 5.5 shows the proportions of households with private lending. It is indicated that compared to 2013, rural areas, urban areas and the whole country all had a significant decline in the proportion of households with private lending in 2015. The proportion of rural households with loans was 8 percentage points higher than the national level.

Figure 5.6 compares the situations of households with private loans and formal loans. The participation rate of rural households in the private loan market was much higher than that in the formal loan market, about three times of the latter, while the participation rate of urban households in the formal loan market was 5 percentage points higher than that in the private loan market.

5.1.3 Inclusive Finance

The development of financial markets in rural areas is an important part of establishing a modern financial system and also one of the key points to examine the present state of China's inclusive finance. Some institutions such as banks, rural credit cooperatives and benefiting-farmers' financial

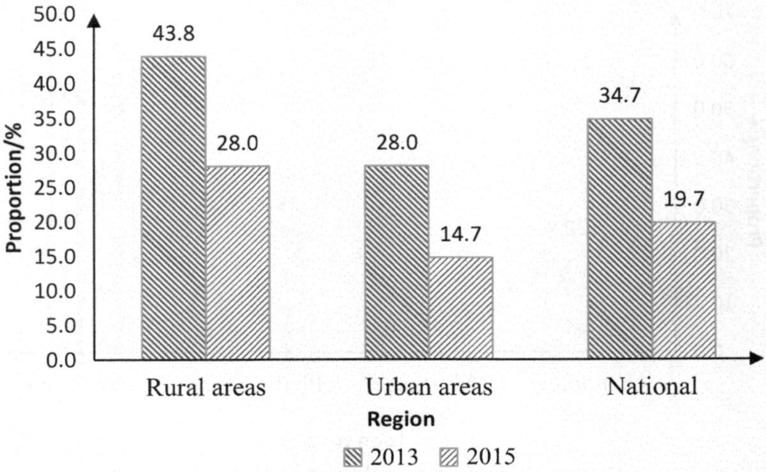

Fig. 5.5 Overall situation of households participating in loan markets in 2015, unit: %

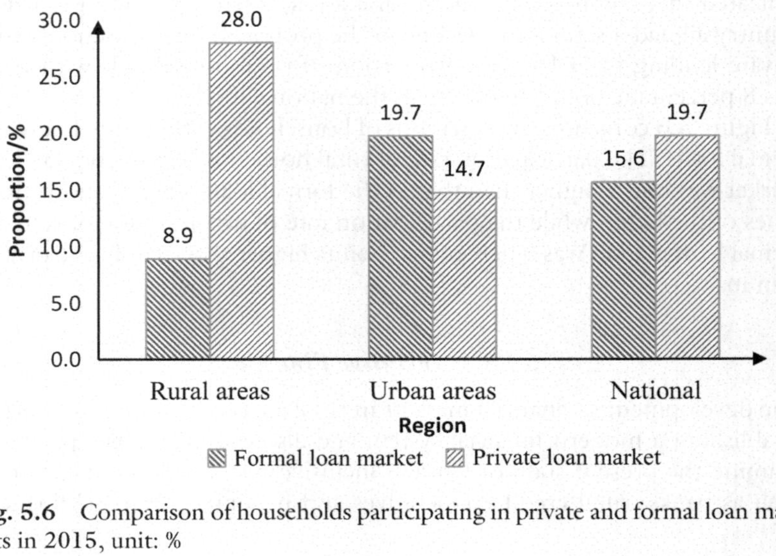

Fig. 5.6 Comparison of households participating in private and formal loan markets in 2015, unit: %

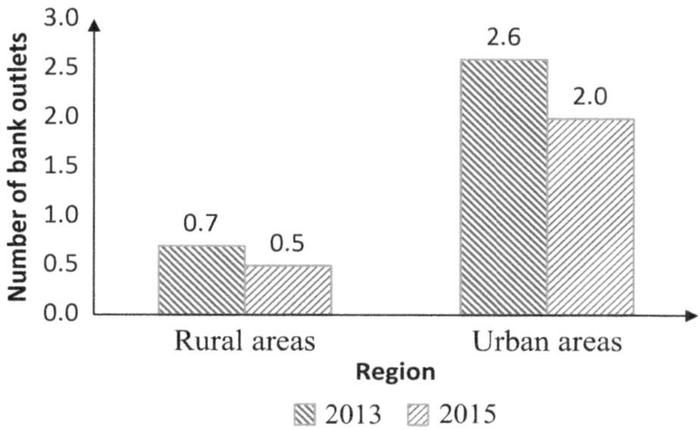

Fig. 5.7 Comparison of the number of bank outlets around urban and rural households

service outlets provide the most basic financial services for rural areas. Therefore, examining the financial services provided by these formal financial institutions will help reflect the development status and trend of financial services in rural areas more accurately and clearly.

5.1.3.1 Financial Service Facilities

CRHPS (2015) investigated the number of bank outlets within the villages/housing estates to measure financial service facilities in villages (housing estates). As can be seen from Fig. 5.7, the average number of bank outlets of each village in the rural areas in 2015 was 0.5, and that in urban areas was 2, which revealed the obvious gap in financial service facilities between rural and urban areas. Compared to 2013, the average numbers of bank outlets in the villages/housing estates in the rural and urban areas were all decreasing.

Table 5.3 shows the distribution of bank outlets[1] in the vicinity of the villages (housing estates). As can be seen in the table, 76.3% of villages in rural areas did not have bank outlets in the vicinity, which was much higher than the ratio of urban areas (32.2%). In terms of the number of villages

[1] The community questionnaires asked the number of bank outlets including rural credit cooperatives and postal savings within the administrative areas of the villages where the respondents were located.

Table 5.3 Distribution of the number of bank outlets near the villages (housing estates), unit: %

Number	*0*	*1*	*2*	*3*	*4*	*5 or more*
Rural areas	76.3	14.0	4.5	2.1	1.5	1.6
Urban areas	32.2	18.1	16.9	14.0	6.7	12.1

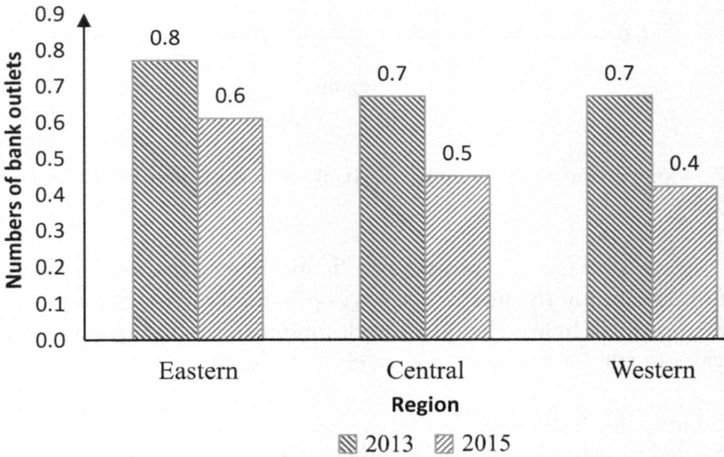

Fig. 5.8 Regional differences in the numbers of bank outlets near the villages/ housing estates

(housing estates) with bank outlets, the ratio of villages with two or more bank outlets in the vicinity was also far lower than that of urban areas.

Figure 5.8 shows the average number of bank outlets near the villages in the eastern, central and western regions of rural areas. It can be seen that in 2015, the number of bank outlets near the villages in the eastern region was 0.6, which was higher than that in the central and western regions. Compared to 2013, the average numbers of bank outlets within the villages/housing estates in the eastern, central and western regions were all decreasing.

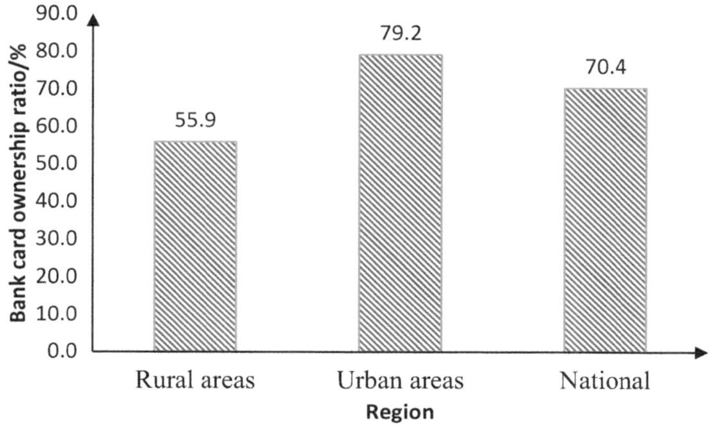

Fig. 5.9 Comparison of bank card ownership ratio of households, unit: %

5.1.3.2 Bank Card Coverage

The bank card is the basic service provided by financial institutions as well as a kind of credit payment instrument with the total or partial functions of consumer credit, transfer and settlement, depositing and drawing cash, and so on, which is issued by formal financial institutions such as banks and rural credit cooperatives to the society. The bank card coverage rate can fully reflect the account coverage in China. Generally speaking, bank cards include debit and credit cards, but in this report, bank cards refer to debit cards. According to the survey data (Fig. 5.9), households with bank cards in rural areas accounted for 55.9% of the total rural households, 23.3 percentage points lower than the national urban households.

Rural households in the country owned an average of 1.7 bank cards, while urban households and national households owned 2 and 2.5 bank cards on average, respectively.

5.1.3.3 Financial Service Evaluation

Financial service coverage and satisfaction evaluation is an important index in measuring the development of inclusive finance. By examining the coverage, forms, content and evaluation of financial services, whether residents have realized the right to obtain financial services can be reflected.

Specifically, forms of financial services include bank (rural credit cooperative) outlet counters, self-help banks (ATM and other self-service ter-

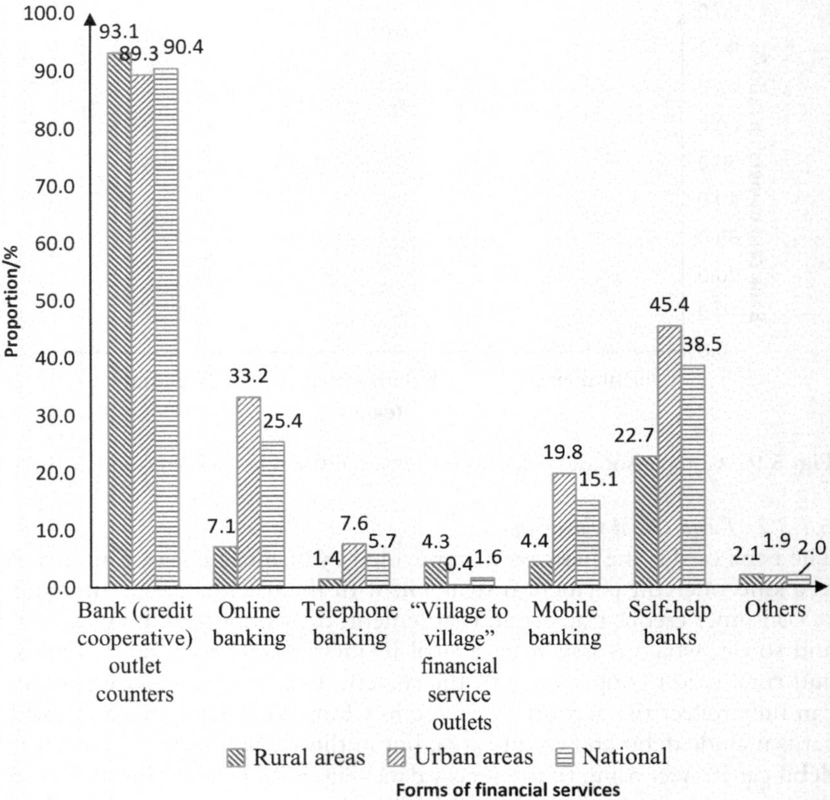

Fig. 5.10 Forms of financial services received by households, unit: %

minals), online banking, mobile banking, and telephone banking and agricultural financial service outlets. As shown in Fig. 5.10, the form of financial services accepted by rural households in the country was mainly counter services (93.1%), followed by self-service banking services (22.7%); the proportions of the uses of online banking, mobile banking and telephone banking in rural areas were far below those in the urban areas.

Figure 5.11 reflects the household satisfaction evaluation of financial services provided by formal financial institutions such as banks, rural credit cooperatives and "village to village" financial service outlets of benefiting farmers. By contrast, rural households express higher satisfaction with

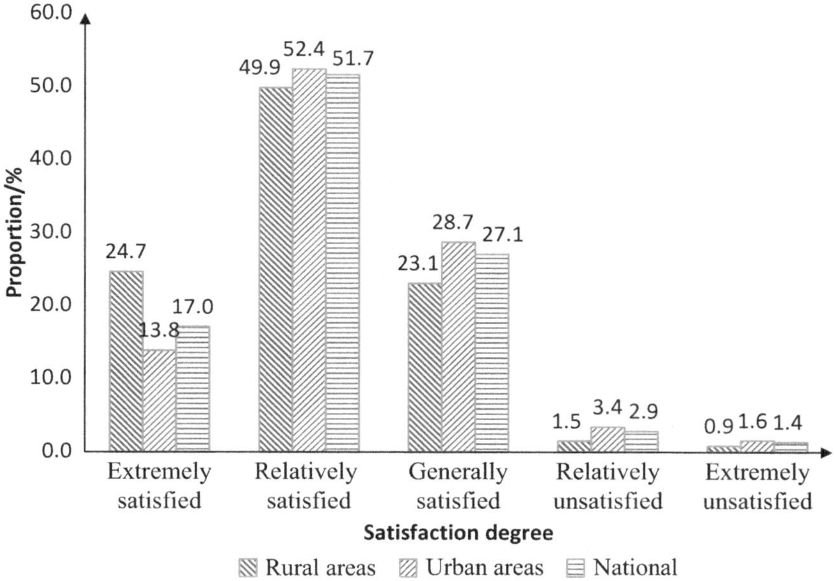

Fig. 5.11 Satisfaction evaluation of financial services, unit: %

financial services provided by formal financial institutions, with a satisfactory rate of 74.6% (including "extremely satisfied" and "relatively satisfied"). Some rural households are not satisfied with bank services mainly because of the poor service and few bank outlets, as shown in Fig. 5.12.

5.1.3.4 Bank Service Convenience

As shown in Fig. 5.13, 87.0% of rural households indicated that the nearest financial services were counter services at bank outlets or credit cooperative outlets, and 7.1% indicated that the nearest financial services were self-help banks, while 3.8% said the nearest ones were "village to village" financial service outlets of benefiting farmers.

Survey data show that the average distance between rural households and their nearest financial service point was 9.8 kilometers and the average time they spent was 22.2 minutes.

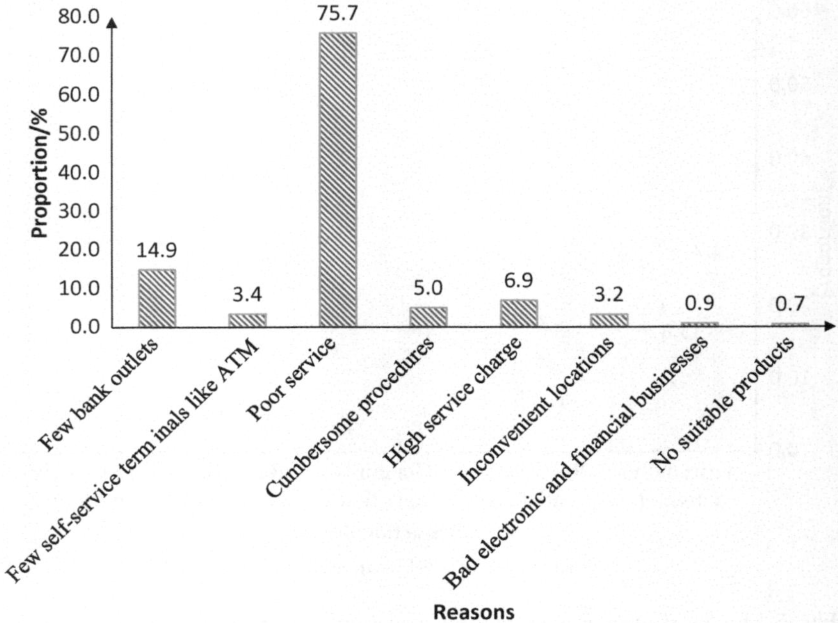

Fig. 5.12 Reasons for rural households' unsatisfaction with bank services, unit: %

5.1.4 *Mobile Internet Finance*

5.1.4.1 The Coverage of Mobile Banking and Online Banking

The development of mobile Internet finance is complementary to formal financial institutions seeing the low coverage rate, high service cost and low efficiency of the latter, so that rural households can obtain the necessary financial services at a lower cost but in more convenient and quicker ways. Information about the ownership as well as the, frequency and main purpose of using online banking and mobile banking accounts of rural households can objectively reflect the current situation of the development of mobile Internet finance in rural China.

Survey data show that (as shown in Fig. 5.14) the proportions of national households owning mobile and online bank accounts were 15.1% and 25.4%, respectively. These proportions in rural areas were only 4.3% and 7.1%, respectively. It can be seen that mobile Internet finance is not

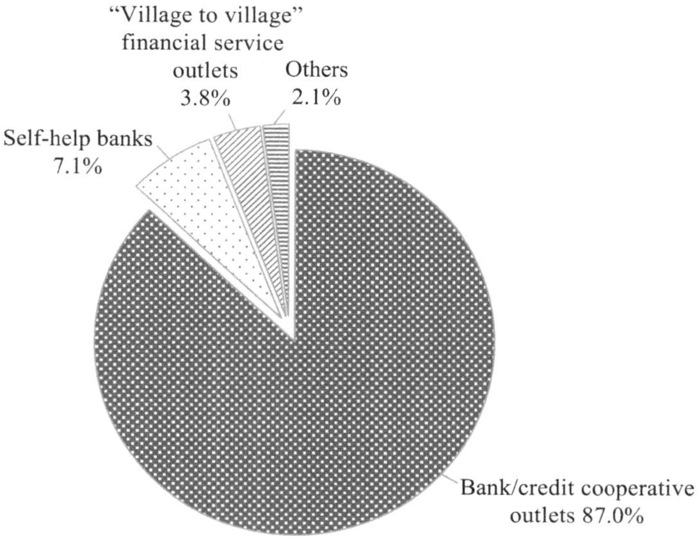

Fig. 5.13 The nearest financial service points to households in rural areas

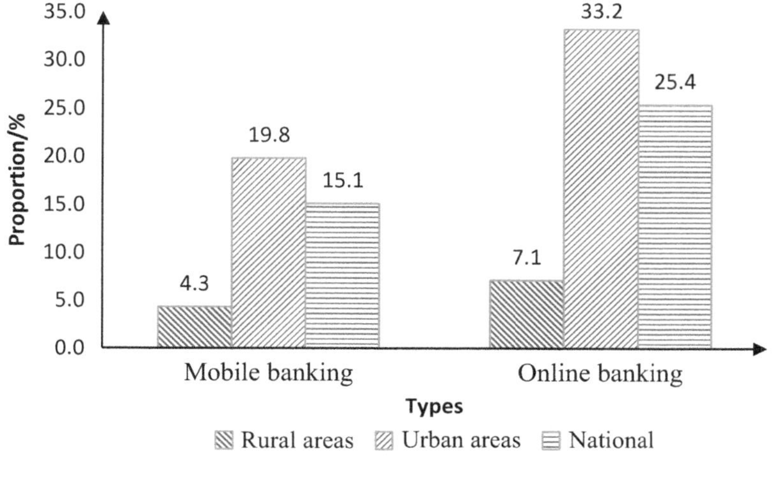

Fig. 5.14 Proportions of owning or using mobile and online bank accounts, unit: %

widely popularized in rural households of China. The proportion of rural households owning or using online bank accounts is higher than that for mobile bank accounts.

5.1.4.2 Comparison of Household Characteristics

According to the characteristics of households, we further analyzed the proportion of households holding Internet financial products. The higher the education level of householders, the higher the proportion of households holding Internet financial products. As shown in Fig. 5.15, among households with higher education, the proportion of households with mobile banking was 38.1%, well above the proportion of those at the secondary education level or below the primary education level (21.1% and 7.4%). At the same time, for households that received higher education, the proportion of owning online bank accounts (62.5%) was almost double that for households that only received secondary education (35.1%).

Comparing the ages of householders, we know that households with householders aged between 18 and 30 had the highest percentage of owning mobile and online bank accounts, 44.9% for mobile banking and 66% for online banking. As the age of the household head increases, the proportions of households owning mobile and online bank accounts decline (see Fig. 5.16).

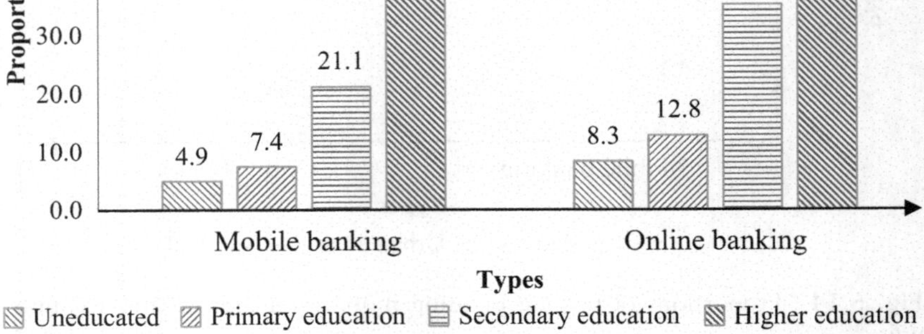

Fig. 5.15 Proportions of households owning mobile and online bank accounts at different educational levels, unit: %

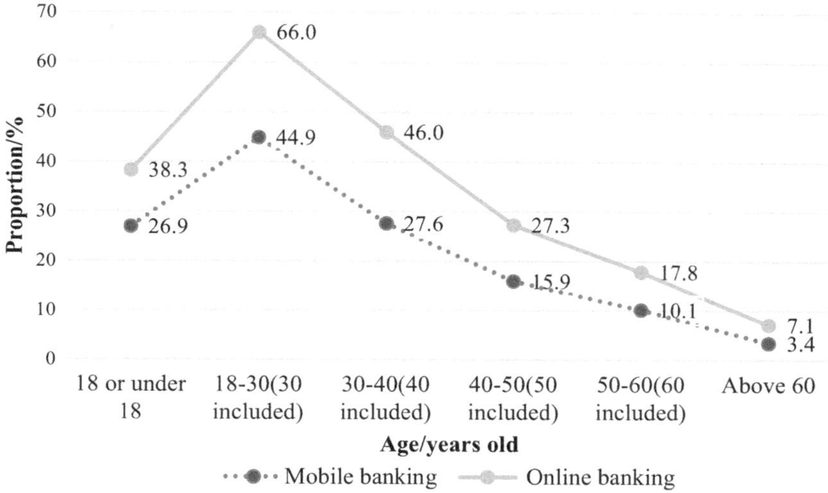

Fig. 5.16 Proportions of households owning mobile and online bank accounts with householders at different ages

5.1.4.3 Frequency of Using Mobile Banking and Online Banking

According to the survey data, as shown in Fig. 5.17, 57.2% of rural households that have opened mobile banking and Internet banking said that they rarely used mobile banking, 33.4% said they frequently used mobile banking and 9.4% never used it; in contrast, 54.7% of rural households said that they seldom used online banking, 40.2% of rural households said they often used it and 5.1% of rural households never used it. It can be seen that the frequency of using mobile banking was higher than that of using online banking.

In terms of the main uses (as shown in Fig. 5.18), rural households opened online banking mainly for "online shopping electronic payment" (54.3%), for "transfer to payment platforms like Alipay and Tenpay" (42%) and for "inter-account and inter-bank transfer services" (30.1%). In addition, the proportion of using "paying phone bills, utilities, etc." service was 11%, and 4.7% for "inquiry" service.

As shown in Fig. 5.19, in contrary to the main uses of online banking, the main purposes of rural households using mobile banking were "inter-account and inter-bank transfer services" (41.1%), "paying phone bills, utilities, etc." (39%) and "transfer to payment platforms like Alipay and Tenpay" (32%). In addition, the ratio of "online shopping electronic payment" was 28.8%.

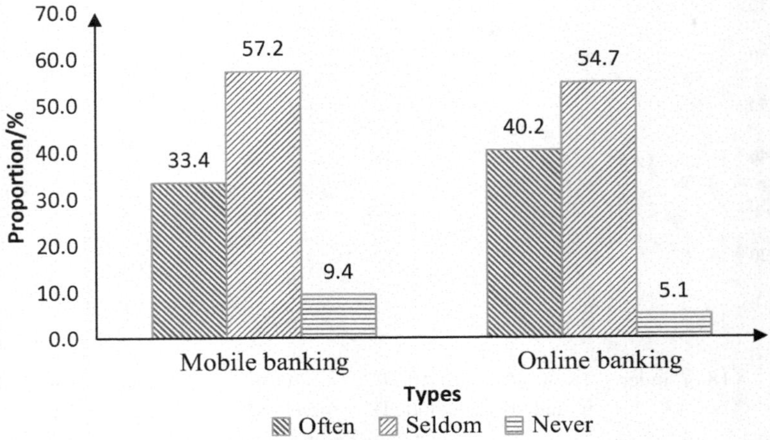

Fig. 5.17 Frequency of using mobile and online banking of rural households, unit: %

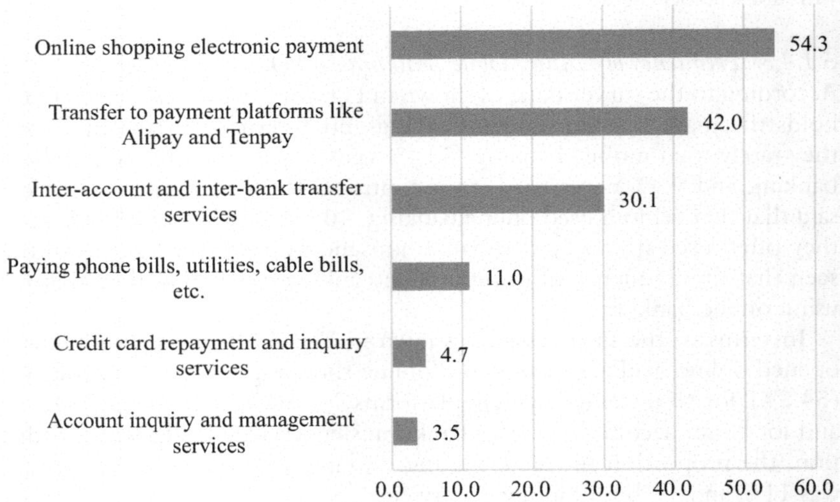

Fig. 5.18 Main purposes of using online banking, unit: %

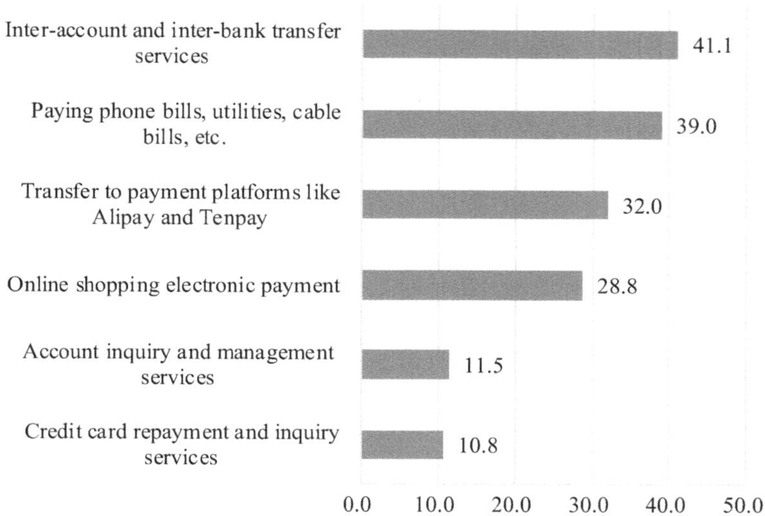

Fig. 5.19 Main purposes of using mobile banking, unit: %

Figure 5.20 shows the reasons why rural households do not use online banking. Of rural households, 40% said that the reason was "no needed functions", and the reason for "worrying about the security of online banking" and "not knowing how to use it" accounted for 22.6% and 14.3%, respectively.

Figure 5.21 shows the reasons why rural households do not use mobile banking. About one-third (30%) of rural households said that the reason was "worrying about the security of funds", while "no needed functions" and "not knowing how to use it" accounted for 20.6% and 20.2%, respectively.

5.1.5 *Financial Planning Products*

Financial planning products include bank financial products, online financial products such as Alipay and Tenpay, P2P Loan and so on. Bank financial products refer to the traditional bank financial products with a subscription of generally more than 50,000 yuan, including financial products with a fixed period of time when the funds are frozen and cannot be cashed in advance, and those which can be redeemed and cashed at any

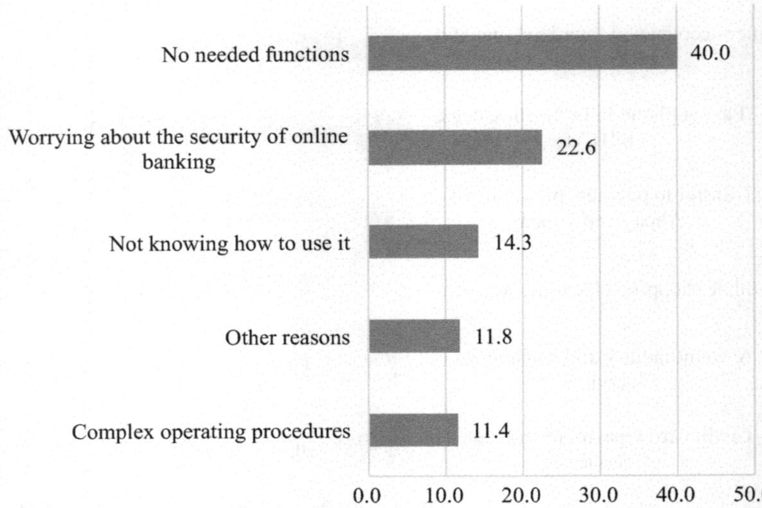

Fig. 5.20 Reasons for not using online banking, unit: %

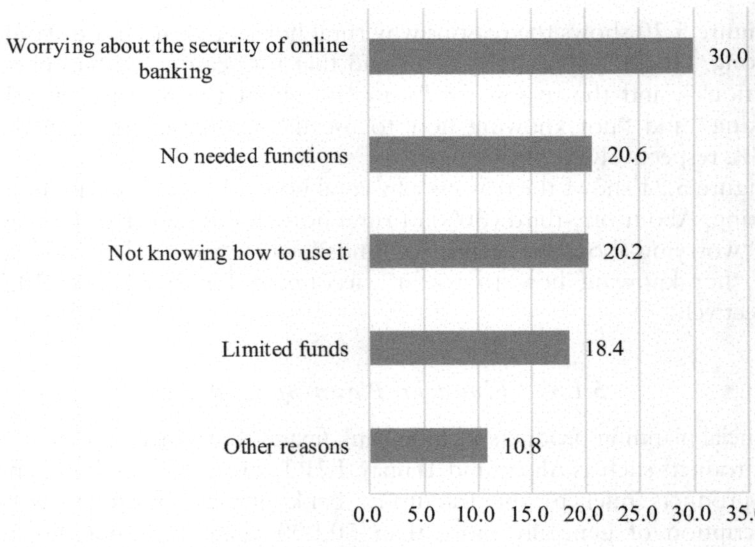

Fig. 5.21 Reasons for not using mobile banking, unit: %

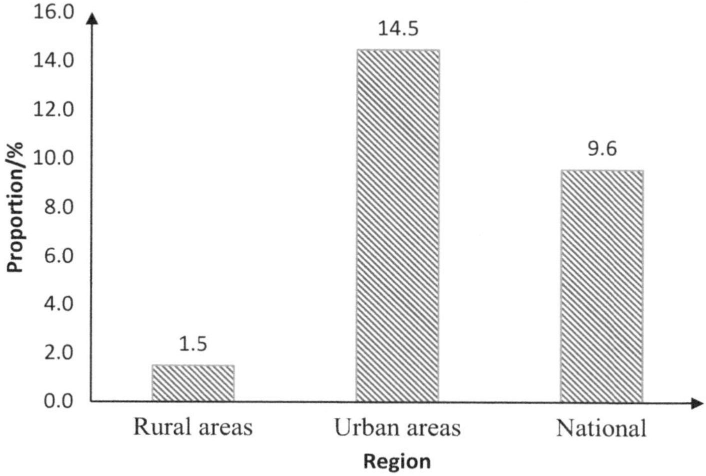

Fig. 5.22 Proportions of households owning financial planning products, unit: %

time. Online financial products refer to products such as Yu'E Bao, WeChat Financing, Jingdong Coffers, Baidu Financing, Treasurers' Treasure and so on. Other financial products refer to financial products that exclude bank financial products and online financial products such as Yu'E Bao mentioned above.

5.1.5.1 Ownership of Financial Planning Products

As shown in Fig. 5.22, China's households with financial planning products accounted for 9.6% of the total households in the country. The proportion of households with financial products in urban areas was 14.5% and the proportion of households with financial products in rural areas was 1.5%.

Financial planning products are divided into bank financial products, online financial products and other financial products. Specifically, Fig. 5.23 shows that the proportion of national households owning online financial products (6.2%) was higher than that of households owning bank financial products (4.2%) and other financial products (0.5%).

Table 5.4 shows the ownership rate of financial products and household assets in China. It can be seen from the table that the ownership rate

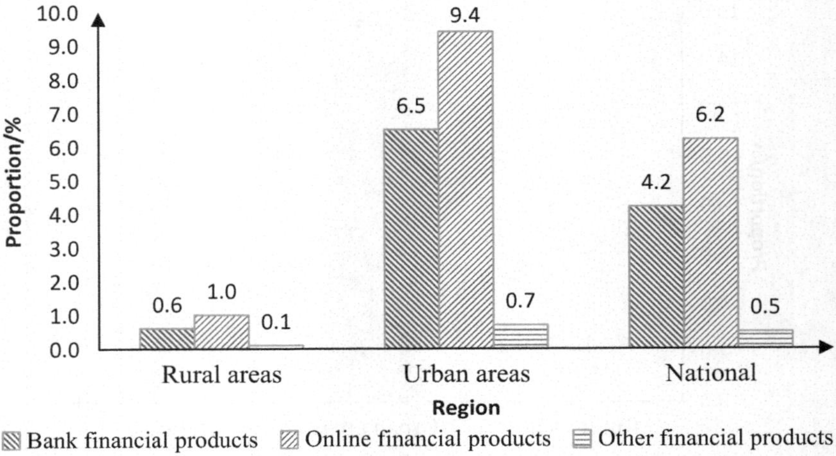

Fig. 5.23 Proportions of households owning various financial planning products, unit: %

Table 5.4 Financial planning products and household assets, unit: %

Assets (¥)	*Financial planning products*	*Bank financial products*	*Online financial products*	*Other financial products*
Below 58,000 yuan	1.57	0.22	1.39	0.01
58,000 yuan (inclusive)—215,000 yuan	3.07	0.76	2.47	0.07
215,000 yuan (inclusive)—483,000 yuan	5.57	1.75	4.09	0.29
483,000 yuan (inclusive)—1.099 million yuan	13.16	5.00	9.00	0.60
More than 1.099 million yuan	26.39	14.73	15.04	1.44

of all kinds of financial products has increased with the quantity of assets, indicating that the participation of households in financial markets is closely related to their own assets.

Table 5.5 shows the relationship between the proportions of households participating in various financial products markets and the annual

Table 5.5 Financial planning products and household income, unit: %

Income	*Financial planning products*	*Bank financial products*	*Online financial products*	*Other financial products*
Below 10,000	3.22	0.88	2.48	0.08
10,000 yuan (inclusive)—31,000 yuan	2.81	0.87	2.12	0.06
31,000 yuan (inclusive)—58,000 yuan	6.28	2.38	4.39	0.06
58,000 yuan (inclusive)—100,000 yuan	11.81	5.84	6.92	0.43
More than 100,000 yuan	24.17	11.42	15.36	1.69

income of households. Like assets, the higher income households have, the more financial products they own.

5.1.5.2 Structure and Returns of Financial Planning Products

Figure 5.24 depicts the structure of financial products owned by China's households. Bank financial products had the most ownership, accounting for up to 80.5%, followed by online financial products, accounting for 11.7%.

It can be seen from Table 5.6 that households with financial planning products own these products with the market value of 86,870.1 yuan on average, of which bank financial products have the market value of 159,490.1 yuan, online financial products 15,638.8 yuan and other financial products 138,655.0 yuan.

More data show that households with financial planning products obtained the average income of 28,913.3 yuan from them last year and the median was 3000 yuan. Rural households obtained an income of 1191.8 yuan and the median was 0, while urban households obtained an income of 31,649.7 yuan and the median was 4800 yuan.

5.1.5.3 Beginning Time of Owning Online Financial Products

The online financial product is a new form of finance based on payment, cloud computing, social networks, search engines and other Internet supplies to achieve intermediary business such as financing, payment and information, which includes Yu'E Bao, WeChat Financing, Jingdong Coffers, Baidu Financing, Treasurers' Treasure and so on. Data show that national households with online financial products accounted for 6.2% and households in rural and urban areas accounted for 9.4% and 1.0%, respectively.

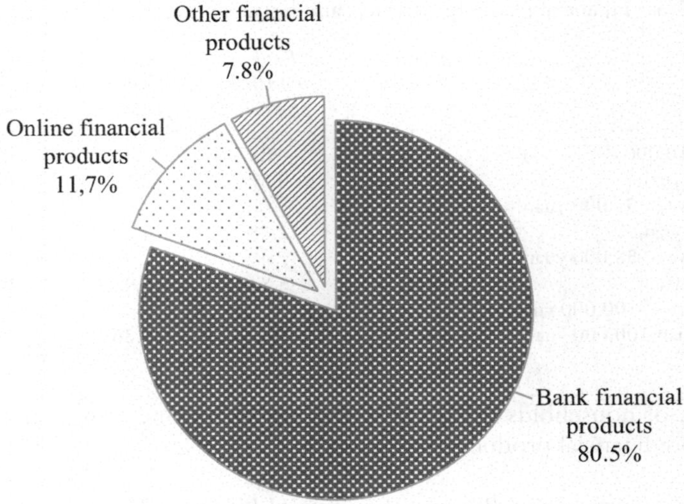

Fig. 5.24 Proportions of financial planning products

Table 5.6 The total market capitalization of financial planning products, unit: yuan

	Rural areas		*Urban areas*		*National*	
	Mean	*Median*	*Mean*	*Median*	*Mean*	*Median*
Financial planning products	47,972.8	10,000.0	89,266.8	20,000.0	86,870.1	20,000.0
Bank financial products	85,272.2	50,000.0	16,3757.8	10,0000.0	15,9490.1	90,000
Online financial products	11,950.2	4000.0	15,867.4	5000	15,638.8	4695.0
Other financial products	71,009.4	30,000.0	14,5099.7	50,000	13,8655.0	50,000.0

Figure 5.25 describes the beginning year of households with online financial products owning such products. As can be seen from the figure, about 4% of households have held online financial products since 2011; households with online financial products since 2014 accounted for 36.3% of households with online financial products, and 12.2% of households

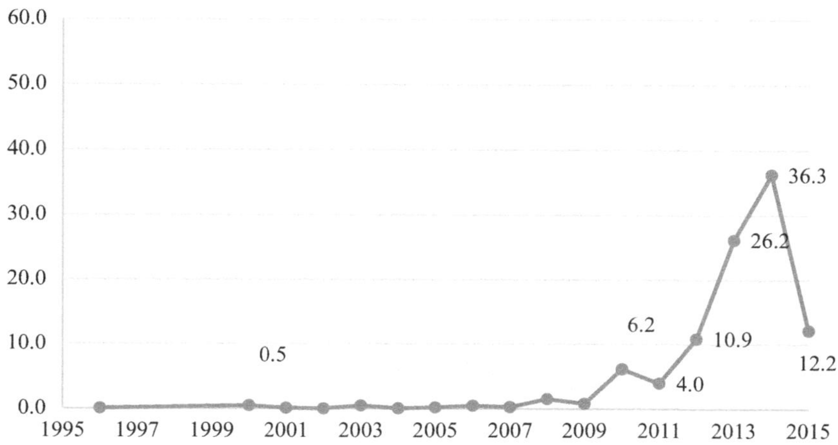

Fig. 5.25 The beginning time of rural households owning online financial products, unit: %

started to own financial products in 2015. Obviously, compared to the proportions from 2005 to 2011, households that have held online financial products since 2014 accounted for the highest proportion of households with online financial products.

5.1.5.4 Reasons for Holding Online Financial Products

Figure 5.26 illustrates the reasons why households hold online financial products. As can be seen from the figure, "convenience for online shopping payment" (82.4%) and "convenience for transfer and remittance" (58.5%) were the main reasons for holding the online financial products. Other reasons included "fund increment" (28.7%), "convenience for living (paying utilities, phone bills, etc.)" (27%), "as another form of household savings" (20.0%) and "convenience for credit card repayment"(18%). In addition, 8.8% of households said that holding online financial products was to diversify investment risks. It can be seen that the main purpose of China's households in selecting online financial products is to facilitate access to payment, followed by fund increment and diversifying investment risks.

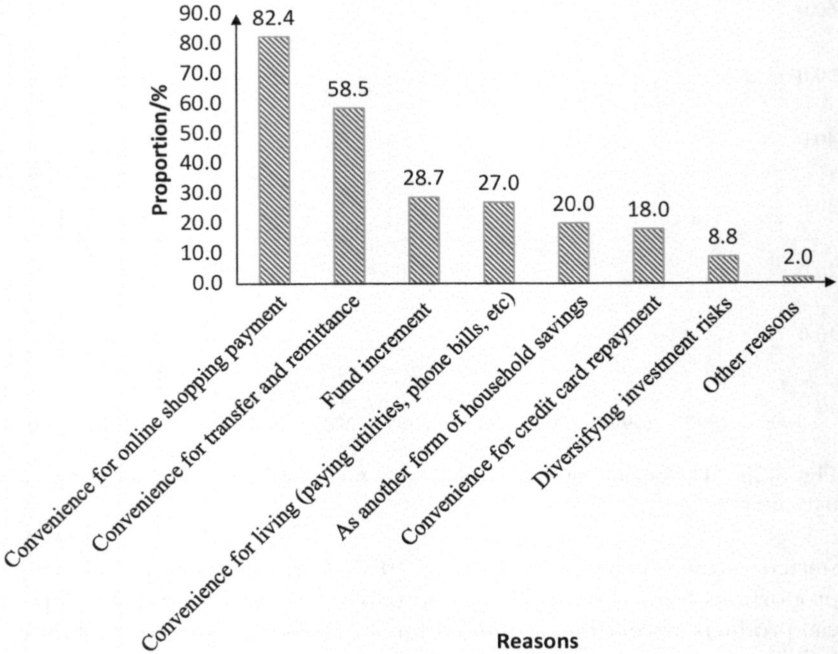

Fig. 5.26 Reasons for holding online financial products, unit: %

For those households that do not choose to buy online financial products, Fig. 5.27 shows the reasons why households do not hold online financial products. About half (49.7%) of households nationwide claimed that they have never heard about online financial products, 18.6% of households said that it was because of limited funds and 15% said that it was because they did not have relevant knowledge. In addition, the reasons also included "high risks of online financial products" (6.9%), "no time and energy to buy" (6.2%) and "not knowing how to buy" (5%).

5.1.5.5 Household Characteristics and Online Financial Products

According to the household characteristics, we further analyzed the proportions of households holding online financial products. The higher the education level of householders, the higher the proportion of such house-

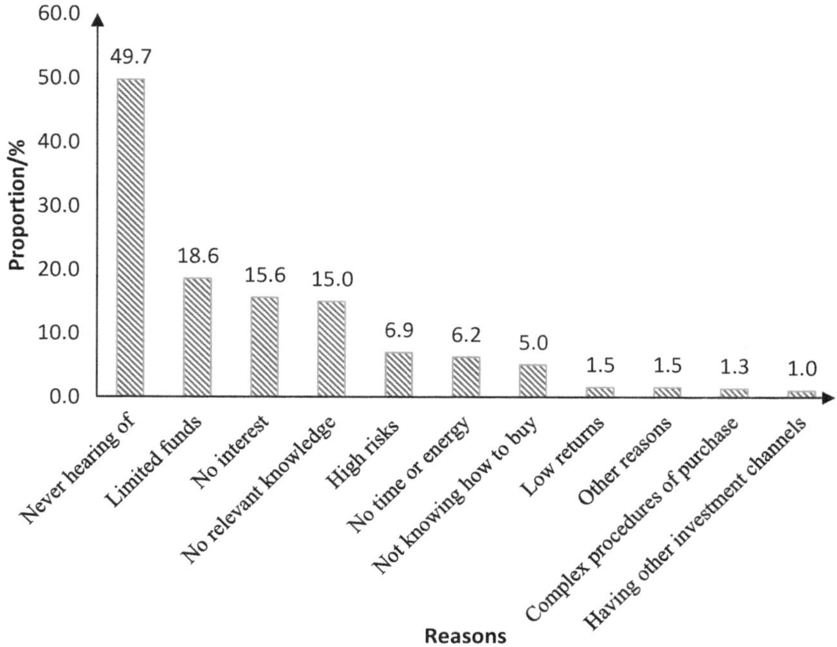

Fig. 5.27 Reasons for not holding online financial products, unit: %

holds holding online financial products. As shown in Fig. 5.28, households with online financial products accounted for 24.4% of households whose heads have received higher education, which was well above the proportions in households with the level of secondary education and primary education (9.8% and 2.4%).

In terms of the ages of householders, householders at the age of 19–30 holding online financial products accounted for the highest proportion of all householders with online financial products (26.1%), followed by householders at the age below 18 (13.7%). With the increase of the age of householders, the proportion of households holding financial products gradually decreased (see Fig. 5.29).

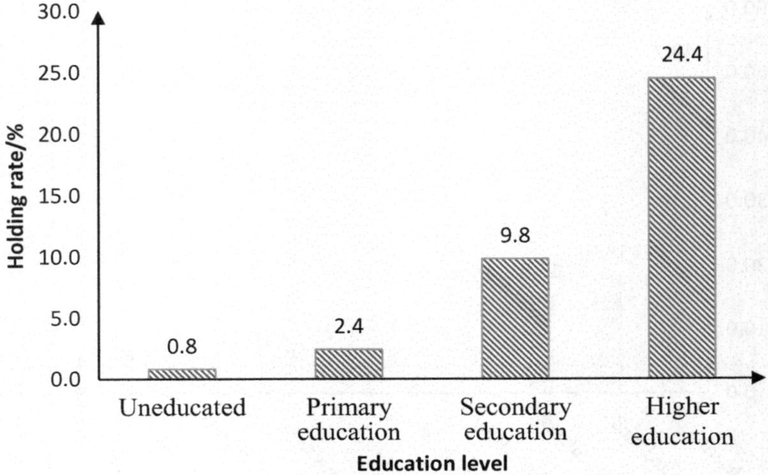

Fig. 5.28 Householders' education level and holding rate of online financial products, unit: %

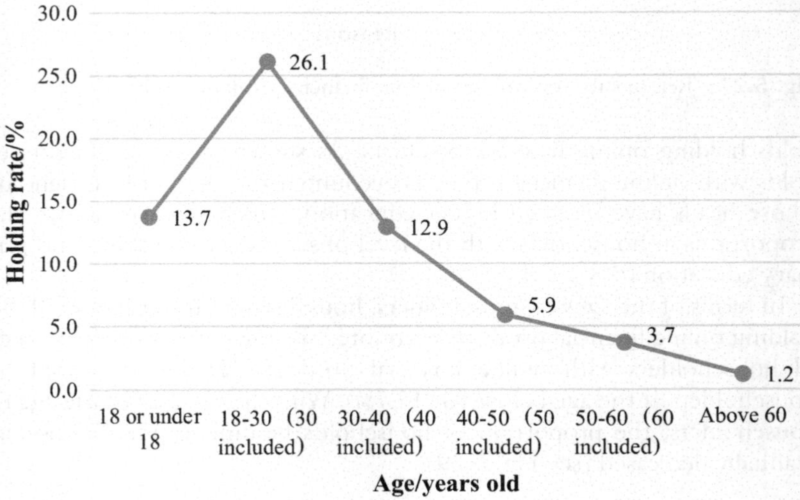

Fig. 5.29 Age of householders and proportions of holding online financial products, unit: %

5.2 Agricultural Production and Management Loans for Farmers

5.2.1 *Credit Needs*

5.2.1.1 The Definition of Credit Needs

Rural households' credit needs refer to the demand of rural households for loans from formal financial institutions, including actual and latent credit needs, due to economic activities such as production and management, purchase of housing or automobiles and daily consumption. Actual credit needs refer to the demand of families for applying for loans to formal financial institutions; latent credit needs refer to the demand for funds without application to formal financial institutions. In this report, according to the design of relevant issues in the CRHPS, families with credit needs are divided into two categories as follows: (1) the families who have obtained bank loans; and (2) the families who have no bank loans due to "demanding for loans but not applying to banks for them", "being rejected when applying for loans" or "being applying for loans".[2]

In this section, we focus on exploring rural households' credit needs arising from agricultural production and management and combine with family characteristics to make an in-depth analysis of financing preference of rural households.

5.2.1.2 An Analysis of Credit Needs

The data of CRHPS show a decreasing trend in the demand for agricultural production and management loans in recent years. The demand ratio in 2015 was only 12.7%, declining more than 14.2% compared with 2013. Credit availability increases year by year, resulting from a rising pass rate of loans[3] over the past years. Now the pass rate is over 50%, which indicates that more than half of the households applying for loans can get them (see Table 5.7).

[2] If one does not get bank loans due to "demanding for loans but not applying to banks for them" or "being rejected when applying for loans", we call this phenomenon "credit constraints". That is, there is demand for credit but people cannot obtain loans for personal or other reasons. Another "credit constraints" refers to a situation where the amount of the loan that is actually received is less than the amount of the loan that is applied for or demanded.

[3] The pass rate of loans is obtained by dividing the number of households that have got loans by the number of households that applied for loans.

Table 5.7 Changes in credit needs, unit: %

	2015	*2013*	*2011*
Demand ratio	12.7	26.9	30.0
Credit availability[a]	29.4	26.8	23.3
Credit accessibility[b]	49.7	53.7	55.3
Pass rate of loans[c]	59.2	49.9	42.2

[a]Credit availability refers to the proportion of households obtaining loans to households demanding for loans. Credit availability = credit accessibility * the pass rate of loans

[b]Credit accessibility refers to the proportion of households applying for loans to households demanding for loans

[c]The pass rate of loans refers to the proportion of households getting loans to households applying for loans

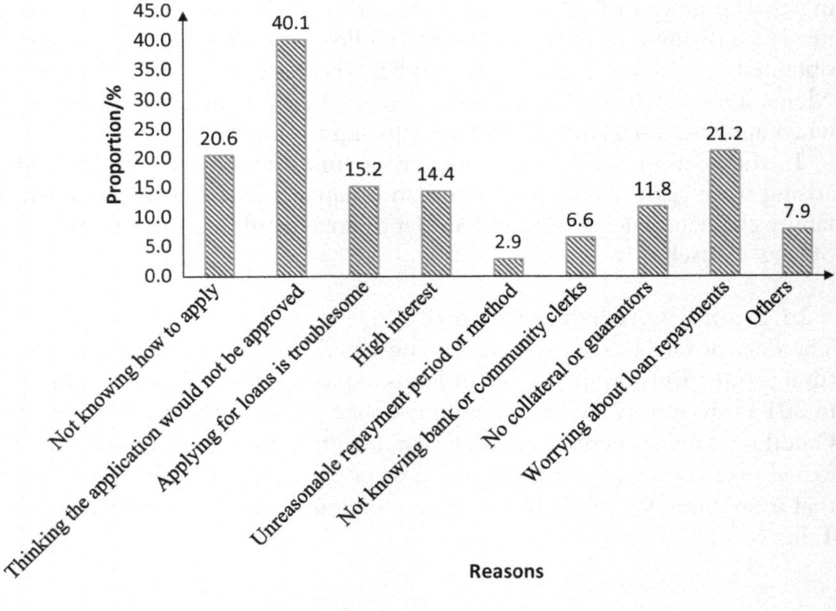

Fig. 5.30 Reasons for not applying for loans, unit: %

As shown in Fig. 5.30, the primary reason for agricultural households having credit needs but not applying for formal loans such as bank loans in rural areas in 2015 is "thinking the application would not be approved", accounting for up to 40.1%, followed by reasons of "worrying about loan repayments", "not knowing how to apply" and "applying for loans is troublesome", accounting for 21.2%, 20.6% and 15.2%, respectively.

Table 5.8 Overview of families thinking their application would not be approved, unit: yuan

	Property	*Income*	*Land values*	*Home values*
Families thinking that their applications would not be approved	267,777.9	29,048.3	73,662.3	182,599.2
Families whose applications were rejected	350,557.3	33,198.8	133,233.9	152,180.6
Families being applying for loans	464,558.7	46,781.1	146,921.2	223,589.5
Families having got loans	440,516.4	158,941.3	117,668.8	184,338.9

According to the survey data, we made a further analysis that the families thinking that their application would not be approved have an average asset of 267777.9 yuan and an annual income of 29048.3 yuan, which does not reach the average level of rural households. Their indicators are closest to those of the families whose applications for loans were rejected and 20% of such families are low-income households, indicating that those families made a reasonable estimation after assessing their actual situation (see Table 5.8).

Figure 5.31 shows the reasons for the failure of rural agricultural families to obtain loans in 2013 and 2015. On the whole, "low income", "no guarantors" and "not knowing bank clerks" are the main reasons why rural households didn't get loans in 2013 and 2015. In 2013, no guarantors was the primary cause, accounting for 30.1%, followed by the reason of low income accounting for 30.0%. However, compared with 2013, the proportion of the reason of "no guarantors" increased by 7.3% (accounting for 22.8%) in 2015, becoming the primary cause of hindering rural households from obtaining loans.

5.2.1.3 Agricultural Loan Structure

Figure 5.32 describes the term structure of rural households' agricultural production and management loans. It can be seen from the figure that the loans obtained by rural households are mainly short-term loans. Loans with a term of one year or shorter have the largest quantity, making up a 70.1% share of the total number of loans. Medium-term loans with its maturity ranging from one to five years account for 26.2%. The proportions of the two types of loans total 96.3%. It suggests that agricultural

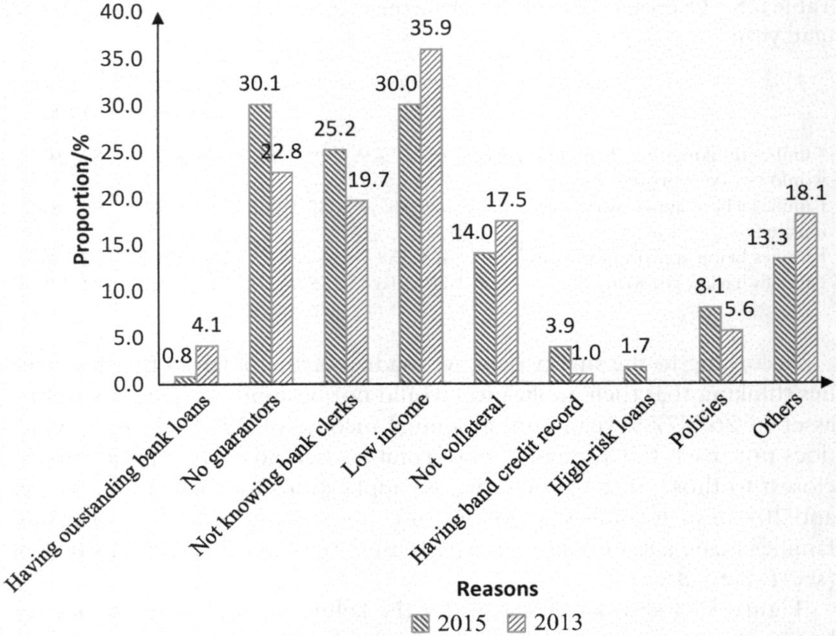

Fig. 5.31 Reasons for rural households not obtaining loans, unit: %

production and management loans in rural areas are mainly short or medium-term loans.

Figure 5.33 reflects the repayment methods of agricultural loans among rural households. Lump sum repayment and Regular interest payment with the principal paid off at maturity become their main choices, accounting for 45.0% and 26.9%, respectively.

5.2.1.4 Loan Service Evaluation

Among rural households with agricultural loans, about 30% of the households are extremely satisfied with loan services (see Fig. 5.34), 38% of the households are relatively satisfied and 27% of households are generally satisfied. Only 5% of the households are dissatisfied, which shows that households having got loans in rural areas are mostly satisfied with the loan services provided by formal financial institutions such as banks and credit cooperatives.

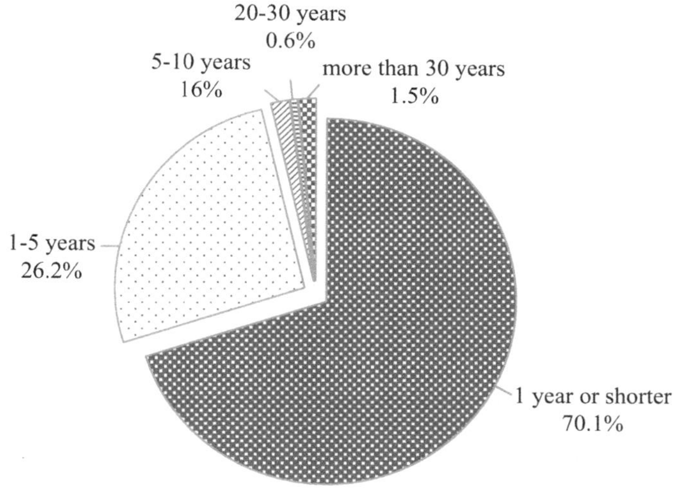

Fig. 5.32 Term of loans

5.2.2 *Financing Preference*

Surveys found that most agricultural households prefer informal financing channels, and only 22.4% of rural households prefer bank credit. At present, China's rural financial market has two obvious characteristics. First, the degree of information asymmetry is high, discouraging profit-oriented financial institutions and making the financial repression caused by insufficient finance supply very serious. Since farmers' production is highly dispersed and susceptible to risks such as weather and market, it is difficult for financial institutions to know information or types of farmers beforehand or to effectively supervise the use of loans by farmers afterward, and they tend to use collateral mechanism. However, farmers generally lack qualified collateral. As a result, a dilemma where people in great need of loans are often unable to get services provided by formal financial institutions comes into being. Second, there is a dual financial supply structure of formal channels and informal channels. Plain differences exist in the level of interest rate, loan scale, collateral requirements and other aspects of formal channels and informal channels. Whether farmers are willing to choose formal financing channels depends largely on the difference of financing costs between the two kinds of channels. The average loan interest rate of

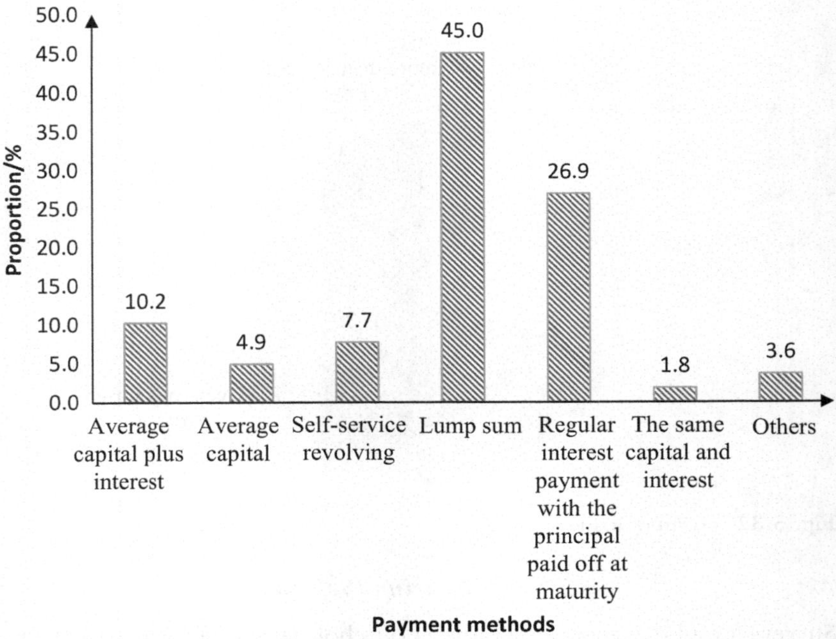

Fig. 5.33 Repayment methods, unit: %

informal channels in rural China is significantly lower than that of formal channels, which may be the main reason why farmers prefer to finance through informal channels.

5.2.2.1 Financing Preference of Rural Households

Table 5.9 shows the proportions of different financing preference of rural households. Most agricultural households in rural areas prefer private lending and it accounts for 65.8%; 22.4% of agricultural households prefer bank loans; for 7.6% of rural households, their choices depend on the amount of money; only 4.2% of rural households think both channels are not bad.

5.2.2.2 Financing Preference and Features of the Head of a Household

Table 5.10 describes the relationship between age and financing preference of rural heads of household. From the table, we can see that the heads of households of all ages prefer private lending, which is related to

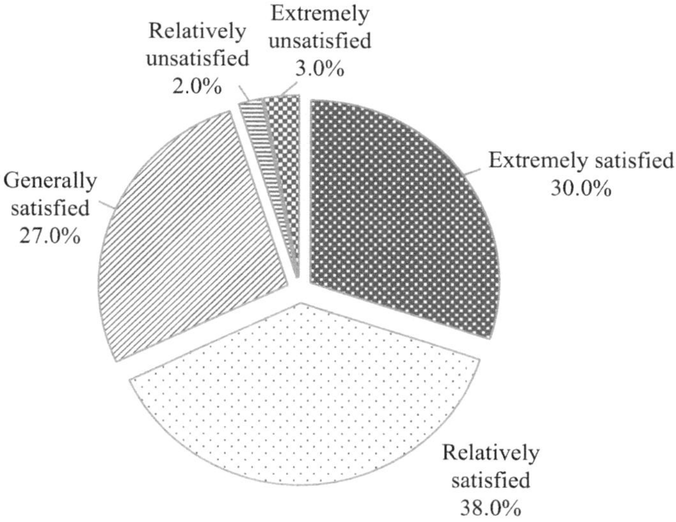

Fig. 5.34 Loan service satisfaction evaluation

Table 5.9 Different financing preference of rural households, unit: %

Financing channels	*Percentage (%)*
Bank loans	22.4
Private lending	65.8
Depending on the amount of money	7.6
Both are OK	4.2

Table 5.10 Age of the head of household and household financing preference, unit: %

Age of the head of household	*Bank loans*	*Private lending*	*Depending on the amount of money*	*Both are OK*	*Total*
18–30	26.5	57.2	10.6	5.7	100
30–40	28.3	55.5	11.4	4.9	100
40–50	22.8	64.9	8.4	3.9	100
50–60	22.9	65.5	7.8	3.8	100
60 or above	20.4	68.9	6.1	4.7	100

Table 5.11 Educational level of head of household and financing preference, unit: %

The educational level of head of household	*Bank loans*	*Private lending*	*Depending on the amount of money*	*Both are OK*	*Total*
No education	20.3	71.2	4.9	3.5	100
Primary education	22.2	66.0	7.4	4.4	100
Secondary education	24.9	60.2	10.9	4.0	100
Higher education	39.6	36.6	18.1	5.7	100

the traditional borrowing habits in rural areas. Heads of household aged from 30 to 40, by contrast, have a preference for credit such as bank loans and the proportion is 28.3%. For heads of household in this age group, the proportion of the household financing preference of "depending on the amount of money" or "both are OK" is relatively large. The older the people are, the more conservative the financing preference is. People aged 60 or above have a preference for private lending.

It is shown in Table 5.11 that the higher the educational level of the heads of rural households is, the stronger their households' preference for bank loans in choosing financing channels is. Among households whose heads are highly educated, 39.6% of them prefer bank credit, surpassing the proportion of preference for private lending. Heads of household who have received higher education are the main group whose choices depend on the amount of money, which means that "depending on the amount of money" is a rational choice of financing channels.

According to Table 5.12, the gender difference of the head of households doesn't have an obvious influence on financing preference. Among households who prefer private lending, the proportion of male heads of households is higher than that of female heads of households.

5.2.2.3 Financing Preference and Family Characteristics

Table 5.13 reflects the relationship among rural family assets, income, financial knowledge level, home values and financing preference. It can be seen that rural households with a preference for bank credit are significantly higher than those preferring private lending in terms of the level of assets, income and financial knowledge. It is noteworthy that the households whose financing choices depend on the amount of money have the highest level of financial knowledge and assets.

Table 5.12 Gender of the head of household and financing preference, unit: %

Gender	*Bank credit*	*Private lending*	*Depending on the amount of money*	*Both are OK*	*Total*
Female	22.2	64.4	7.7	5.8	100
Male	22.5	65.9	7.6	4.1	100

Table 5.13 Family characteristics and financing preference

	Assets (yuan)		*Income (yuan)*		*Financial knowledge level*		*Home values (yuan)*	
	Mean	*Median*	*Mean*	*Median*	*Mean*	*Median*	*Mean*	*Median*
Bank loans	417,952	179,000	64,947	27,633	34	31	229,557	100,000
Private lending	249,778	120,900	38,738	21,710	24	15	154,869	80,000
Depending on the amount of money	457,219	199,300	47,456	26,400	39	32	340,534	100,000
Both are OK	456,836	157,340	51,255	22,215	28	15	324,496	100,000
Total	312,007	137,700	45,807	23,276	28	26	192,835	100,000

5.2.3 *Credit Gap*

The credit gap in this section refers to rural households' unmet demand for credit funds (including formal loans like bank loans and private lending) which are used for agricultural production and management. Specifically, four categories of households are included, namely, rural households that have credit needs but fail to get loans, rural households having obtained formal loans which don't fully meet their demand, rural households that have demand for borrowing from private lenders but fail to obtain it and rural households having obtained funds from private lenders but still in need of funds.

5.2.3.1 Credit Funding Gap of Rural Households

Table 5.14 presents the capital amount lacked for meeting the demand for lending. As is shown in the table, the funding gap of formal loans is significantly wider than that of private lending. The capital amount of

Table 5.14 The capital amount of unmet needs for lending for agricultural production and management among rural households, unit: yuan

	Mean	*Median*
Getting no loans, having demand for them	57,892	25,000
Getting loans, not fully satisfied	144,840	30,000
Getting no funds borrowed from private lenders, having demand for them	27,091	5000
Getting funds borrowed from private lenders, not fully satisfied	76,106	15,000

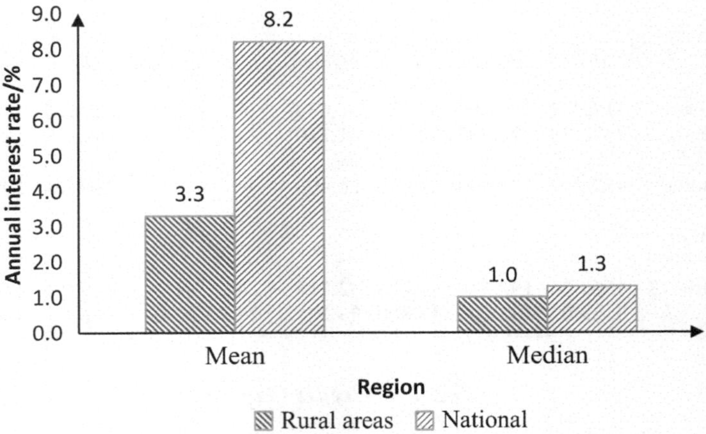

Fig. 5.35 The highest acceptable annual interest rate, unit: %

unmet needs for credit among rural households that have obtained agricultural loans is up to 145,000 yuan, far bigger than that of rural households that have obtained funds from private lenders; the average capital amount of credit needed by households without agricultural loans is 58,000 yuan, 30,000 yuan or so higher than the capital amount of unmet needs for private lending.

5.2.3.2 Acceptable Interest Rate

It can be seen from Fig. 5.35 that for unmet capital demand, the highest annual interest rate that rural households can accept on average is 3.3%, far lower than the national average, which indicates that rural households are less tolerant toward borrowing rate.

5.3 Private Lending of Rural Households

The lending and borrowing behavior among farmers is an important part of the rural financial market, which can not only increase farmers' income, but also reduce rural poverty and narrow the gap between the rich and the poor. In rural areas, since serious information asymmetry exists in the lending market, the private financial market is an effective supplement to the formal financial market. In 2015, more than 28% of rural households borrowed money from private lenders, far higher than the national level, and private borrowing is mainly used for housing as well as production and management projects.

5.3.1 Private Lending Participation Rate

Private lending in this chapter refers to the form of borrowing by individuals through channels other than the formal financial institutions such as banks or credit unions, and it includes borrowing from parents and other relatives, friends and colleagues, as well as private financial organizations. In the case of serious information asymmetry existing in the lending market, the private financial market is an effective supplement to the formal financial market. This is especially so in rural areas, where since it is difficult for banks to obtain information on the potential borrowers' repayment ability, most rural people meet their demand for loans by borrowing from private lenders. The lending and borrowing behavior among farmers is an important part of the rural financial market, which can not only increase the farmers' income, but also reduce rural poverty and narrow the gap between the rich and the poor.

Private lending participation rate refers to the proportion of households borrowing funds from private lenders. As Table 5.15 shows, 19.7% of households in the country participated in private lending in 2015, and the rural private lending participation rate was as high as 28%, indicating that China's rural households' private lending activities were flourishing.

Table 5.15 Private lending participation rate, unit: %

Region	*Private lending participation rate*
National	19.7
Rural areas	28

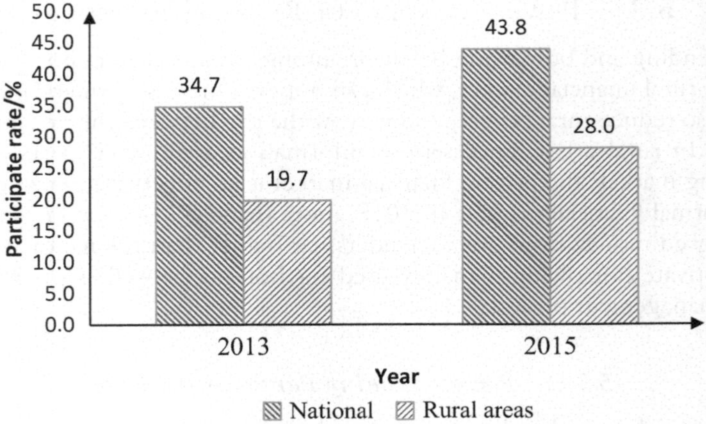

Fig. 5.36 Comparison of private lending participation rate, unit: %

As Fig. 5.36 shows, compared with the data of 2013, in 2015, the household private lending participation rate declined both in the country as a whole and in rural areas, and the national private lending participation rate has decreased by 15%, while the private lending participation rate in rural areas has decreased by 15.8%.

Table 5.16 reflects the private lending participation rate of Chinese households in agriculture/industry and commerce, real estate, automobile and education. According to the table, in the country, 8.5% of households borrowed funds from private lenders for the purchase or building of housing, 5.2% for the production and management of agriculture/industry and commerce, 2% for education and 1.1% for the purchase of cars. Among rural households, 11.2% of households borrowed funds from private lenders for the purchase or building of housing, 8.8% for the production and operation of agriculture/industry and commerce, 3.3% for education and 1.1% for the purchase of cars. In summary, households in our country have a higher private lending participation rate in housing and agricultural/industrial and commercial projects, especially in rural areas.

5.3.2 *The Scale of Private Lending*

The scale of private lending refers to the current capital amount of outstanding private debt held by households. Table 5.17 shows the scale of private lending per household among households in debt in 2015. It can

Table 5.16 Private lending participation rates of different loans, unit: %

	Agricultural/industrial and commercial loans	*Housing loans*	*Car loans*	*Educational loans*
National	5.2	8.5	1.1	2
Rural areas	8.8	11.2	1.1	3.3

Table 5.17 The scale of private lending

Area	*Private lending (10,000)*	*The proportion of private lending to total liabilities (%)*
Rural areas	4.5	77.8
Eastern rural areas	5.3	71.9
Central rural areas	4.7	86.2
Western rural areas	3.6	73.6
National	7.3	54.3

be seen from the table that in rural areas the scale of private lending per household among households in debt was 45,000 yuan and the proportion of private lending to total liabilities was 77.8%. In eastern rural areas, the scale of private lending per household among households in debt was 53,000 yuan, and the proportion of private lending to total liabilities was 71.9%; in central rural areas the scale of private lending per household among households in debt was 47,000 yuan, and the proportion of private lending to total liabilities was 86.2%; in western rural areas the scale of private lending per household among households in debt was 36,000 yuan, and the proportion of private lending to total liabilities was 73.6%. In the country as a whole, the scale of private lending per household among households in debt was 73,000 yuan, and the proportion of private lending to total liabilities was 54.3%. Data show that in 2015, the proportion of private lending to total liabilities of rural households was large, especially in rural areas, indicating that rural households' borrowing mainly comes from private lenders.

Table 5.18 describes the scale of private lending for different uses of rural households. From the table, we can see that funds borrowed from private lenders in the country or in rural areas are mainly used for industry

Table 5.18 Private lending for different uses, unit: 10,000 yuan

	Agriculture	*Industry and commerce*	*Real estate*	*Vehicle*	*Education*	*Health care*
National	3.7	17.3	6.4	11.2	1.9	2.6
Rural areas	2.8	8.5	4.6	3.6	1.5	2.2

Table 5.19 The scale of private lending per household in different regions, unit: 10,000 yuan

	Eastern	*Central*	*Western*
Agriculture	3.6	2.8	2.3
Industry and commerce	6.2	10.7	7.3
Real estate	4.9	5.1	3.6
Vehicle	4.0	3.8	2.9
Education	1.9	1.3	1.3
Health care	2.5	2.1	2.0

and commerce, real estate and vehicles. In rural households, the average amount of capital borrowed from private lenders for industrial and commercial uses was 85,000 yuan, for housing use 46,000 yuan and for vehicle use 36,000 yuan. It can be concluded from the above data that in rural areas, the industrial and commercial production and management produce the highest scale of private lending per household.

Table 5.19 describes the scale of private lending of rural households in different regions. According to the table, in eastern, central or western China, funds borrowed from private lenders are mainly used for industry and commerce, real estate and vehicles. Central rural areas have the largest scale of private lending used for industry and commerce (107,000 yuan) and for housing (510,000 yuan). Eastern rural areas have the largest scale of private lending used for vehicles (40,000 yuan). In terms of private lending used for agricultural production and management, eastern rural households are the biggest borrowers, followed by central and western rural households. The amount of private lending of eastern rural households is 13,000 higher than that of western rural households.

5.4 Financial Knowledge and Financial Behavior of Rural Households

In order to better understand the level of financial knowledge of Chinese households and study the impact of financial knowledge on household financial and economic behavior, we have designed a series of questions about financial knowledge to measure the level of financial knowledge of Chinese households. According to the households' answers to those questions, we construct the index of financial knowledge by applying the technique of factor analysis.

In the analysis of the Chinese households' financial knowledge, we found that the overall level of financial knowledge of households in our country is low and the gap among regions and between urban and rural areas is huge. The study also found that the level of education greatly influences financial knowledge and that economic and financial training courses have a significant impact on it. In the study of financial behavior of households with different levels of financial knowledge, we found that the higher the level of financial knowledge is, the higher the households' proportion of participation in the financial markets is, and that these households hold riskier assets. Among households with a higher level of financial knowledge, their proportion of obtaining loans is larger while their proportion of participation in private finance is smaller. In addition, financial knowledge has a huge impact on the consumption patterns of households. Among households with a higher level of financial knowledge, their proportion of paying by debit or credit card is larger and so does their proportion of online shopping. Thus, financial knowledge has an enormous impact on the various economic activities of households. However, at present, there is a relatively low level of financial knowledge of households in China and a big difference among regions and between urban and rural areas. Therefore, it is necessary to increase financial knowledge of households in our country, especially in western China and rural areas, so as to promote the participation of families in economic activities and boost economic development.

5.4.1 The Overall Level of Financial Knowledge

5.4.1.1 Answers to Questions About Financial Knowledge

Questions About Interest and Computing Capability

Suppose you now have 100 dollars and the bank's annual interest rate is 4%. If you put the 100 yuan in a five-year term deposit account, how much principal and interest will you get in five years? _____

□ <120 yuan □ >120 yuan

□ =120 yuan □ I don't know

Regarding the simple question on interest rate calculation, Table 5.20 shows that in 2015, only 28.5% of households gave the right answer while the proportion of households saying they didn't know was as high as 48.5%. By contrast, in 2013, 14.1% of households gave the right answer and the proportion of households saying they didn't know was up to 52.5%. Thus, although households in our country were greatly lacking in simple calculation capacity of deposit interest rate, the situation has improved compared with 2013. But in 2015, the lack of knowledge in this field of China's rural households was more serious. The proportion of rural households that gave the right answer in 2015 only reached 16.4%, 5.8% higher than in 2013; the proportion of households saying they didn't know was as high as 65.6%, no significant improvement being made compared with 2013. Therefore, we know that although most rural households in our country put money in the bank, they have little knowledge about the calculation of interest.

Questions About Inflation

Suppose now you have 100 dollars. The current bank rate is 5% per year and inflation rate is 3% per year. What you can buy with the 100 yuan and its interest after you put it in the bank for one year will be _____?

Table 5.20 Answers to questions about interest and computing capability, unit: %

	True		*False*		*I don't know*	
	2013	*2015*	*2013*	*2015*	*2013*	*2015*
National	14.1	28.5	33.4	23.0	52.5	48.5
Urban areas	16.7	35.8	40.0	26.0	43.3	38.2
Rural areas	10.6	16.4	24.4	18.0	65	65.6

☐ more than what you can buy at present
☐ the same as what you can buy at present
☐ less than what you can buy at present
☐ I don't know

Regarding the answers to the inflation problem, in 2015, the ratio of the right answer was 16.2%, the ratio of the wrong answer 37.9% and the ratio of the answer of "I don't know" 45.9%. Compared with 2013, the ratio of households that gave the right answer increased by 0.6% and the ratio of households that gave the wrong answer declined. And in 2015, the ratio of the right answer among rural households was lower than the national average by 3.8%, while the ratio of the answer of "I don't know" was higher than the national average by 15.6%. It can be concluded that most rural households cannot understand the problem of inflation (see Table 5.21).

Questions About Risks in the Financial Market
Do you agree that it is generally riskier to buy a company's stock than to buy a stock fund?

1. Yes
2. No
3. Having no idea of stocks
4. Having no idea of stock funds
5. Having no idea of both things

Table 5.21 Answers to questions about inflation, unit: %

	True		*False*		*I don't know*	
	2013	*2015*	*2013*	*2015*	*2013*	*2015*
National	15.6	16.2	40.6	37.9	43.8	45.9
Urban areas	16.0	18.5	49.7	45.1	34.3	36.4
Rural areas	15.2	12.4	28.3	26.1	56.5	61.5

In 2015, the proportion of households with the correct answer to the question in the country was 51.4%, the proportion of households with wrong answers 4.4% and the proportion of households with the answer of "Having no idea" 44.2%. The three indicators were all improved compared with 2013. In 2015, the ratio of the correct answer to the question about the risks in the financial market was higher than that to the question about calculation of interest or about inflation, but the ratio of the answer of "Having no idea" to the question about risks in the financial market was as high as 44.2%. Thus, among households that know about the financial market, there is a higher rate of correct answers and the low overall ratio of the correct answer is due to households' lack of knowledge about the financial risk market. The gap between rural and urban areas is huge. In rural areas, the proportion of the correct answer was only 27.3% while the proportion of the answer of "Having no idea" was up to 70.9%, which shows that rural families extremely lack knowledge about the financial market (see Table 5.22).

Attention to Economics and Finance in Daily Life
How much attention do you pay to economics and finance in your daily life?

☐ very high attention
☐ high attention
☐ moderate attention
☐ little attention
☐ no attention

It can be seen from families' answers to questions about the level of attention to economic and financial programs that only 11% of families pay much attention and 66.8% of families usually pay no attention to eco-

Table 5.22 Answers to questions about risks in the financial market, unit: %

	True		*False*		*Having no idea*	
	2013	*2015*	*2013*	*2015*	*2013*	*2015*
National	26.9	51.4	21.8	4.4	51.3	44.2
Urban areas	38.0	66.2	24.0	5.9	38.0	27.9
Rural areas	11.8	27.3	18.9	1.8	69.3	70.9

Table 5.23 The level of attention to economics and finance, unit: %

	Much attention	*Moderate attention*	*No attention*
National	11.0	22.3	66.8
Urban areas	12.8	26.3	60.9
Rural areas	8.0	15.5	76.5

nomic and financial issues. Therefore, the low rate of correct answers to the above three questions is owing to the general lack of economic and financial concerns among residents in our country. The answers show that a lack of knowledge about finance among families is the main reason why a large proportion of Chinese households gave the answer of "I don't know". In addition, there is an enormous difference in answers to this question between rural and urban areas, which indicates a huge rural-urban gap in financial knowledge (see Table 5.23).

5.4.1.2 Construction of Financial Knowledge Index

In order to measure the level of financial knowledge of each family more accurately, we gave grades based on their answers to the questions. According to their answers to the above questions, we construct the financial knowledge index by applying the technique of factor analysis to measure the level of financial knowledge of each household. The answers to the above four questions were split into seven small questions (except for the question about the attention to economics and finance, each question is divided into two "Yes or No" questions). One question is about whether the respondent gives a direct answer. If a household says it doesn't know the answer, the household is regarded as not answering directly and its answer is marked as "0"; otherwise its answer is marked as "1". It is generally believed that there is a significant difference between the household saying it doesn't know the answer and the household giving a direct answer in the level of financial knowledge. The former may have no idea of the knowledge that the question involves; the latter may know about some knowledge of this part, which, however, is not enough. The other question is about whether the direct answer is correct. The correct answer is marked as "1" while the wrong answer is marked as "0". Obviously, the level of financial knowledge of households with the correct answer is higher than that of households with the wrong answer.

Table 5.24 The load of each factor

Questions	*Answers*	*Factor 1*	*Factor 2*
Whether attention is given to economic and financial information	Yes	0.488	−0.056
Whether the question on the calculation of interest rate is answered	Yes	0.805	0.273
The answer to the question on the calculation of interest rate	Correct	0.639	0.355
Whether the question on inflation is answered	Yes	0.758	0.309
The answer to the question on inflation	Correct	0.443	0.502
Whether the question on risks in the financial market is answered	Yes	0.792	−0.548
The answer to the question on risks in the financial market	Correct	0.759	−0.582

Factor Analysis

Table 5.24 shows the factor loading obtained by applying the method of factor analysis to these questions. From the result of the factor analysis, we can see that there are six common factors. The larger the coefficient of factor loading is, the more powerful the explanation of the factor for the question will be. Comparing the factor loading of different factors, we know that the loading coefficients of Factors 1, 2 and 3 are larger. Since we mainly focus on the financial knowledge of households, it is more important to identify the factors that affect the level of financial knowledge.

By observing the load of each factor, it is found that Factor 1 has a positive effect on each question. That is to say, Factor 1 can make households pay more attention to economic and financial programs in daily life and let them directly and correctly answer all kinds of economic and financial questions. Thus, it can be assumed that Factor 1 reflects the ability of households to correctly answer financial questions—the level of household financial knowledge. Next, we calculate the factor score to measure the specific level of financial knowledge of households.

The Calculation of Factor Score

According to the coefficients of factor score and the answers to the questions, the household factor scores of Factors 1 and 2 are obtained (see Table 5.25).

Table 5.25 Score coefficients on Factors 1 and 2

Questions	*The score coefficient on Factor 1*	*The score coefficient on Factor 2*
Whether attention is given to economic and financial information	0.139	0.072
Whether the question on the calculation of interest rate is answered	0.012	0.335
The answer to the question on the calculation of interest rate	−0.072	0.341
Whether the question on inflation is answered	−0.019	0.347
The answer to the question on inflation	−0.202	0.393
Whether the question on risks in the financial market is answered	0.496	−0.154
The answer to the question on risks in the financial market	0.509	−0.182

Formula (5.1) gives the calculation method of factor score:

$$\text{Factor\_score}_i = \sum_{n=1}^{7} \beta_{in} Q_{in} \tag{5.1}$$

According to the answers to the questions and the factor score coefficients of households, the factor score of each household can be calculated by applying Formula (5.1). In order to reflect the level of financial knowledge of households more directly, the factor score of each family is standardized, and Formula (5.2) gives the method of standardization:

$$\text{Index\_finance} = \frac{\text{Factor\_score}_i - \text{Min}(\text{Factor\_score}_i)}{\text{Max}(\text{Factor\_score}_i) - \text{Min}(\text{Factor\_score}_i)} \times 100 \tag{5.2}$$

The standardized index is the financial knowledge index used to measure the level of financial knowledge of households. The calculated household financial knowledge index ranges from 0 to 100. "0" indicates that the financial knowledge of the household is at the lowest level in the sample; "100" indicates the highest level in the sample. Table 5.26 shows the distribution of family financial knowledge index:

Table 5.26 Distribution of family financial knowledge index

	10th percentile	*20th percentile*	*30th percentile*	*40th percentile*	*50th percentile*	*60th percentile*	*70th percentile*	*80th percentile*	*90th percentile*
Financial knowledge	0.0	0.0	0.0	30.6	37.9	47.8	63.2	75.3	87.9

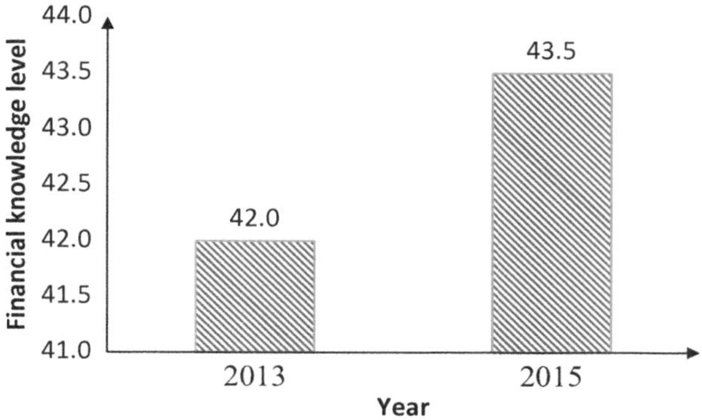

Fig. 5.37 Household financial knowledge level in China

It can be seen from the distribution of family financial knowledge index that more than 30% of households got a score of 0, that is to say, these families did not answer all the above questions or all of their answers were wrong. Thus, it is clear that there is a huge difference among households in our country in the level of financial knowledge.

5.4.1.3 Financial Knowledge Level

China's Overall Level of Financial Knowledge

It can be seen from Fig. 5.37 that the overall level of household financial knowledge in our country in 2015 was 43.5, slightly higher than that of 2013. This shows that the overall level of household financial knowledge in China has been slightly improved.

The Rural-Urban Difference of Household Financial Knowledge in China

The rural-urban difference in household financial knowledge in China is huge. The average level of financial knowledge of urban households is 53.8 while that of rural households is only 26.8, which indicates that the financial knowledge of China's rural households is fairly lacking (see Fig. 5.38).

According to Table 5.27, nearly 40% of households in rural areas have a knowledge level of zero, and their knowledge level is significantly lower than that of urban households' in each percentile.

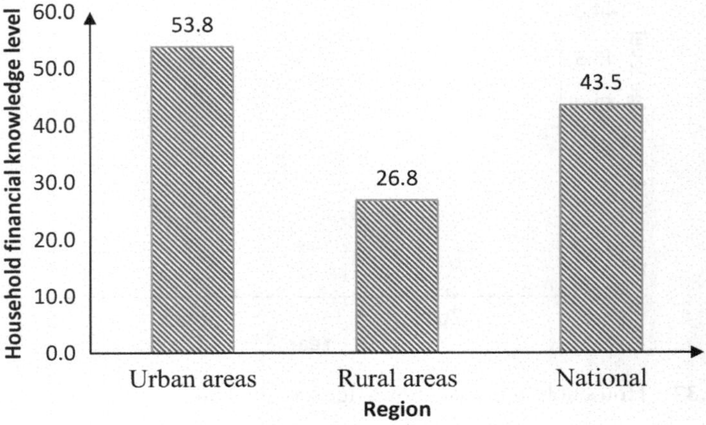

Fig. 5.38 The overall level of China's household financial knowledge

Inter-regional Differences of Family Financial Knowledge in China

From the perspective of regions, households in eastern China have the highest level of financial knowledge (47.8), followed by households in the middle (40.9) and households in western China have the lowest level (39.3). Thus, there is a positive correlation between the level of household financial knowledge and the level of economic development. The more developed the economy is, the higher the level of knowledge will be (see Table 5.28).

5.4.2 *Distribution of Financial Knowledge*

This section mainly discusses the distribution of the household financial knowledge levels on demographic characteristics and gives the financial knowledge levels of people with different educational levels, at different ages and of different genders, respectively.

5.4.2.1 Educational Level and Financial Knowledge

As Fig. 5.39 shows, the financial knowledge level of illiterate households is 16.8 and that in rural areas is 13.5; the financial knowledge level of households with high school education is 51.8, and that in rural areas is 35.7. It can be observed that there is a very strong correlation between

Table 5.27 Comparison of Chinese household finance knowledge level between urban and rural areas

	10th percentile	*20th percentile*	*30th percentile*	*40th percentile*	*50th percentile*	*60th percentile*	*70th percentile*	*80th percentile*	*90th percentile*
National	0.0	0.0	0.0	30.6	37.9	47.8	63.2	75.3	87.9
Urban areas	0.0	0.0	31.5	41.9	57.3	63.2	73.6	77.5	87.9
Rural areas	0.0	0.0	0.0	0.0	10.4	30.6	41.0	54.2	73.6

Table 5.28 Comparison of the overall level of household financial knowledge among eastern, middle and western regions

	Eastern	*Central*	*Western*
National	47.8	40.9	39.3
Urban areas	56.6	51.4	50.5
Rural areas	28.0	26.8	25.3

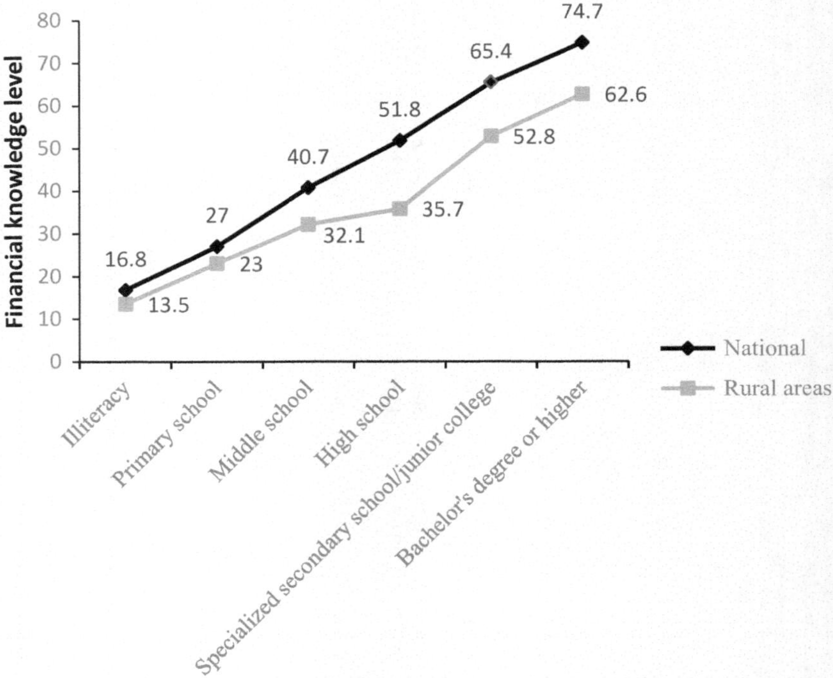

Fig. 5.39 Financial knowledge level of people with different educational levels

the educational level and household financial knowledge level. Thus, the higher the educational level is, the higher the household financial knowledge level will be.

It can be seen from Fig. 5.40 that the financial knowledge level of households having taken economic and financial courses is 76.1, higher than that of households not taking these courses (41). In rural areas, the

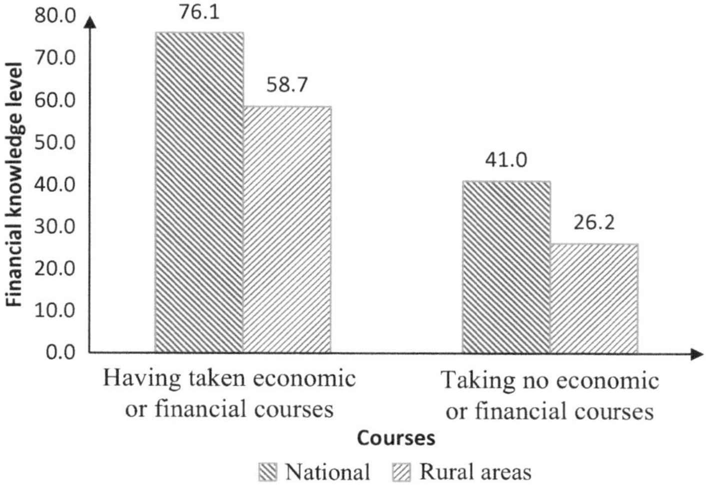

Fig. 5.40 The impact of economic and financial courses on financial knowledge

financial knowledge level of households having taken economic and financial courses is 58.7, also higher than that of households not taking these courses (26.2). Therefore, economic and financial training has a significant impact on the promotion of family financial knowledge.

As shown in Fig. 5.41, the impact of economic and financial courses is greater on households with a low educational level. In other words, the financial knowledge training has a more significant effect on people with a low educational level.

5.4.2.2 Age and Financial Knowledge

In Fig. 5.42, the financial knowledge level of people aged between 18 and 30 is 64.8 and that in the rural area is 36.7; the financial knowledge level of people aged 60 or above is 32.3, and that in the rural area is 19.6. It can be observed that both in rural areas and in urban areas, the younger the group is, the higher the level of financial knowledge will be.

Combining Fig. 5.43, we can see that the younger group receives higher level of education, thereby having higher knowledge level. Therefore, the different levels of knowledge among age groups are due to their different years of schooling.

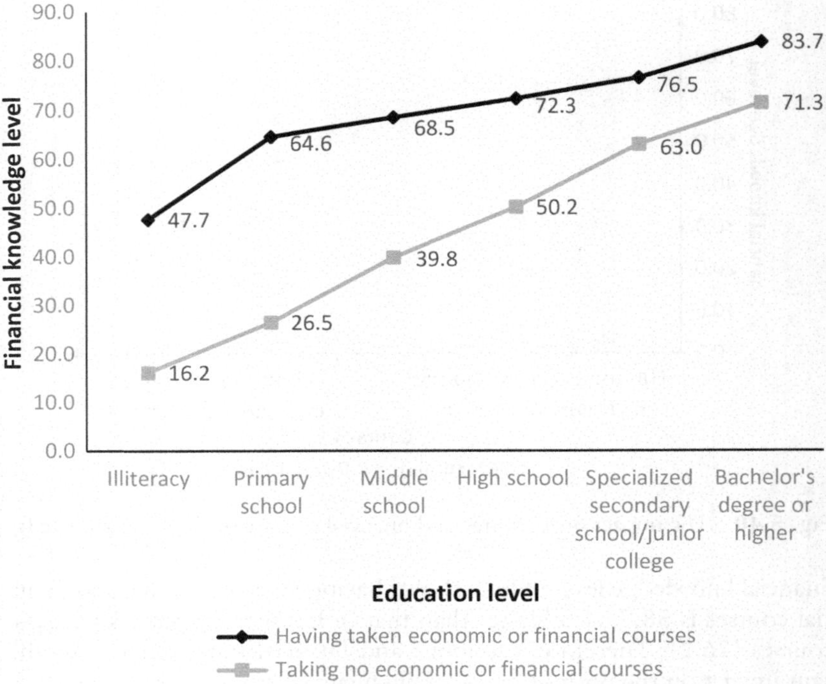

Fig. 5.41 The impact of economic and financial courses on people with different educational attainment

5.4.2.3 Gender and Financial Knowledge

As Table 5.29 shows, the level of financial knowledge of women in the country is higher than that of men while in rural areas the level of financial knowledge of men is significantly higher than that of women. From the perspective of educational level, men and women in the country have the same level of knowledge while in rural areas the educational level of men is greatly higher than that of women. Hence the gender difference in the level of financial knowledge in rural areas is due to the different educational level.

So it can be seen that the improvement of the educational level will increase the level of family financial knowledge. At the same time, the training of financial knowledge also has a significant impact on increasing family financial knowledge, especially among households with a low educational level.

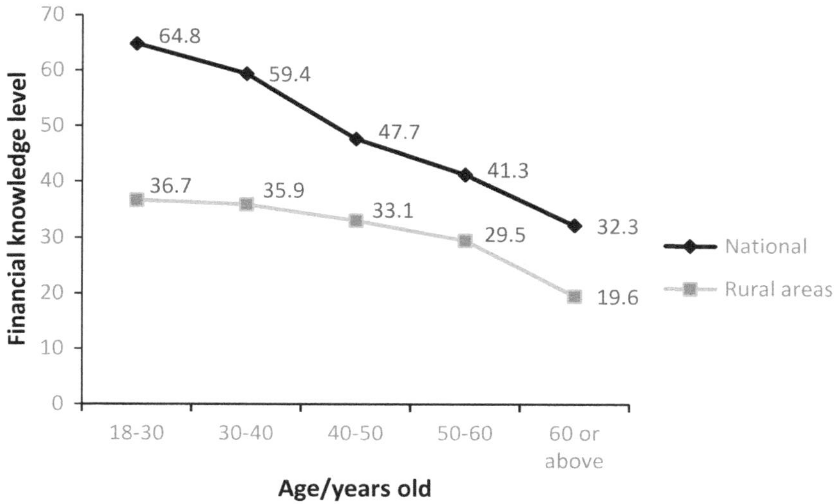

Fig. 5.42 Financial knowledge level of people at different ages

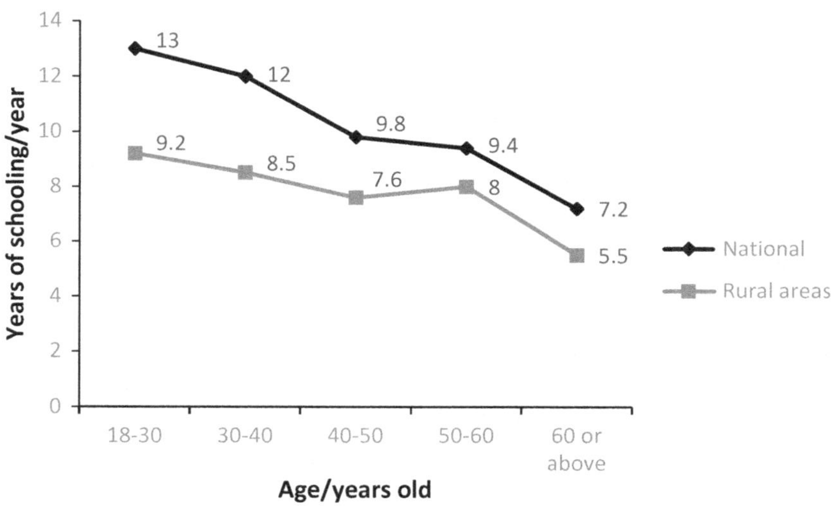

Fig. 5.43 Years of schooling of different age groups, unit: year

Table 5.29 Financial knowledge level of different genders

	Financial knowledge		*Years of schooling (year)*	
	National	*Rural areas*	*National*	*Rural areas*
Male	42.5	27.5	9.3	7.2
Female	46.8	21.4	9.3	4.7

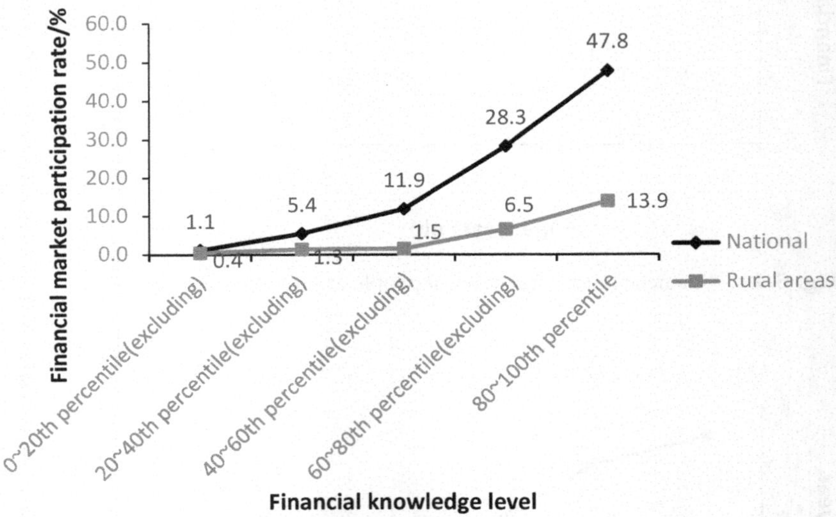

Fig. 5.44 The impact of financial knowledge level on household financial market participation, unit: %

5.4.3 *Financial Knowledge and Household Financial Behavior*

5.4.3.1 The Impact on Financial Market Participation

Figure 5.44 shows the impact of financial knowledge on household financial market participation. Financial market participation refers to whether the family participates in risk markets of stocks, funds, bonds, financial products, derivatives, gold and so on.

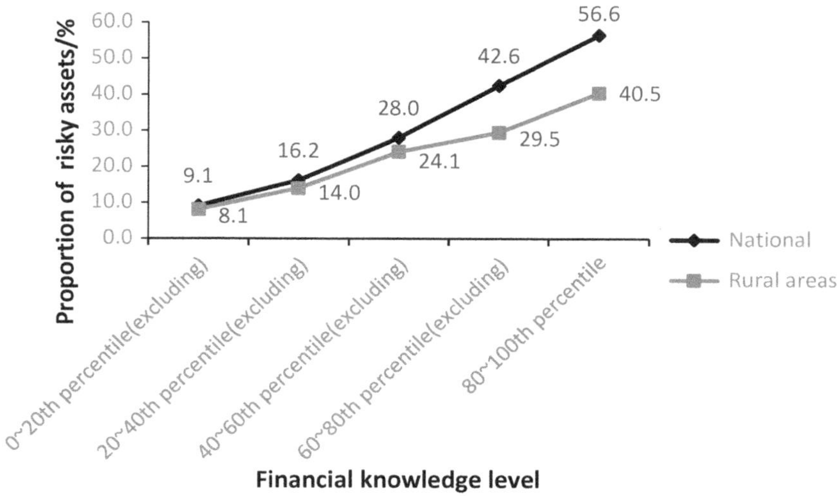

Fig. 5.45 Financial knowledge level and percentage of households holding risky assets, unit: %

As the figure shows, the financial market participation rate of households in the bottom 20th percentile of financial knowledge level is only 1.1% and that in rural areas is 0.4%; the financial market participation rate of households in the top 20th percentile of financial knowledge level is 47.8% and that in rural areas is 13.9%. Thus, the higher the level of family financial knowledge is, the higher the household financial market participation rate will be.

5.4.3.2 The Impact on the Allocation of Risky Assets

In Fig. 5.45, the percentage of households who hold risky assets is 9.1% among households in the bottom 20th percentile of financial knowledge level and that in rural areas is 8.1%; the percentage of households who hold risky assets is 56.6% among households in the top 20th percentile of financial knowledge level and that in rural areas is 40.5%. Therefore, the higher the level of household financial knowledge is, the higher the percentage of households holding risky assets will be.

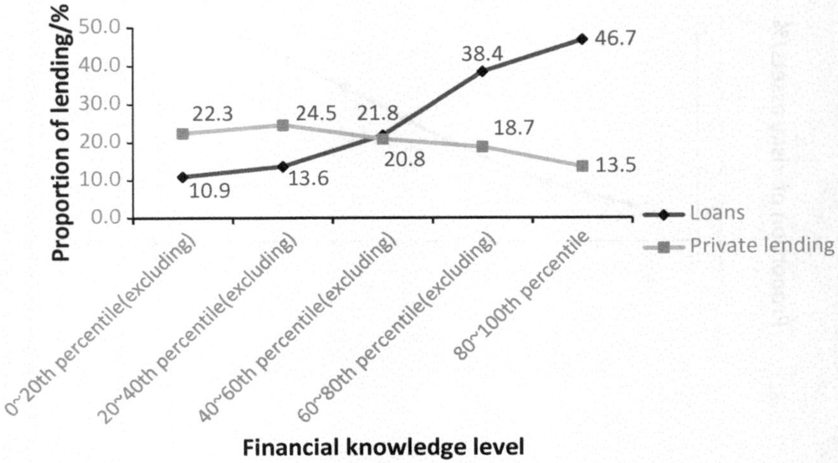

Fig. 5.46 National household finance knowledge level and lending, unit: %

5.4.3.3 The Impact on Household Borrowing Behavior

In the figure, among households in the bottom 20th percentile of financial knowledge level, 10.9% of them have loans and 22.3% of them have funds borrowed from private lenders; among households in the top 20th percentile of financial knowledge level, 46.7% of them have loans and 13.5% of them have funds borrowed from private lenders. It can be seen that families with higher levels of financial knowledge are more likely to obtain loans, thereby reducing the demand for private lending. Thus, the higher the knowledge level of households is, the higher the proportion of households obtaining loans and the lower the participation rate of private finance will be (see Fig. 5.46).

It can also be seen that the higher the knowledge level of households is, the higher the proportion of households obtaining loans is by observing the impact of financial knowledge on rural households' credit. In the figure, among rural households in the bottom 20th percentile of financial knowledge level, 7.4% of them obtain loans; among rural households in the top 20th percentile of financial knowledge level, 25.3% of them obtain loans. However, financial knowledge has no significant impact on the participation of rural households in private lending, which may be due to social relations of rural households (see Fig. 5.47).

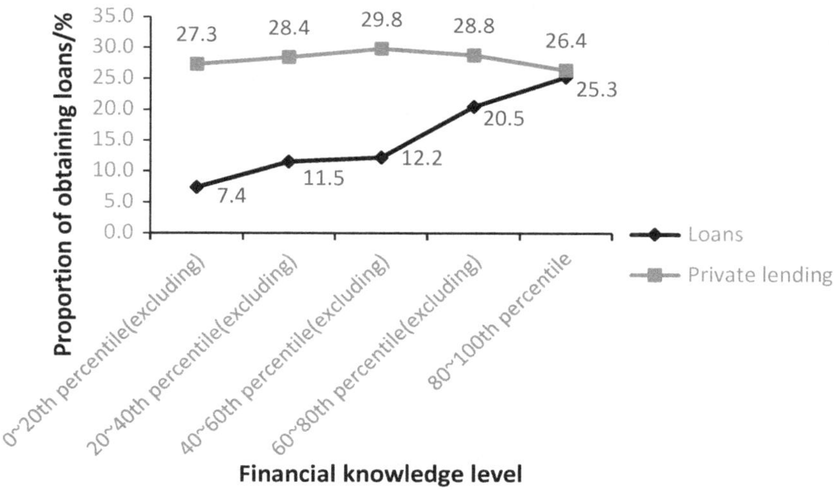

Fig. 5.47 Rural household financial knowledge level and lending, unit: %

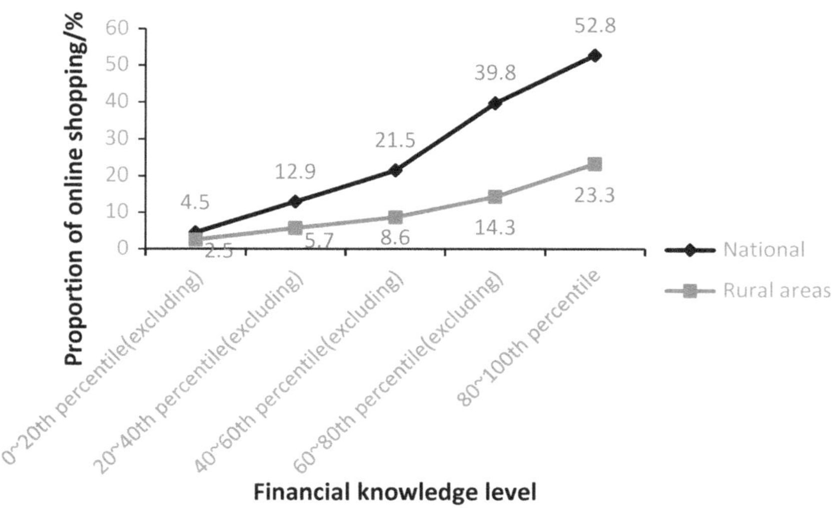

Fig. 5.48 The impact of financial knowledge level on household online shopping, unit: %

5.4.3.4 The Impact on Online Shopping

As Fig. 5.48 shows, the percentage of households who shop online is 4.5% among households in the bottom 20th percentile of financial knowledge level and that in rural areas is 2.5%; the percentage of households who shop online is 52.8% among households in the top 20th percentile of financial knowledge level and that in rural areas is 23.3%. Therefore, the higher the financial knowledge level is, the higher the percentage of households shopping online will be.

CHAPTER 6

Research Conclusions

Based on the analysis of previous chapters, this chapter further uses the China Rural Household Survey (CRHPS) data to carry out systematic analysis and comprehensive research, as well as to sum up and refine the new features, trends and issues of China's rural families.

(1) The expansion of household cultivated land management is obvious, and the proportion of agricultural machinery social service is high.

In the context of the government making great efforts to promote a modest scale of various forms of agriculture, the expansion of China's rural household agricultural production and management is obvious (Fig. 6.1). In 2015, the average size of Chinese agricultural families' cultivated land reached 1.9 acres, which was 0.25 acres larger than that in 2013. Compared with the total area of agricultural production and operation in 2013, the area of cultivated land for agricultural production and management in 2015 increased visibly. Urban agricultural families' cultivated land area reached 3.4 acres, and the agricultural cultivated land area of rural families was 1.7 acres. The difference of rural families' cultivated land area is obvious in different regions, with the cultivated land area of northeast rural households reaching 6.9 acres.

With the expansion of agricultural households' production and operation, a higher proportion of agricultural households have purchased agricultural machinery services (Fig. 6.2). In 2015, agricultural households

© Zhejiang University Press 2020

W. Qian et al., *The Economy of Chinese Rural Households*,
https://doi.org/10.1007/978-981-13-8591-9_6

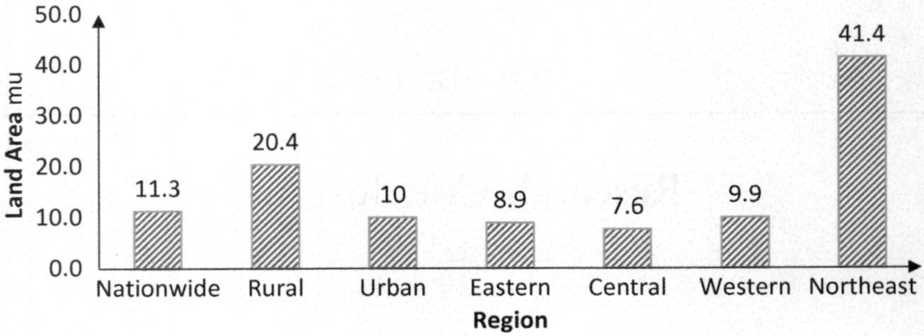

Fig. 6.1 Land area for agricultural production and management

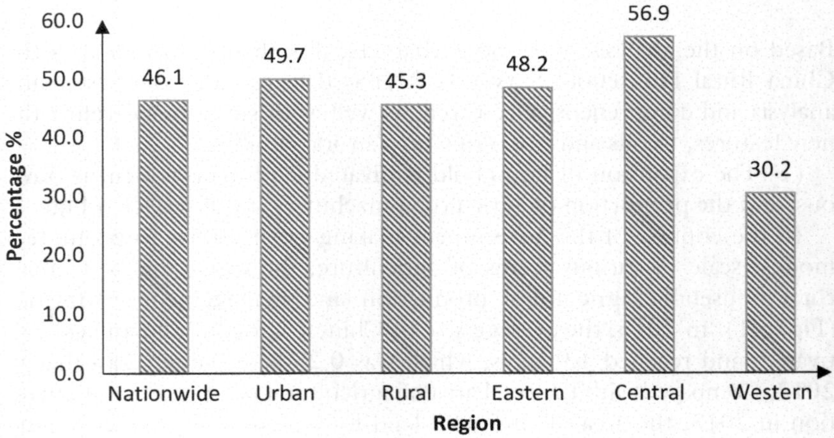

Fig. 6.2 The machinery hiring and renting ratio of agricultural families

who purchased agricultural machinery services through employment or leasing in the production process made up as high as 46.1%. Statistics show that agricultural households in different regions purchase agricultural services differently. The percentages of agricultural households who purchased agricultural machinery services in the eastern and western regions are 48.2% and 56.9%, respectively, while only 30.2% of western agricultural households hired or leased machinery. The above regional differences may be related to the relatively high proportion of agricultural production machinery (36.1%) and agricultural production livestock

(21.8%) in western agricultural households. It is worth mentioning that the proportion of agricultural household livestock ownership in the western region is as high as 21.8%, much higher than that in the eastern region (4.5%) and the western region (6.6%).

(2) The percentage of long-term cultivated land circulation increased significantly, and the inter-period circulation increased.

There has been an obvious increase in the proportion of China's agricultural families taking part in land circulation (Fig. 6.3). In 2015, 32.9% of Chinese agricultural families took part in land circulation, which was an increase of 8.8 percentage points over 2013. In 2015, 18.9% of agricultural households moved out of agricultural lands, 13.7% moved in, and only 0.4% shared both activities. Agricultural households who did not take part in land circulation went down from 75.9% in 2013 to 67.1%. It is worth mentioning that the progress of urbanization promoted the circulation of cultivated land. Statistics show that the percentage of land sold or leased by rural families who had purchased houses in urban districts was 35.7%, which was 21% higher than those who had not purchased houses in urban districts.

The rents for circulated cultivated lands in 2015 had various degrees of increase compared to 2013. The rent for agricultural cultivated land increased in 2015, with the rent for transferred-out land averaging 425 yuan/mu (1 mu ≈ 0.165 acres) and transferred-in land averaging

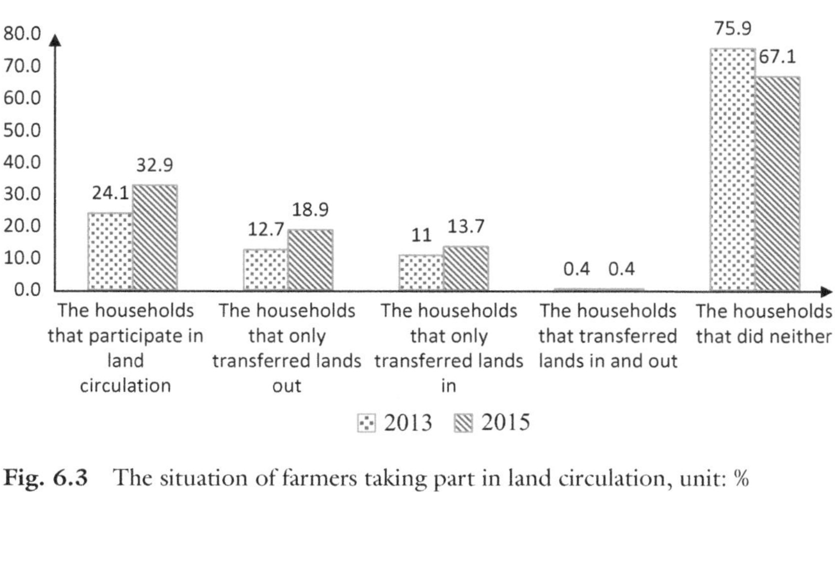

Fig. 6.3 The situation of farmers taking part in land circulation, unit: %

443 yuan/mu. In 2013, the rent for transferred-out land was 383 yuan/mu and transferred-in land 298 yuan/mu. The statistics show that the average rent will increase significantly if the village committee is involved in the process of farmland transfer, whether the land is transferred in or out. For the transferring-out of farmland, the average rent was 590 yuan/mu if the village committee was involved and was 388 yuan/mu if the village committee was not involved. For the transferring-in of farmland, the average rent was 629 yuan/mu if the village committee was involved and was 434 yuan/mu if the village committee was not involved.

The increasing trend of long-term land circulation is obvious. In 2015, the average outward transferring time limit of cultivated land used for agriculture was 6.1 years, while the average inward transferring time limit was 5.5 years, 1 year more than that in 2013. However, statistics show that 15.3% of cultivated land's circulation period exceeded 30 years (Fig. 6.4), which does not comply with Article 14 of the *Land Administration Law of the People's Republic of China*, which stipulates that "farmers' collectively owned land should be managed by the members of the collective economic organizations under contracts, and the time limit for engagement in farming, forestry, animal husbandry, fishery production and land contract management is 30 years".

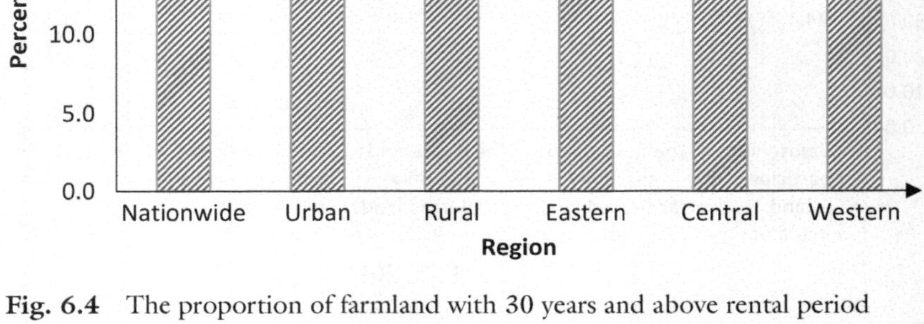

Fig. 6.4 The proportion of farmland with 30 years and above rental period

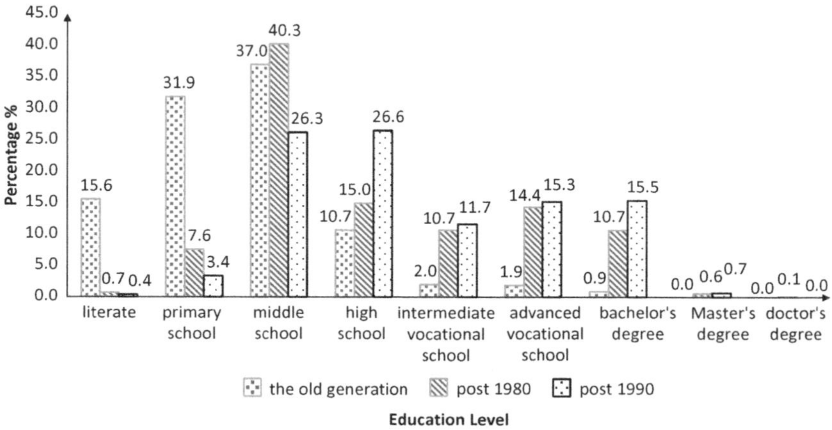

Fig. 6.5 The educational attainment comparisons between the old and new generation of migrant workers

(3) The new generation migrant workers' qualities obviously improved, and there is a considerable change in citizens' manners.

The overall improvement of new generation migrant workers' qualities is first manifested in educational attainment (Fig. 6.5).

Figure 6.5 shows that there is a significant improvement in educational attainment from the old generation to the generations of "post-1980s" and "post-1990s". The proportion of people with primary school and lower qualifications decreased visibly, from 47.5% (the old generation) to 8.3% (the "post-1980s"), to 3.8% (the "post-1990s"); the percentage of people with a high school diploma and above increased significantly from 15.5% (the old generation) to 51.4% (the "post-1980s"), and then to 69.9% (the "post-1990s"), and the percentages of people graduated from high school, intermediate vocational school, vocational senior high, university and postgraduate schools all showed an increasing trend.

The improvement of the new generation migrant workers' moral characters also has an impact on their citizenization. They began to "get out of agriculture" and gradually "fit into" towns and cities. First of all, the proportion of the new generation of migrant workers participating in the New Rural Pension Scheme decreased, and the proportion of those participating in urban employees' pension scheme greatly improved (Fig. 6.6).

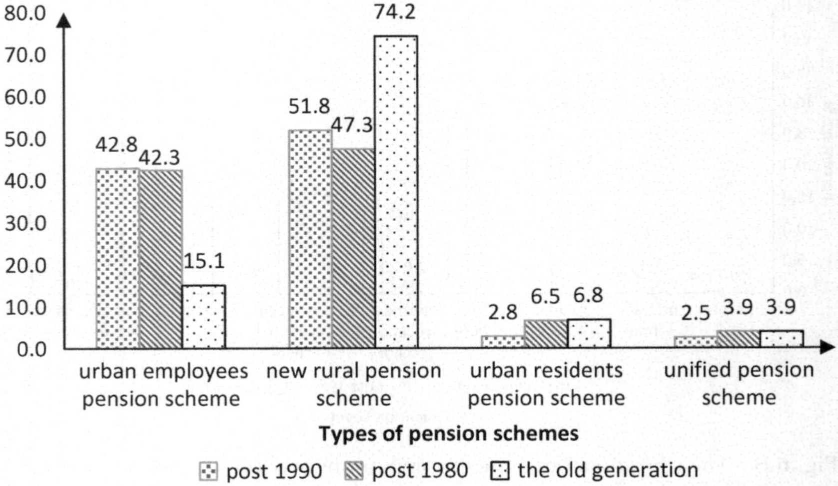

Fig. 6.6 The distribution of the enrollment in various pension schemes of migrant workers in different age groups, unit: %

From Fig. 6.5, it can be seen that the proportion of the post-1980s' and post-1990s' migrant workers who participated in the urban employees' pension scheme was 42.3% and 42.8%, respectively, which were much higher than the 15.1% of the old generation, while the proportion of the two groups who participated in the New Rural Pension Scheme was 47.3% and 51.8%, respectively, significantly lower than the old generation's 74.2%.

Second, the proportion of the new generation of migrant workers who participated in the new rural cooperative medical insurance decreased, while the proportion of those who joined the basic medical insurance for urban workers increased significantly (Fig. 6.7).

It can be seen from Fig. 6.7 that the proportion of new generation farmers participating in the new rural cooperative medical insurance is declining, with the old generation making up 79.7%, the "post-1980s" 64.5% and the "post-1990s" 74.1%. The proportion of migrant workers participating in basic medical insurance for urban workers increased significantly, with the old generation making up 8.9%, the "post-1980s" 23.90% and the "post-1990s" 10.9%. It is worth noticing that although the proportion of post-1990s' migrant workers who participated in the new rural cooperative medical insurance is lower than the old generation,

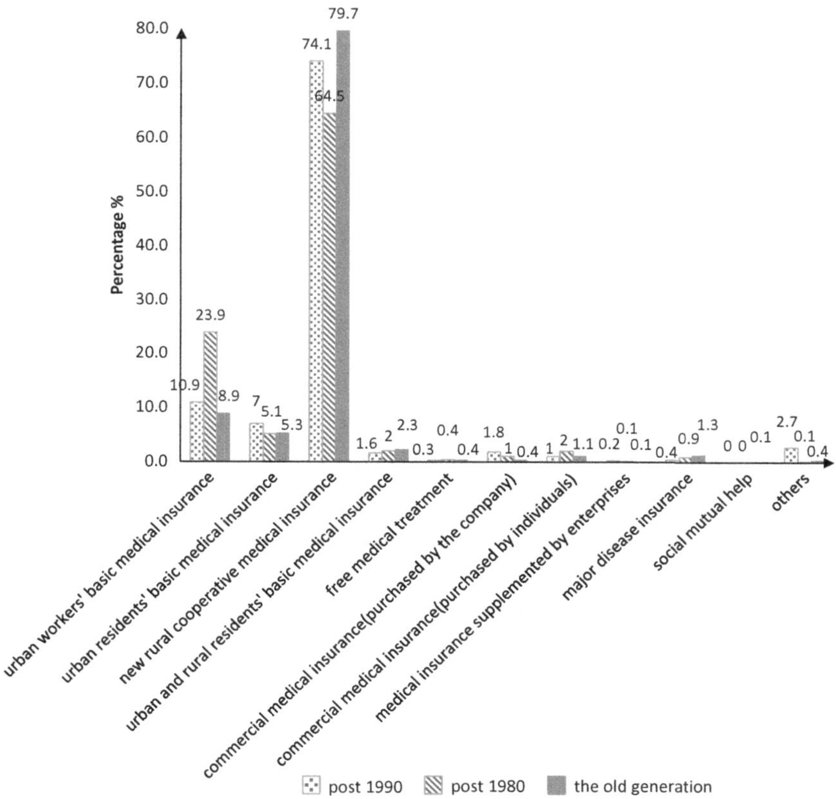

Fig. 6.7 Distribution of medical insurance varieties of migrant workers in different age groups, unit: %

it is higher than the post-1980s' generation. The reason that less post-1990s' migrant workers joined the basic medical insurance than the "post-1980s" is probably that the post-1990s' migrant workers had not spent much time in the city. The transition of mind and the process of joining in the basic urban workers' medical insurance both require a period of time, so there are still many people who have not had enough time to "get out of agriculture" and join in the basic urban workers' medical insurance.

Therefore, it can be considered that the new generation of migrant workers has begun to change the situation of the old generation that overly relies on the social security provided by their rural place of origin, and is gradually integrating into the urban social security system, which will certainly promote the process of farmers transitioning into urban residents.

(11) The new generation of migrant workers' labor supply time declined obviously, which accelerates the shrinkage of demographic dividends.

Demographic dividend refers to the positive effect on a country's economic growth brought by the high proportion of working-age population and high labor participation rate, which lead to the surplus of labor force, and then a lower labor cost and lower production cost, in the demographic transition process. The CRHPS data shows that in recent years, the proportion of China's urban and rural working-age population in the total population is on the decline (Table 6.1).

As can be seen from Table 6.1, from 2011 to 2015, the proportion of working-age population in the total population dropped from 74.14% to 71.25%. The proportion of working-age population in rural areas decreased from 73.18% in 2011 to 69.2% in 2015. The proportion of working-age population in urban areas dropped from 74.9% in 2011 to 72.4% in 2015, and the declining of the proportion of working-age population in rural areas was greater than that in urban areas. According to the National Bureau of Statistics, the total population in rural areas dropped from 657 million in 2011 to 603 million in 2015, and the total urban population increased from 691 million in 2011 to 771 million in 2015. We can deduce from this that between 2011 and 2015, the working-age population in rural areas decreased by 62.84 million, and the working-age population in urban areas increased by 40.97 million, which means that the total working population reduced by 19.35 million. This once again confirms the trend of declining demographic dividends in China.

The CRHPS data further show that the trend of declining demographic dividend is not only manifested in the decline in the working-age population, but also in the decline in labor supply time of the new generation of workers (Fig. 6.8).

Table 6.1 The proportion of China's urban and rural working-age population in the total population, unit: %

Year	*Rural*	*Urban*	*Average*
2011	73.18	74.87	74.14
2013	71.52	74.05	73.11
2015	69.20	72.38	71.25

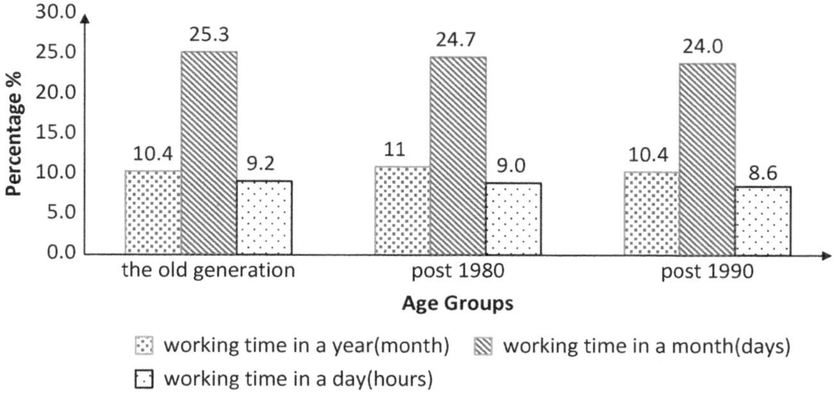

Fig. 6.8 Working time of migrant workers in different age groups (2015)

From Fig. 6.8 we can see that from the old generation to post-1980s' and post-1990s' migrant workers, there was a decreasing trend of working time every month and every day. The number of working days in a month dropped from 25.3 days of the old generation to 24.7 days of the "post-1980s" and then down to 24.0 days of the "post-1990s". The weekly working hours decreased from 9.2 hours of the old generation to 9.0 hours of the "post-1980s", to 8.6 hours of the "post-1990s". This means that the younger generation of migrant workers knows better how to protect themselves, and their working time is more and more close to the provisions of the labor law. On the other hand, it also means that the labor supply time of the new generation of migrant workers will decline, which, combined with the shrinking of the working-age population, will further accelerate the decline of population dividends.

(4) The trend of migrant workers "leaving agriculture" is obvious, and the circulation of land and increase of the farmland scale are gaining speed.

In recent years, the phenomenon of migrant worker households working in agriculture as a part-time job has been gradually reducing, and the trend of farmers "leaving agriculture" has become obvious. What Fig. 6.9 shows is the evolution of migrant worker households' participation in agricultural production from 2011 to 2015.

From Fig. 6.9, it can be seen that from 2011 to 2013 and then to 2015, the correlation between migrant workers and agriculture had obviously weakened. The proportion of migrant workers involved in agricultural

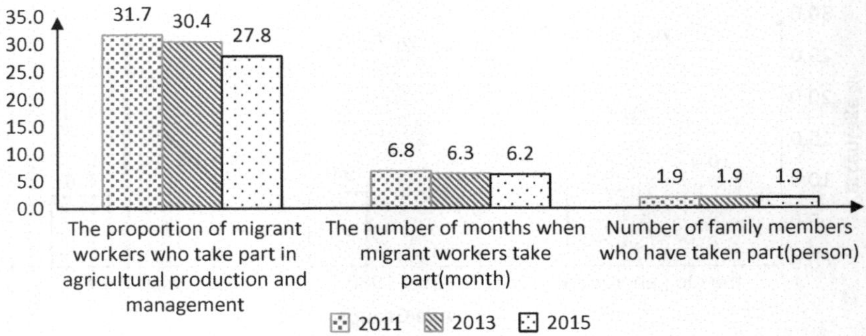

Fig. 6.9 Migrant workers' participation in agricultural production and management, unit: %

production and management decreased from 31.7% in 2010 to 30.4% in 2012 and then down to 27.8% in 2014, and the number of months for agricultural production and management dropping from 6.8 to 6.3 months, and then down to 6.2 months.

From the comparison between the new generation and the older generation of migrant workers, we can further discover the trend of "leaving agriculture" in migrant workers' families (Fig. 6.10).

Figure 6.10 shows that from the older generation to the post-1980s' and to the post-1990s' migrant workers, the proportion of migrant workers engaged in agriculture declined constantly, as the proportion of the older generation, the "post-1980s" and the "post-1990s" was 23.7%, 4.5% and 4.0%, respectively.

This trend of migrant worker families "leaving agriculture" also contributed to the circulation of land and the large-scale operation of farmlands. Figure 6.11 shows the comparison of farmland transfer between migrant workers' families and rural households.

From Fig. 6.11 we can see that since 2011, the speed of migrant worker families transferring out lands has been quite fast. In the 2011 survey, the proportion of migrant workers transferring out lands was 12.9%, which is 6.9 percentage points higher than the 6.0% of rural households. In 2013, the proportion of migrant workers transferring out lands was 16.4%, 6% more than rural families' 10%. By 2015, 30.9% of migrant worker households had had some lands transferred out, 19.6% higher than the 11.3% of rural households. By 2015, the average area of land transferred out by

Fig. 6.10 The employment structure of migrant workers in different age groups (2015), unit: %

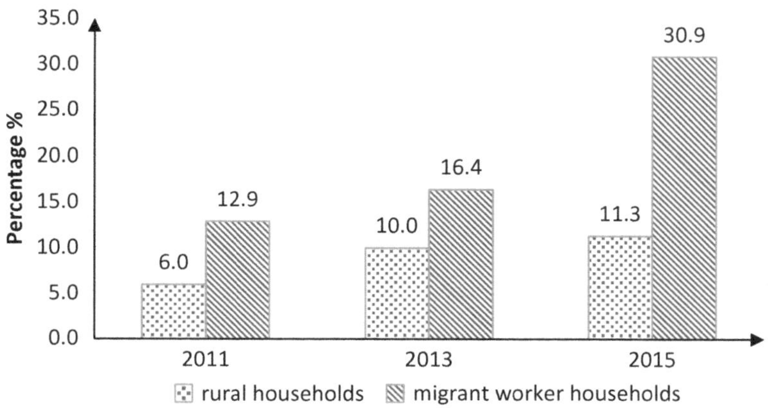

Fig. 6.11 Proportions of lands transferred out by migrant worker families and rural families

migrant worker households was 0.85 acres, 15.9% higher than the 0.73 acres of rural households. The main reason why more and more migrant workers transferred out their lands is that they no longer engaged in agricultural production, which accounts for 66.7% (Fig. 6.12).

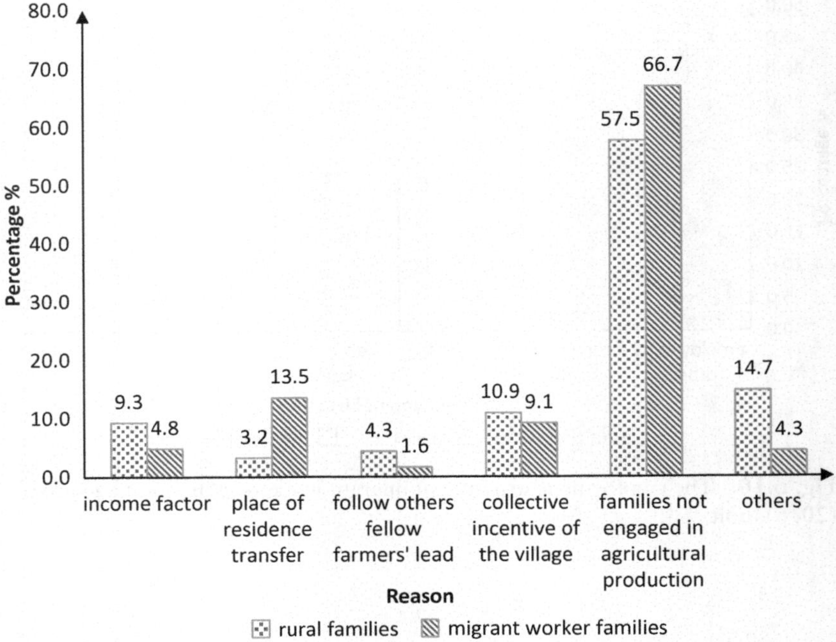

Fig. 6.12 Reasons why migrant worker families and rural families transferred lands out

At the same time, a small number of migrant worker families started to purchase or rent lands to implement large-scale farmland management (Fig. 6.11).

From Fig. 6.13, it can be seen that the proportion of migrant workers acquiring transferred lands was 4.7%, which is lower than the 15.0% of rural families, and far lower than the proportion of 30.9% that migrant workers' families transferring out land as mentioned above. However, the average household rent area reached 2.65 acres, which is 29.27% larger than the 2.05 acres of rural families. Therefore, it can be argued that as more and more migrant workers are "leaving agriculture", more lands start to be owned by a small number of competent agricultural managers, thus promoting the scale of agricultural land management.

(5) Use and configuration of housing of migrant worker families are dislocated, and housing vacancy in rural areas is serious.

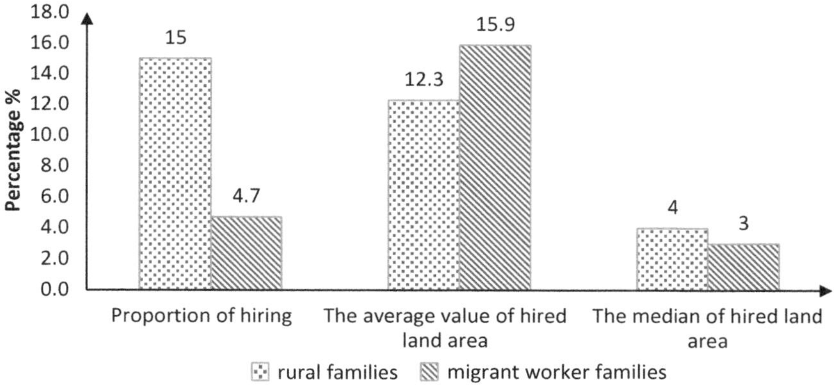

Fig. 6.13 The comparison between hired lands of migrant worker families and rural families

At present, the living conditions of migrant workers in urban areas are generally poor. According to the National Bureau of Statistics' *Survey of Migrant Workers in 2015*, of all migrant workers, 28.7% lived in the dorms of their companies, 11.1% living in the sheds of their construction sites, 4.8% living in their places of management and operation, 18.1% living together with others, 18.9% renting residences on their own, which was increased by 0.4 percentage points and 14% working outside of the rural areas but living at home. The CRHPS surveyed migrant workers who lived in residential buildings and had relatively stable jobs in urban areas. The CRHPS' samples of migrant workers have the following characteristics. First, it only surveyed the migrant workers who lived in urban residential buildings. Second, it only surveyed those who lived in urban areas for more than 6 months. Third, it only surveyed those whose main consumptions were in the urban areas. Thus, it can be argued that the sample of migrant workers in the CRHPS represents a relatively stable group of migrant workers working in urban areas. However, even the living conditions of this group are not ideal. First of all, the homeownership rate is low (Fig. 6.14).

From Fig. 6.14 we can see that even for a group of migrant workers whose living conditions are the best among their cohorts, their homeownership rate was only 55.6%, 40.6% of which came from leasing. Besides, most of the houses were rough or simply decorated (Fig. 6.15).

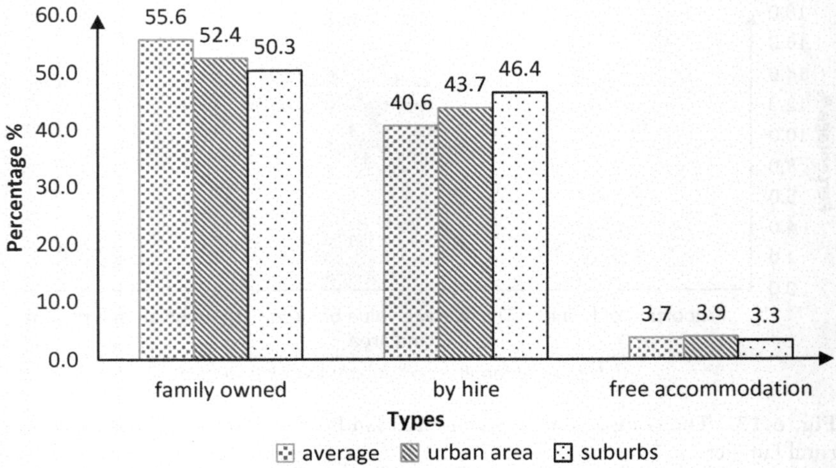

Fig. 6.14 Nature of housing of migrant workers

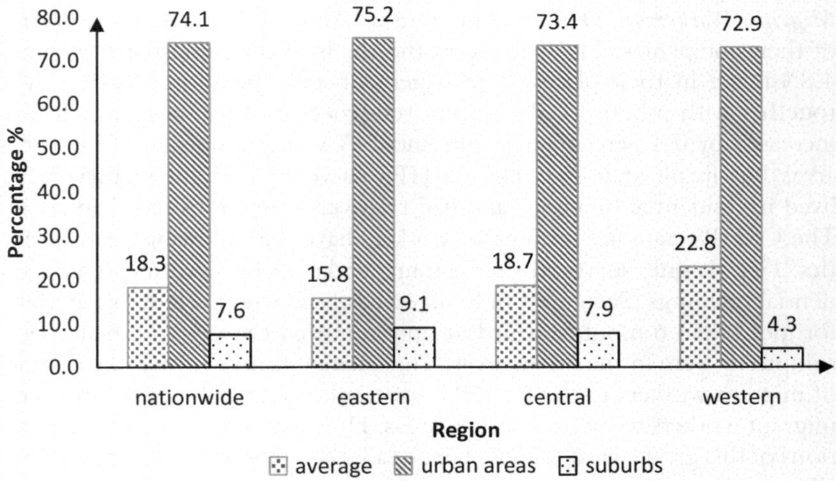

Fig. 6.15 Furnishing of migrant workers' housing

Although the majority of migrant workers have low homeownership rates and poor living conditions in urban areas, most of them have their own houses in rural areas, and the overall homeownership rates are higher (Fig. 6.16).

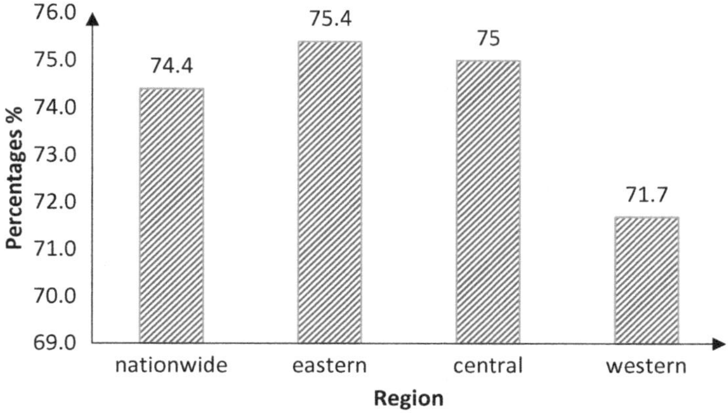

Fig. 6.16 Ownership of migrant workers' housing

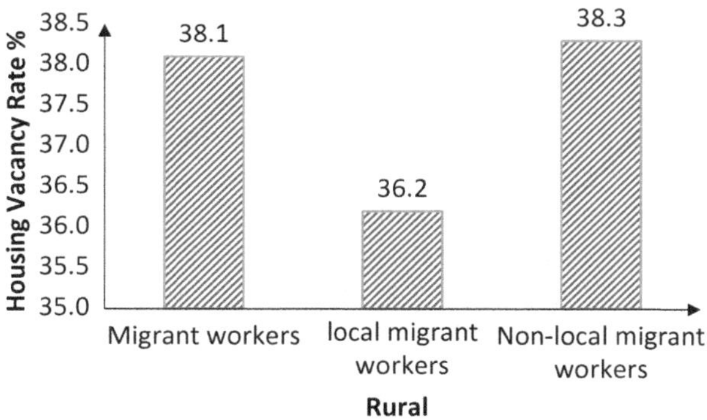

Fig. 6.17 Vacancy rate of migrant workers' rural housing

However, the majority of migrant workers' housing in rural areas cannot be transferred. Therefore, the housing of the migrant workers whose families moved frequently has to be vacant (Fig. 6.17), which not only wastes resources, but also reduces migrant workers' ability to purchase apartment in urban areas. In terms of the national average, the housing vacancy rate of migrant workers in rural areas was 38.1%. The rate was 36.2% for local migrant workers and 38.3% for non-locals.

(6) Rural households' needs for formal loans are hard to meet, and private lending becomes the main channel.

Demands for formal loans refer to rural families' needs for loans because of production management, housing purchases, daily consumptions and

Table 6.2 The satisfaction of rural families' demands for proper fiduciary loans, unit: %

	2015	*2013*	*2011*
Reach of fiduciary loans	49.7	53.7	55.3
Pass rates of fiduciary loans	59.2	49.9	42.2
Availability of fiduciary loans	29.4	26.8	23.3

other financial activities. Statistics show that rural families' satisfaction rates of proper fiduciary loaning channels are quite low (Table 6.2).

As can be seen from Table 6.2, the availability of fiduciary loans of rural households is low, which means the proportion of households with loaning needs actually applying for loans is low, and this rate had been declining since 2011 to 49.7% in 2015. This has also resulted in the low actual availability of rural household credit which is 29.4%.

Figure 6.18 shows that the main reason why some rural agricultural families who had the needs for loans but did not apply for proper loans such as bank loans in 2015 is "not expect it to be approved", which accounts for as much as 40.1%, followed by "worry about being not able to pay back" "not know how to apply" and "applying is troublesome", which account for 21.1%, 20.6% and 15.2%, respectively.

The low availability of formal loaning channels leads to rural households preferring to rely on private lending markets. Private lending refers to the fact that individuals borrow money from relatives, friends or colleagues, as well as private financial organizations other than financial institutions such as banks or credit unions. In fact, private lending markets are more likely to meet demands than formal channels. Figure 6.19 summarizes the amount of money that rural households demand for but have not been met.

As shown in Fig. 6.19, the funding gap of formal loans is significantly larger than that of private loans. The amount of money that had been demanded by the rural families who had agricultural loans but was not loaned was as high as 145,000 yuan, much higher than that demanded by the rural families with private loans. The average demanded amount of money by families without agricultural loans was 58,000 yuan, about 30,000 higher than the private funds that had not been met. However, the rural families' private lending scale is much bigger than that of the formal loaning channels. The scale of private lending refers to the current number of loans that have not been paid back.

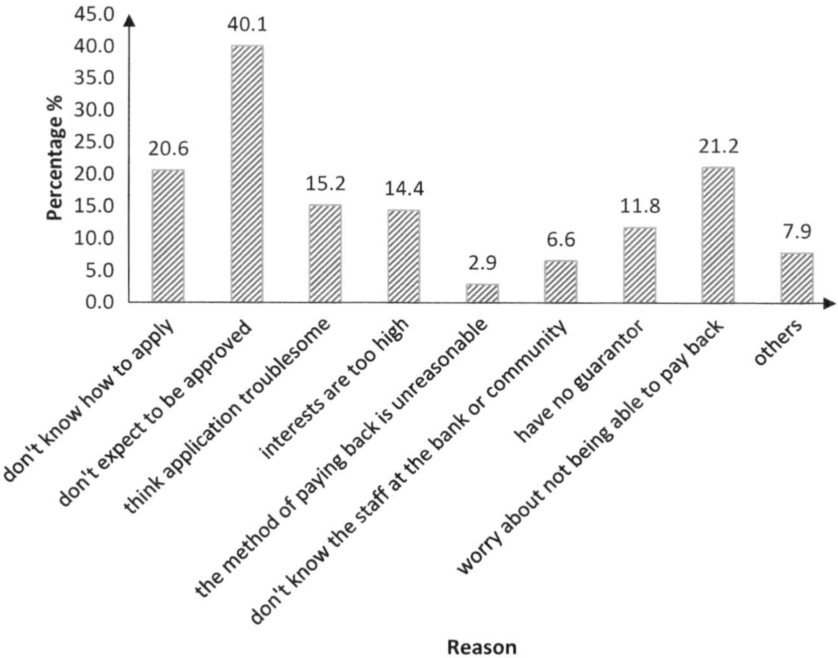

Fig. 6.18 Reasons for not applying for loans

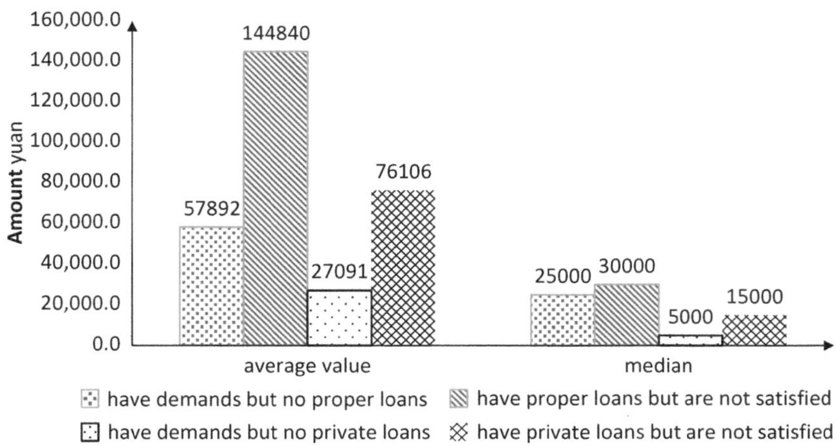

Fig. 6.19 The amount of loans for rural household agricultural production and management that have not been met

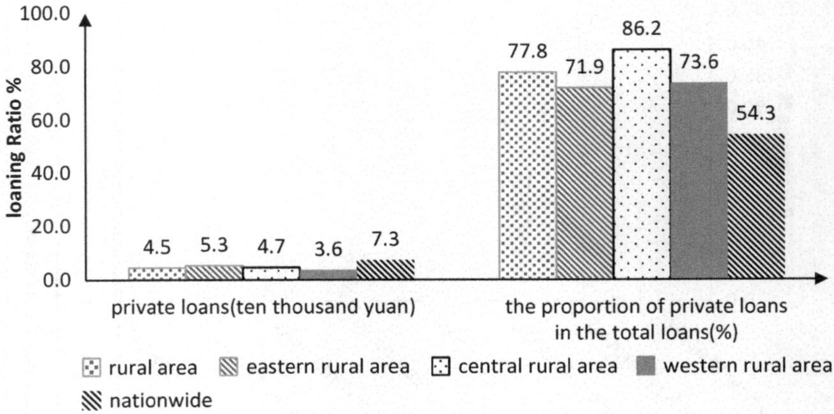

Fig. 6.20 The scale of private loans

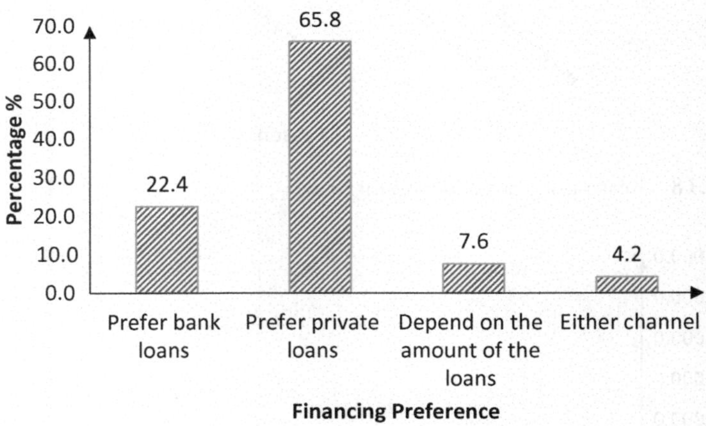

Fig. 6.21 Financing preferences of rural families

Figure 6.20 shows the average household loaning scale in 2015.

As can be seen from Fig. 6.20, the average rural household loan was 45,000 yuan, of which 77.8% was private lending. Of all this, the average eastern rural household loan was 53,000 yuan, of which 71.9% was private lending; the average central rural household loan was 47,000 yuan, of which 86.2% was private lending; the average western rural household loan was 73,000 yuan, of which 54.3% was private lending. Statistics show that in 2015, rural households' private lending made up a large part of the total liability, which was especially prominent in rural areas. This indicates that rural household loaning mainly came from private lending.

In fact, most rural families' financing preferences leaned toward private lending. Figure 6.21 shows the proportions of agricultural families' financing preferences. A majority of agricultural families in rural areas preferred private lending, accounting for 65.8%; 22.4% of agricultural families preferred bank loans; 7.6% of the families chose according to the amount of loans; and only 4.2% would use either channel of loans.

The manufacturer's authorised representative in the EU is Springer Nature Customer Service Centre GmbH, Europaplatz 3, 69115 Heidelberg, Germany. If you have any concerns regarding our products, please contact ProductSafety@springernature.com

Printed and bound by CPI Group (UK) Ltd, Croydon, CR0 4YY

25/09/2026

02222897-0006